# CAMBRIDGE STUDIES IN LINGUISTICS

*General Editors*: W.SIDNEY ALLEN, B.COMRIE, C.J.FILLMORE
E.J.A.HENDERSON, F.W.HOUSEHOLDER, R.LASS, J.LYONS
R.B.LE PAGE, F.R.PALMER, R.POSNER, J.L.M.TRIM

*Referential–semantic analysis*
*Aspects of a theory of linguistic reference*

# In this series

*Issued in hard covers and as a paperback

# REFERENTIAL– SEMANTIC ANALYSIS

*Aspects of a theory of linguistic reference*

## TORBEN THRANE

*Lecturer in English Language and Literature*
*University of Copenhagen*

CAMBRIDGE UNIVERSITY PRESS

CAMBRIDGE

LONDON   NEW YORK   NEW ROCHELLE
MELBOURNE   SYDNEY

Published by the Press Syndicate of the University of Cambridge
The Pitt Building, Trumpington Street, Cambridge CB2 1RP
32 East 57th Street, New York, NY 10022, USA
296 Beaconsfield Parade, Middle Park, Melbourne 3206, Australia

First published 1980

Printed in Great Britain by
University Press, Cambridge

*Library of Congress Cataloguing in Publication Data*

Thrane, Torben.
Referential–semantic analysis.

(Cambridge studies in linguistics; 28)
Bibliography: p.
Includes index.
1. Reference (Linguistics) 2. English language –
Semantics. I. Title. II. Series.
P325.5.R44T5    415    79-17405
ISBN 0 521 22791 7
ISSN 0068-676X

BIRGITTE
MARIE
LOUISE

# Contents

# *Preface*

The present work is intended as a contribution towards the clarification of one of the problems with which man has preoccupied himself at all times: the relationship between words and things. It is not a philosophical work although the problem is often considered to be primarily philosophical in nature. But the problem has many aspects. Some of these are philosophical, some are pragmatical, some are sociological – and some are linguistic. It is the latter aspects that will be treated here, although some notice will be taken of what philosophers have had to say on the question.

My interest in the problem was first awakened when I participated in a research seminar on the problems of 'linguistic representation', instigated and led by Professor Gunnar Bech, in 1968. Owing to his sad illness, which to the detriment of us all has since forced him to retire prematurely, no very clear conclusions emerged from the seminar, so when a few years later the British Council and the Danish Research Council for the Humanities made it financially possible for me to devote three years to full-time research, I began to explore the area on my own. I am grateful to these two bodies for their support. I am likewise grateful to the Department of English at the University of Copenhagen for supporting my application for such a long leave of absence from my departmental duties.

I spent the three years 1973–6 at the Department of Linguistics, University of Edinburgh, submitting towards the end of that time a thesis for the degree of PhD under the title *A study in the referential functions of English noun phrases*. I consider these three years the happiest and most fruitful period of my professional life, and I would like to thank all the teachers and fellow-students who contributed to it. There are two persons I would like to thank personally for this period: Dr John M. Anderson, with whom I had – and have since had – many a good discussion, and whose theories have played an important part in my own work; but most of all Professor John Lyons, who took an active interest in my work which far exceeded the call of duty, and who has continued to do so.

Although the present work, like so many others in linguistics these days, has grown out of a PhD thesis, it is not identical to the thesis, mainly owing to the points of constructive criticism raised against the thesis by two anonymous readers for the Cambridge University Press. I am grateful to them both for forcing me to rethink some of the fundamental principles of the work.

Throughout the last two years I have been sorely trying the patience of my colleagues, friends and students at the Department here with questions and discussions. My thanks are due to them for keeping their patience, and especially to Dr Graham Caie, Peter Harder, Arnt Lykke Jakobsen, Christian Kock, Dr Ingeborg Nixon, and Svend Erik Rosenberg (the last of the Department of Linguistics).

I am also very grateful to Annette Götzsche and Tora Schou for typing the manuscript in record time, while at the same time tending their normal secretarial duties for the Department.

Yet over and above all others, I want to thank my wife and two daughters, to whom the work is dedicated. It is my wife's patient understanding and support more than anything that has carried me through the various crises I have undergone during the long history of the work. And it is my daughters who have provided, though unwittingly, much of the stuff that has gone into it.

*Mørkøv, January 1979.*                                            T.T.

# Introduction : the functions of language

Language may perform a variety of functions. We employ it to make statements, ask questions, express our emotions, order someone else around, etc. No serious objection can be levied against the view that language performs functions. However, a number of objections can be raised against specific proposals as to what functions language performs, how many, how they should be distinguished, which is the basic one and other proposals of a similar concrete nature. Also, disagreement is fierce over the nature of the relationship between language functions and linguistic form and structure, over the question as to whether an investigation of linguistic structure should take account of language functions, or, if it should, to what degree.

If we have a plank that we, for some reason or other, wish to hammer a nail into, we look around for a hammer. Failing to find one, we look for a suitable stone, an axe, even the leather heel of a shoe. We do not look for a feather, a handful of soil, not even for another plank, for we know that these would all be unsuited to the task of getting the nail in the plank. In our choice of tool we rely on our knowledge of the properties of things; those will do, these will not do for the job in hand. There is an important relationship between the structural properties of things and the functions that we wish these things to perform. So too, with language. If we want to enquire into the structural properties of language we must take heed of the functions that language may perform.

The first serious discussion of language functions is that by Bühler (1918; 1934: 24ff), although he credits Plato with the original insight of language as an *organum*. Bühler's 'organon-model' is the linguistic correlate of Martin Buber's virtually contemporary philosophical model of religious experience, based as it is on *Ich* (the speaker), *Du* (the hearer), and *Es* (the thing). Seen in relation to these three factors, the linguistic sign – which to Bühler is explicitly 'concrete phenomena of sound' – is, respectively a *symbol*, a *symptom*, and a *signal*. Each of the

1

three relations that the sign may contract corresponds to a separate linguistic function. The relation between speaker and sign corresponds to the expressive (*Ausdruck*) function of language, that between hearer and sign to the stimulative (*Appell*) function, and that between thing and sign to the descriptive (*Darstellung*) function.

He does not query the priority of the descriptive function, but he does argue that independent status can be given to the other two, conceding, however, that no sharp lines of demarcation can be drawn between the three functions. For reasons that will become abundantly clear I am in general sympathy with the view that priority should be accorded the descriptive function. In order further to substantiate this view, I should like to point to the fact that it is the only function on which there is substantial agreement among a number of scholars who have all dealt specifically with the problem of the functions of language:

| (1) | Bühler | Lyons | Halliday | Jakobson | Popper |
|-----|--------|-------|----------|----------|--------|
| | *Ausdruck* | expressive | inter-personal | emotive | expressive |
| | – | social | | phatic | – |
| | *Appell* | – | | conative | stimulative |
| | *Darstellung* | descriptive | ideational | referential | descriptive |
| | – | – | textual | – | – |
| | – | – | – | metalingual | – |
| | – | – | – | poetic | – |
| | – | – | – | – | argumentative |

Lyons (1977: 50ff) gives a comprehensive account of Bühler's, Halliday's, and Jakobson's functions, but for his own purposes he adopts the three ascribed to him above. This is not to say, of course, that these are the only functions of language recognized by Lyons, but they are presumably those that he takes to be the most important.

As far as can be gleaned from his article, Halliday (1970) collapses Bühler's *Ausdruck* and *Appell*, further expanding this composite function to be defined as the function whereby 'language serves to establish and maintain social relations' (Halliday 1970: 143). The textual function is supposedly the function whereby we are able to construct and understand coherent stretches of speech. Insofar as this can be properly described as one of the functions of language, I suspect that it correlates, to some extent at least, with Popper's argumentative function (see below).

The largest number of functions is offered by Roman Jakobson (1960), and he, like Bühler, has a principled basis for them, namely, the six necessary and sufficient components of a comprehensive utterance situation. These are, in the order comparable to the equivalent functions listed in (1)[1] under Jakobson, the addresser, the contact, the addressee, the context, the code, and the message. The basis of the functions is explained in terms of orientation. When an utterance is primarily orientated towards the code – i.e. the language in which discourse is held at the moment – then the utterance is an instance of a predominantly metalingual function, to take just one example. Like Bühler, Jakobson is careful not to regard the functional classification of particular utterances as an all-or-nothing affair.

Popper (1963: 134f, 295) follows Bühler for three of his four functions, but in addition he proposes what he calls an argumentative function. As the name implies, this is the function of language which enables us to construct valid arguments. Insofar as this function is characterized morphologically, I take it to subsume Halliday's textual function.

It could perhaps be argued that there is no argumentative function. Popper might be held to have perversely confused the semantic structure of language, which is the linguistic reality that permits *us* to draw inferences from one set of sentences to another along lines which are defined by the temporal linearity of speech, with unnecessary and damaging considerations of what language 'does'. But surely such an argument is confused. Language is a tool. *We* employ it, for a variety of purposes, and it is the nature of these purposes we are investigating at present. One of these purposes is, clearly, to convince our interlocutor, to leave him no alternative but to accept what we say. When we engage in an act of convincing by uttering a sequence of semantically inter-related sentences, then we employ language in a predominantly argumentative function.

Popper's account is interesting for yet another reason. He explicitly states that the functions are ordered hierarchically (in the order given

---

[1]   Arabic numerals in parentheses refer to 'chapter-internal' examples. Thus (1) here refers to example (1) in the Introduction. Reference to 'chapter-external' examples will be given by the number of the relevant example preceded by the number of the chapter; thus (5:30) refers to example (30) in chapter 5.

under Popper in (1)). An utterance may be expressive without being argumentative, or, in general, an utterance may be used to perform a function of any level without performing the functions at lower levels, but not vice versa. He sees in this hierarchical order a means of characterizing human language as against other, e.g. animal, semiotic systems. The two lowest functions, the descriptive and the argumentative, are peculiar to human language. Reflecting on the relationship between these two functions and various types of meaning, we note that the descriptive function correlates with referential (denotative, descriptive) meaning, whereas the argumentative function correlates with meaning conceived of as a set of sense-relations, or sense in Lyons' terms. The connection between these two types of meaning shall occupy us at a later stage (cf. §2.0). Suffice it here to say that they complement each other, in that they represent two different viewpoints of the same phenomenon.

It is the main purpose of the present work to enquire into various aspects of what I shall call, following Jakobson, the referential function of language. As I hold the view that language structure and language function are inter-related, particular investigations will be undertaken of ways and means of acquiring insight into linguistic structure by way of considerations of language functions. Before we can go on to these matters, however, one or two pertinent contemporary assumptions need attention.

# PART I: THE PRELIMINARIES

For, what is worse, knowledge is made by oblivion; and to purchase a clear
and warrantable body of Truth, we must forget and part with much we know.
SIR THOMAS BROWNE *Pseudodoxia Epidemica*

# 1 *The linguistic preliminaries*

## 1.1 Pronominalization

Among the clearly defined areas of contemporary linguistic research, that of pronominalization is the only one to subsume matters of reference in any consistent way.

There are two fundamental aspects involved in the linguistic analysis of pronouns. Although they are interrelated they call for a distinction which is not always clearly drawn. One aspect is concerned with the internal analysis of pronouns; another is concerned with the function of the pronouns in linguistic utterances. Moreover, it is not immediately obvious what the relationship between these two aspects is in inferential terms: can the internal make-up of pronouns be inferred from a consideration of the functions they (may) perform, or is the range of functions performed by a given pronoun dependent in some way upon its internal make-up? In the present section I shall enquire into these questions on the basis of a number of more-or-less recent treatments of the pronoun in the linguistic literature.

It would appear to be the case that within each aspect three different views are in contention. Thus within the functional aspect we can distinguish (I) 'co-reference', (II) 'substitution', and (III) 'indication'; and within the aspect of internal composition, (A) their composition as NP, (B) as non-derived, and (C) as involving syncretism/segmentalization. These may not be absolutely clear-cut distinctions, particularly with respect to (A) and (C), and they may not cover the whole field of pronominalization. Yet if we simplify the issue somewhat and regard the personal pronouns as constituting the paradigm instances of pronominalization on the basis of which the distinctions are drawn, they at least are not misleading. Table 1 shows how a number of studies pertaining to pronouns and pronominalization reflect these distinctions.

The position AI, I suppose, is what could be called the classical transformational position, most ably defended by Karttunen (1971)

Table 1

|   | I | II | III |
|---|---|---|---|
| A | Lees & Klima (1963)<br>Karttunen (1971)<br>Kuroda (1971) | Lakoff (1968a) | |
| B | Jackendoff (1972)<br>McCawley (1971) | Crymes (1968)<br>Harweg (1968)<br>Bloomfield (1933) | Collinson (1937) |
| C | Postal (1966)<br>Sommerstein (1972) | Hjelmslev (1937) | |

against the rival position BI, the two holders of which differ among themselves in matters which need not concern us at present.

What is of immediate interest about the classical position (AI) is that it is reached from the point of view of the functional aspect. Since (personal) pronouns may be used instead of a 'full' NP, the implication drawn is that the internal structure of a (personal) pronoun can be assessed on the basis of the internal structure of NPs. This inference relies on what since Chomsky (1965: 145ff) has been known as the referential index convention: deep structure NPs are assigned a referential index of some form.

However, a further requirement is imposed on pronominalization. Not only should the referential indices on two (or more) NPs be identical for pronominalization to occur, the NPs should also be lexically identical. If both conditions are met we have what Chomsky (1965: 196) calls 'strictly identical Nouns'. Pronominalization is held to depend on strict identity in this sense.

On the assumption that 'co-reference' has something to do with the notion of reference as this has been developed by linguists and philosophers since Strawson (1950), the requirement of lexical identity is strange. Not only does it contravene the basic principle of reference, namely, that a great variety of linguistic forms may be used to refer to the same entity *salva veritate* (cf. also Sampson 1969: 18), it also creates problems for the analysis of 'co-referential epithets' in which the noun is not the same as the noun in the antecedent NP. This point is mentioned by Jackendoff (1972: 110), and it constitutes one of the major reasons for

Lakoff's abandonment of the referential index approach (cf. G. Lakoff 1968a: 16ff; also 1968b). Jackendoff and Lakoff thus seek to establish TG-parallels to Harweg (1968) in which this principle is of crucial importance. Consequently, both lay themselves open to criticisms of arbitrarily delimiting the domain of grammatical description to the sentence (cf. Delisle 1973), since such a view in order to be consistent must acknowledge that it is essentially the same processes that operate across sentence boundaries as within.

The referential index convention itself, i.e. divorced from the condition of lexical identity, is the formulation of the assumption that the internal structure of proforms can be assessed on the basis of the internal structure of NPs. Yet here, too, there are difficulties. It is, for example, not always clear which determiner is involved in (one or both of) the two NPs between which relativization is supposed to hold. Cf. in this connection Kuroda (1971: 184 fn 6) where this point is dismissed as not constituting a 'serious drawback' for the argument advanced (in support of Karttunen (1971)), because the apparent violation of the constraint on backwards pronominalization (disallowed when two indefinite NPs are involved) is avoided since 'eventually [the trigger of backwards pronominalization] is replaced by a relative pronoun, *which one can reasonably assume to be definite*' (my emphasis). In other words, a deep structurally indefinite NP is 'replaced' by something which is assumed to be definite. Moreover, it is not even clear that this 'replacement' can occur since, presumably, it presupposes the application of a process which, however, is blocked by the presence of two indefiniteness markers.

Disregarding such difficulties, the classical position rests on the assumption – not always fulfilled, cf. Partee (1970: 370) – that there is a relation (of reference) between words and things, to put it informally and somewhat simplistically. If this relation holds between two words (in the same sentence) and only one thing, then a secondary, parasitic relation (of co-reference) is said to hold between the two words.

In order to be able to state these matters in a slightly more sophisticated manner, let us establish a distinction between entities of various levels. We shall say that an entity of level zero is a non-linguistic entity (a thing, a person, a thought, an emotion, etc.), and that an entity of level one is a linguistic entity (a word, a sentence, a NP, a VP, etc.). See Sørensen (1958: 17ff) for a more detailed discussion of the notion of 'level' in this connection, including an expansion of this simple, basic scheme to cover a level 2 (a metalinguistic level), and a discussion of the possibilities for restricting the number of 'metalevels'.[1] Dependent on this distinction we shall say that an *inter*-level relation is a relation holding between entities of different levels, whereas an *intra*-level relation holds between entities of the same level.

With these points in mind we can now reformulate the classical position. In order to account for pronominalization, advocates of position AI assume the existence of an inter-level relation (of reference). If two entities of level one contract an inter-level relation with the same entity of level zero, then an intra-level relation (of co-reference) is inferred between the two level one entities in question. Schematically the situation is as follows:

(1)    the dog chased its tail

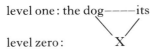

Investigation into co-reference is to be conducted within the syntactical and/or the semantical framework. Therefore the inferred (intra-) relation is promoted to primary status, and the inter-relations are left for philosophers and logicians to explore.

In contrast, the advocates of position B – and particularly of BII – are engaged in describing a 'purely' linguistic relationship. The diagram which reflects this position is:

(2)    level one: the dog[2]_____its

Substitution is an intra-level relation which holds between entities of

---

[1] The relevant problems of *suppositio materialis* (or *hypostasis*), among which is the prominent notion of 'reflexive' reference, will not be gone into here. As for my views on these matters they tally with the conclusions reached by Jakobsen (1977), one of which is that hypostasis-forms are material objects *without* meaning (in fact belong to the object level). Adopting this view we can restrict our attention to just the two levels mentioned above without needing to postulate the existence of an infinite number of metalevels. At the same time it is not altogether an uncontroversial view.

[2] This is not quite correct as far as Harweg is concerned. To him *the dog* would be a pronoun, or a two-dimensional syntagmatic substituens. Substitution holds between *a dog* and *the dog* in precisely the same manner as between *a dog* and *its*. This imprecision does not affect the point being made, however.

level one, and no consideration is given to what possible inter-level relations entities of level one may contract. Such a view is in many ways attractive, and the results it gives rise to are both powerful and interesting. Yet it fails to account exhaustively for many aspects of pronominal usage. To mention but one point, it cannot account for first and second person personal pronouns. If we want to give an account of the functions of pronouns we must take note of the inter-level relations contracted by them.

This, precisely, is what Collinson does in his largely neglected study of 'indicaters' in various languages. Collinson's starting-point is notional, and his aim is to describe the semantic field of *indication*. This latter term is explained as the notional content of those linguistic items that either 'point' to entities (occurrents) or 'mark' them as foci of continued interest for the benefit of the listener. Under this approach a number of traditionally rather disparate items are brought together (articles, pronouns, case-, tense-, and aspect-markers, prepositions, adverbials of certain semantic types, and an assortment of isolated phrases and constructions). The work is, in fact, an early attempt to explicate (what is now called) deixis from a semantic point of view, and it contains a number of shrewd and original observations. However, it does not attempt to explicate the relationship between pronominal function and internal composition. Furthermore, although the basic notion is 'indication' (i.e. in my terms (one of) the relation(s) between entities of levels one and zero), it in fact foreshadows the classical TG-position AI with respect to third person personal pronouns. These are seen as primarily anaphoric. My reason for classifying Collinson's work as a work of type III is then that the anaphoric relation itself is conceived of as a specific kind of indication, namely, *indication within a context, or referential indication* (title of Collinson's chapter 3).

Apart from the complexities arising from failure to distinguish the two aspects of pronominal analysis alluded to above, matters are further complicated by consideration of what might at first sight appear to be yet a third aspect, the syntactic *process* of pronominalization. Langacker (1966) and Postal (1971) seek to pinpoint the *conditions* under which pronominalization occurs or does not occur. Though seemingly of a quite fundamental syntactic nature, such investigations presuppose acceptance of a particular view on the relationship between antecedent and pronoun, in both instances the notion of co-reference (see especially Postal 1971: 8 fn 8). But since the intricacies of co-reference as such have not yet been unravelled, and since reasonable doubts can be raised as to the importance of the notion as a tool for an exhaustive analysis of pronouns (cf. Partee 1970), it may be considered a somewhat slender basis for the analysis of the syntactic process of pronominalization.

The problems of pronominalization and the various concomitant phenomena behind the tabulation of approaches above are highlighted by Stockwell, Schachter & Partee (1973: ch. 4) partly by the fact that their treatment of pronouns would fall within almost every compartment of table 1, dependent as it is not only on Postal's segmentalization theory, but also on co-reference (reflexives) and substitution (their anaphora) (simple pronouns),[3] partly in a more explicit form:

It seems, then, that our attempt to push the L[ees] K[lima] approach to pronominalization to its limits, while not entirely successful, has uncovered some interesting and non-trivial problems which have counterparts in the referential indexing approach. Solution to these problems does not appear to be imminent, *since the conditions do not appear to be syntactic in any familiar sense of the word.* (Stockwell, Schachter & Partee 1973: 184; my italics)

Although the sentiment expressed in this passage is often implicit, it is rarely found so explicitly stated as here. I take it to be an expression of the authors' awareness of the limitations of syntactic analysis as currently enforced, and at the same time as an invitation to explore what other possibilities there might be for coming to grips with the problems of pronouns and pronominalization.

As will become clearer I shall seek to establish an approach to pronominal analysis that would fall into CIII, that is, a position whereby a pronoun is regarded as a linguistic item the basic function of which is to *refer*, and the internal composition of which may be described as a syncretism of such syntactic and semantic features as are elsewhere spelled out as noun phrases.

## 1.2   Linguistic relations and linguistic models

Since the beginning of the present century a predominant part of the

---

[3]   They regard the part of their approach which is based on substitution as a continuation of the Lees & Klima position which is here considered to be co-referential – rather than substitutional – because, to me, it seems rather to be a precursor of the referential indexing approach than an alternative to it. It just so happens that the referential index had not yet been introduced in discussions of these phenomena when their paper was written. Cf. this with the parallelism between the two approaches commented upon in the quoted passage above.

writing on language has been implicitly or explicitly structuralist, in the sense that it has approached the description and classification of linguistic entities through investigations of the relations obtaining among them. This holds for the various (European and American) structuralist schools proper, for stratificational, systemic, and relational grammar, and, to a smaller extent, for transformational-generative grammar as the latter was originally conceived by Chomsky. I shall not go into an account here of all of these schools, nor of the various relations proposed by them. I want rather to restrict myself to a brief and general survey of just one well-known grammatical relation and the treatment it receives in the general framework of two models for grammatical description. The relation in question is, in Bloomfield's terms, the endocentric relation of subordination.

Subordination is the name of a binary, grammatical relation with the properties transitive, asymmetric, irreflexive and non-inclusive. This means that

(3)   (a) if x is subordinate to y, and y is subordinate to z, then x is subordinate to z;

(b) if x is subordinate to y, then y cannot be subordinate to x;[4]

(c) if x is subordinate to y, then y $\neq$ x;

(d) if x is subordinate to y, then x cannot be included in y, nor can y be included in x.

Those models for grammatical analysis in which this relation plays a prominent part may be called *dependency grammars* (DG).[5] The class of DG is set off against a class of *constituency grammars* (CG), the basic relation of which is *be a constituent of*. The properties of this relation are transitive, asymmetric, and inclusive. This means that

(4)   (a) if x is a constituent of y, and y is a constituent of z, then x is a constituent of z;

(b) if x is a constituent of y, then y cannot be a constituent of x;[6]

---

[4]   A symmetric subordination-relation is not entirely unheard of. It forms part of Hjelmslev's (1939; 1943: 23f) set of relations, where it is given the name *interdependence*.

[5]   Various aspects of such models are developed and discussed by Anderson (1971a, b; 1977); Bauer (1979); Baumgärtner (1970); Dahl (1971); Gaïfmann (1965); Happ (1976); Hays (1964); Helbig (1971); Hjelmslev (1939); Kunze (1975); Robinson (1970a, b); Tesnière (1959); Vater (1975).

[6]   It is in general not true that whenever x is a constituent of y, then y is a constituent of x. However, in certain cases special – optional choice – rules permit a particular occurrence of a constituency rule to be symmetric, or partially so: S $\rightarrow$ NP VP; NP $\rightarrow$ NP (S). Cf. also footnote 4.

(c) if x is a constituent of y, then x is included in y.[7]

Among the class of CG the type developed by Chomsky and discussed in detail by Postal (1964) has been particularly influential. It is generally known as Phrase Structure Grammar (PSG).

It is a widely held belief that the grammatical description of a natural language should be of the constituency variety, constituency being assumed to reflect the organization and structure of natural languages (cf. Sampson (1975: ch. 5, also 129ff) for a good discussion of this point which he accepts without question). However, as appears from a comparison of the predicates which define their basic relations, DG and CG are not entirely dissimilar (they are, in fact, weakly equivalent; Gaifmann 1965).

Yet one disparity, flowing from their difference with respect to the property of inclusiveness, merits some attention. It is possible in a DG directly to identify the *head* of a construction on the basis of the non-inclusive nature of the subordination-relation. No such direct identification is possible in CG, where the (constituents counting in DG as) head and modifier are simply co-constituents of the construction that contains them, and no direct relation can be postulated between them. If the notions of 'head' and 'modifier' play any significant role in the grammatical description of natural languages, DG is superior to CG to the extent to which it allows identification of these notions. That importance is attached to them, even among proponents of CG, appears from the fact that the 'head' is referred to in certain proposed constraints on transformations (Ross' *Complex NP Constraint* – Ross 1967: 70; also the constraints (2.26) (p. 17), and (4.206) (p. 119)), and from the notational (X-bar) revisions proposed by Chomsky (1970), the most immediate result of which is that the head of a construction can now be legitimately identified in CG (cf. Robinson 1970b: 274, Akmajian & Lehrer 1976). I return to this issue in §4.3.2 when I have narrowed down the field of enquiry.

Apart from the immediate question of 'headship', the insistence on employing a pure CG-model for grammatical description has had a

---

[7]   The inclusive nature of the constituency relation makes the property of reflexiveness redundant. It has been discussed whether a category, x, should be permitted to be rewritten as xy, where y might be null, or as $x_i x_j \ldots x_n$. It is clear that any constituent, z, may be regarded as 'containing' any number of identical constituents. Such a description would appear to be needed for co-ordination, at least. It seems to me to be empty, however, to permit also the 'pure' reflexive relationship whereby x might be rewritten simply as x.

more far-reaching consequence. If we compare the set of relations described by Bloomfield with the set of relations that find a place in CG – excluding as irrelevant in this context Langacker's command-relation (Langacker 1966) – we notice that only two of Bloomfield's relations are accommodated within CG: one corresponding to Bloomfield's relation of exocentricity, and one corresponding to his relation of endocentric co-ordination. Since these are the only syntactic relations defined by a phrase-marker, it follows that also those constructions that Bloomfield would call subordinate must be described on the basis of one or both of these. This point brings us to the topic of the next section.

## 1.3 Predicational structure and explanatory adequacy

One of the most sweeping trends in the recent development in linguistic analysis has been the adoption of what might be called the V-centred view of the sentence. Such an approach to linguistics can be compared to – and is in many instances directly inspired by – the predicate calculus of logistics. It has superseded the earlier, S-P-structured view held by Chomsky and many others, which bears a resemblance to classical subject-predicate logic. Even explicit followers of Chomsky, like Jackendoff (1972), have abandoned the latter strategy in favour of the former.

One of the reasons for the recent predominance of V-centricity is the contention that lexical selection based on primacy of the selection of nouns may have awkward consequences for the eventual choice of verb, whereas the reverse does not hold – at least not if modification is made of Chomsky's general ideas about lexical insertion, as suggested by Seuren (1969: §3.2, particularly 64–6). Furthermore, the abandonment of the notion of deep-structure subject – as first proposed by Fillmore (1968) – solves many of the problems envisaged by Chomsky if verbs were selected independently of nouns since his arguments for independent noun-selection involve reference to the notions of subject and object (Chomsky 1965: §2.3.4, esp. 92f). Cf. on this point also Chafe (1970: 97ff).

In conjunction with the lack of the subordination relation, this trend has in turn led to considerable uniformity in the analyses proposed for a number of more or less disparate syntagms: almost all linguistic data, from straightforward sentence (or clause) constructions and down to matters of quantification, negation, interrogation, etc. are being viewed in terms of a hierarchy of *predications* (i.e. exocentric constructions), all of which are to be interrelated, embedded, pruned, and reduced – indeed, even annulled – in a great variety of ways.

The methodological principle behind this uniformity is dictated by an attempt to satisfy the requirements of the evaluation-criterion known as explanatory adequacy.

The originator of this phrase is Chomsky (esp. 1964). There three levels of adequacy for linguistic description are introduced and discussed, *observational adequacy*, *descriptive adequacy*, and *explanatory adequacy*. I disregard the first of these.

The level of success attained by a descriptively adequate analysis is measured by the degree to which it accounts for the native speaker's intuitions concerning observational linguistic data, and to which it allows for the making of significant generalizations about the data it presents. A great number of different analyses are descriptively adequate in this sense.

The level of success attained by an explanatorily adequate theory is measured by the degree to which it provides a well-motivated and principled basis for selecting one particular descriptively adequate analytic framework against (all) others.

Since we are left in no doubt that the level of explanatory adequacy is 'higher' than both the levels of observation and description, the emphasis has been not so much on giving a merely descriptively adequate analysis of linguistic data as on specifying a principled way in which a *particular* descriptively adequate analysis may be chosen against others. Consider, for example, Lakoff's underlying structure for (one interpretation of ) *100 soldiers shot two students* (G. Lakoff 1970: 179):

(5)

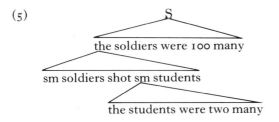

The basis for this analysis is the intuitive semantic affinity between one member of a given construction-type, *BA*, and one member of a different construction-type, *A is B*. But instead of these two construction-types being regarded as equipollent, derivational directionality has been imposed on the formula $BA = A$ *is* $B$, turning it into $A$ *is* $B \Rightarrow BA$.

In this way Lakoff not only seeks to instantiate a significant generalization at the descriptive level, but also to explain the intuitive semantic affinity between the two types of structure.

What is of especial interest to us in the present context is the relationship between these two evaluation measures and the form of language.

Let me first distinguish between a *grammar* ( =a system of rules designed for the analysis of a particular language), and a *theory* ( =a hypothesis concerning the nature and organization of possible grammars, formulated in such a way that it may at the same time serve as a means of comparison between and evaluation of various grammars). Of these it is the grammar that may (or may not) be descriptively adequate, whereas it is the theory – and hence, secondarily, the grammar – that may (or may not) be explanatorily adequate (see esp. Chomsky 1964: 29, 32, 34, 36; 1965: 25ff).

Chomsky's theory may be characterized by the predicates 'creative', 'neutral' (as between production and understanding of utterances), and 'ontogenetic'. The grammar may be described as transformational, generative, and compartmentalized. Our main concern is the creativity imputed to the theory.

The creative aspect of the theory is the basis for the transformational nature of the grammar; it is the aspect that covers the fact that we are able to produce and understand utterances never heard by us before – and one of the factors of this ability is the transformational relationships holding between various sentences.

With these points in mind we may now look into the relationship between explanatory adequacy and the form of language. The explanation involved is supposed to be an explanation of the 'inner form of language' (in a Humboldtian sense), to verify a given assumption about the form of language (Chomsky 1965: 26–7; cf. also the passages quoted by Derwing (1973: 61) from Chomsky & Halle (1965)).

It follows from this that the formal properties of the grammar are supposed to reflect, in greater or less detail, the formal structure of *language*. Consequently, when one of the formal properties of the grammar is to analyze certain superficially non-predicational structures as transforms of underlying predications, it would seem to suggest that the inner form of language *is* structured more or less uniformly in terms of predications, or at least that predicational structure is basic in some sense.

This, of course, is a fallacy. The starting-point was a given *assumption* about linguistic form. Any demonstration of the validity of this assumption on the basis of formal properties growing out of it is therefore (malignantly – cf. Bar-Hillel 1953) circular.

Furthermore, the theoretical characteristics impose no requirement on the grammar to the effect that it should operate on the basis of predicational analysis. That it should do so on a number of occasions is obvious, but the basis for the recognition of this fact lies within the scope of descriptive (and observational) adequacy.

One more factor is relevant to the present topic. A theoretical principle of some historical standing appears both to include and also in some sense to oppose Chomsky's principle of creativity. I am thinking of Hjelmslev's principle of translatability (1943: 97), Searle's principle of expressibility (1969: 19ff), and Katz' principle of effability (1972: 18ff), the origin of which is traced by Katz to Frege (Katz 1972: 19). Let me first show what I mean by saying that Chomsky's principle of creativity is included in (what I shall call, following Searle) the principle of expressibility:

> The hypothesis that the speech act is the basic unit of communication, taken together with the principle of expressibility, suggests that there are a series of analytic connections between the notion of speech act, what the speaker means, what the sentence (or other linguistic element) uttered means, what the speaker intends, what the hearer understands, and what the rules governing the linguistic elements are. (Searle 1969: 21)

Insofar as the principle of creativity is the theoretical basis for the transformational capacity of the grammar, it is included among the various notions between which 'a series of analytic connections' holds, in particular in the last one of those listed. Obviously, linguistic rules – and among them transformational rules – constitute an important factor in the availability of linguistic material for the expression of a particular meaning, and thus in the performance of a speech act. But they are – equally obviously – not the *only* deciding factor. The point is made more explicitly by Katz in his demonstration of the inadmissibility of formulating the principle of expressibility (his effability) on the basis of the principle of creativity (Katz 1972: 22), especially by reference to the fact that creativity is a feature of the (recursive nature of the) *rule-*

system which governs a language, artificial as well as natural, rather than of the *language*.

This observation at the same time constitutes what amounts to what I called the opposition between the two principles of expressibility and creativity. Whereas the principle of expressibility is a characteristic of natural language – cf. in this connection Hjelmslev's (1943: 97) definition of 'everyday language' as the semiotic into which all other semiotics can be translated – the principle of creativity is a characteristic of the *rules* that govern language use, and only some of the rules at that.

We can illustrate this difference by reference to an example not dissimilar to the one quoted from Lakoff above (5), which his analysis should cover:

(6)   (a) many soldiers died in vain
      (b) the soldiers who died in vain were many.

According to Lakoff (1970: 178) a quantified subject NP may be ambiguous; hence (6)(a) may derive from either of

(7)   (a)

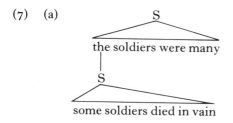

(b)

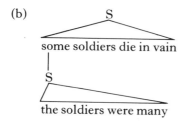

whereas (6)(b) presumably may derive only from (7)(a).

Even if it is conceded that (6)(a) and (b) may be cognitively synonymous, there are several minor details which such an analysis leaves unclear, especially with respect to the assignment of definiteness and indefiniteness in the determiner and the assignment of tense to the verbs. Whichever interpretation is given to (6)(a) or (b) it should be clear that the set of soldiers that died in vain and the set of soldiers that were many should be the same set. Lakoff does not avail himself of referential indices for this purpose, and it is not clear that set-identity can be achieved by an analysis in which both definites and indefinites may be either superordinate or subordinate. Furthermore, it is not clear why the superordinate verb in (7)(b) should be non-tensed (or present?) while it is tensed (past) in (7)(a) (cf. Lakoff's phrase-markers F-77 and F-78, 1970: 178). As will be appreciated, all of these details are of a referential nature.

What Lakoff does in his discussion of examples such as these is to avail himself of the principle of expressibility – the fact that natural language provides a precise expression for a given content – but pretends that it is the principle of creativity. In this way a transformational connection is posited between pairs of sentences whose cognitive similarities are due to the principle of expressibility with which the transformational component is not connected in any inferential manner.

The point I have been trying to make can perhaps be made in the following more direct manner. Due to Chomsky's demand for explanation in linguistic theory, a large amount of attention has been devoted to analyzing observable linguistic data in as uniform a way as possible; and since predicational analysis is needed anyway in a grammar that purports to be descriptively adequate it has come to play an increasingly important role in the analysis of syntagms that are not superficially predicational. By the interrelation between explanatory adequacy and linguistic form, the stage seems to have been reached where 'explanation' is considered to be tantamount to demonstrating a – more or less plausible – predicational source for non-predicational syntagms. An inferential link has been assumed between the explanatory adequacy of the theory and the predicational structure of the descriptive framework. This link is spurious on two counts. Firstly because it rests on an assumption which it cannot itself verify (or falsify); secondly because it rests on an unjustifiable equation of the two distinct principles of expressibility and creativity.

The main argument advanced in the present work is that certain linguistic data, although capable of analysis within a predicational framework – in virtue of the principle of expressibility – are in fact more readily amenable to a different kind of analysis, the nearest parallel to which outside linguistics is the calculus of classes in logic. What is presented here is an alternative analysis of certain kinds of linguistic data to the (by now almost standard) predicational analysis that they have received. The spirit in which this alternative is presented owes much to the following formulation:

Examples that lie beyond the scope of a grammar are quite innocuous unless they show the superiority of some alternative grammar. They do not show that the grammar as already formulated is incorrect. Examples that contradict the principles formulated in some general theory show that, to at least this extent, the theory is incorrect and needs revision. Such examples become important if they can be shown to have some bearing on alternative conceptions of linguistic structure. (Chomsky 1964: 54–5)

# 2 *The philosophical preliminaries*

## 2.0 Introductory comments on 'meaning'

It is the ultimate task of semantics to describe the meaning of the words, phrases and sentences in particular languages and in language generally. This ultimate goal can only be achieved through the achievement of various intermediate goals: (a) a definition or explanation of the term 'meaning'; (b) the development of a notational system in which meanings may be articulated; and (c) the development of a system of general rules matching the meanings of given words, phrases and sentences with particular notational specifications. The achievement of these intermediate tasks would enable us to fill in statements of the following form: (a) 'meaning is __', or 'meanings are __'; (b) 'the notational specification x is a specification (representation) of a meaning'; and (c) 'the notational specification x is a specification (representation) of the meaning of y, because __'. The issues relating to (a) will be considered under the general heading of different *approaches* to the notion of meaning, those pertaining to (b) under *semantic representation*, and those that come under (c) under the term *semantic analysis*.

Although many diverse answers have been given to the question 'What is meaning?' throughout the history of linguistics and philosophy (e.g. physical entities, modes of signifying, mental images, concepts, ideas, the uses of words, speaker's stimulus/hearer's response) it appears that only two answers need be taken seriously: (1) meaning is a *set of conditions*; and (2) meaning is a *set of relations*.

The approach to meaning whereby it is seen as a set of conditions is the foundation of any truth-based semantics. The meaning of a word, w, is said to be the set of conditions to be satisfied by a non-linguistic entity, e, for e to be properly denoted by w. The set of conditions is here called denotative conditions (Sørensen 1967). In the same vein, the meaning of a sentence, s, is the (necessary and sufficient) set of

22

conditions that a state of affairs must satisfy in order for (the proposition, p, expressed by) s to be true. The set of conditions is called truth-conditions (Kempson 1974: 32; 1977: ch. 3). It is quite clear that this approach to meaning avails itself of the inter-level relationships in the sense explained above (p. 10).

On the other valid approach, the meaning of a word, w, is the set of paradigmatic (and syntagmatic) relations of sense that w contracts with other words (Lyons 1968: 428; 1977: 204), and the meaning of a sentence, s, is the set of inferential relationships contracted by s (Kempson 1977: §3.4.3). This approach exploits intra-level relationships.

Priority may be claimed for one or the other of these two approaches over the other, the limiting cases being represented by Sørensen (1967), who would explain any aspect of meaning in terms of denotative conditions, and Bar-Hillel whose scorn for what he calls the dictionary approach to semantics is manifest in much of his writing (e.g. 1967a,b, and 1969).

In stating that there are just two approaches to the notion of meaning I appear to be excluding from consideration what is seemingly a valid third kind of approach, which enjoys widespread support at present, namely, speech acts semantics. This is not so. Speech acts semantics is one embodiment of a functional view of language and it takes in elements from both of the two approaches outlined above in various ways. Austin's wish to play Old Harry with, especially, the true/false fetish has been detrimental to semantics in that it has invited the view that speech acts semantics is an alternative to truth-conditional semantics, whereas in fact it is an *addition* to, or general framework for, it.[1]

If this seems to be a rather too sweeping statement, consider just one line of argument. Is the English verb *to lie* a performative verb? Well . . . We are told by Austin that *to state* is *not* a performative (Austin 1962: 61, 65), so *to lie* is probably not one either. Yet *stating* is an illocutionary act (Austin 1962: Lecture XI), so *lying* might be considered to be one also. This is borne out by the test for verbs defining illocutionary acts (Austin 1962: 126f). Now *if* lying is an illocutionary act we should want

[1] The most consistent and most well-documented attempt to establish speech acts semantics as an alternative to truth-dependent semantics since Searle (1969) is that by Mortensen (1972). This work, unfortunately, is only accessible in Danish, but it contains a summary in English. The recurrent argument is based on the Austinian notion of speaker's commitment.

the general theory of speech acts to characterize the salient points of lying, for example along the lines adopted by Searle for the analysis of promising (Searle 1969: 54ff). But this would mean that all the usual problems of truth and falsehood must be accounted for (or accountable for) in speech acts terms.

Austin nowhere considers the verb *to lie*. But he does give a number of indications throughout that the problems of truth and falsehood are important to speech acts semantics. What he aims his major guns at is not truth and falsehood *in abstracto*, but rather the all-or-nothing status they have been given in discussions of meaning. And this point is hardly in dispute.

The theoretical framework to be developed in Part II is not inspired by the Austinian brand of speech acts semantics. Yet I suppose it might be called a version of speech acts semantics if only because it relies heavily on what speakers, signs, and hearers *do*.

Before continuing, let me state explicitly that a sign, to me, is a linguistic entity consisting of a phonic (graphic) *expression* which has a *meaning*. Although the biplane sign of Saussure and Hjelmslev is by no means universally accepted – due to understandable qualms about what sort of things meanings are – it seems to me uncontroversially true that nothing can be a sign unless it expresses a meaning. This view does not, however, commit me to an explication of a psychological *nébuleuse* in terms of which meanings are to be described.

Let us now look at the question of semantic representation, or the establishment of a notational system whereby meanings can be articulated. Again, a number of widely different proposals have been made, but they all fall into one of three general types: (a) a 'formal' type which exploits only mathematical and/or logical symbols; (b) a 'natural' type which avails itself of (what in other circumstances would count as normal) natural language signs; and (c) a 'mixed' type, drawing on (a) and (b).

An important point now is that the adoption of a particular approach to meaning does not invite a specific type of semantic representation. The statement of this obvious point might appear to be superfluous were it not for the fact that it is sometimes not given due credit. Thus componential analysis – which is a 'natural' type of semantic representation – is sometimes presented as if it is, in itself, a form of semantic analysis. Yet componential analysis is neutral with respect to the approach to meaning for which it serves as a notational device, and hence it may be part of any kind of semantic analysis.

Semantic analysis is a general procedure for describing the meaning of words, phrases and sentences in language. The form of particular semantic analyses depends on various combinations of emphasis on one or more of the following three factors: (a) the approach taken to meaning; (b) the form of semantic representation adopted; and (c) the reliance placed on the particular framework designed to account for the syntactic properties of language.

In chapter 3 I shall go into a more detailed discussion of some of these issues, establishing a distinction between syntactico-semantic and referential–semantic analyses. The form of semantic analysis to be developed here will be of the latter variety. That is, it emphasizes the inter-level relationships of meaning such that its statements of meaning indicate what non-linguistic entities we, as speakers, may mention by means of particular words and phrases. It avails itself of a natural form of semantic representation in terms of semantic components. And it relies on a form of syntactic description that incorporates the subordination-relation.

The key notions in this form of semantic analysis will be the equipollent, primitive notions of *location* and *existence*. To say that existence and location are equipollent notions is by no means non-controversial. Throughout the history of (philosophical) semantics various attempts have been made, explicitly or implicitly, to accord primacy to one or the other of these notions relative to the other. Thus the Modists of the Middle Ages had existence as a basis for their realistic models of various modes by which they explained meaning. This tradition is followed most clearly by Russell in 'On Denoting' (1905). Searle (1969: ch. 4) takes location as the primitive notion on which existence is to be explained, whereas Linsky (1967: ch. 8) disallows even the presence of existence as a significant notion in discussions of referentiality. Only Strawson (1950), although paying relatively more respect to location, recognizes the equipollent nature of the two notions. See Thrane (1976: ch. 2) for a rather more detailed discussion and justification of these conclusions.

I am aware that I walk into a jungle of philosophical controversy by invoking especially the notion of existence. The remainder of this chapter will therefore be devoted to an explication of the sense in which I propose to take it and of some of the consequences of that particular view.

## 2.1  Existence and location

In the Aristotelian account of the categorial system the major distinction is between ὀυσία and συμβεβηκός, between substance and accidence. Substances are characterized as having 'being' in some sense; indeed that is what makes them substances. But substances may also be ascribed to the accidental categories of space and time, or – differently formulated – being at a particular place at a particular time may be predicated of (primary) substances. Although in this way there appears to be a distinction between 'existence' on the one hand, 'location' (spatio-temporal) on the other, the slogan 'Whatever is, is somewhere' indicates some sort of interdependence between the two.

One of the critical points in philosophy is the question as to whether 'exist' is a predicate, or, equivalently, whether existence is a property of non-linguistic entities.

Intricately connected with the determination of this question is another point, namely the fact that the verb 'exist' is inherently ambiguous. Moore (1936) and, following him, Pears (1963), though admitting that 'exist' behaves differently from e.g. 'growl' in identical surroundings (*some tame tigers exist* vs. *some tame tigers growl*), avails himself of this fact in order to point out that

(1)   some tame tigers do not exist

both is and is not meaningful. If it is meaningful it is equivalent to *some tame tigers are fictitious tigers*.

This inherent ambiguity is of importance to us since it reflects the basic distinction between existence and location, in the following sense. What Moore's meaningful interpretation of (1) implies is that some entities cannot be spatio-temporally located despite the fact that they can be called tigers, and that some entities can both be spatio-temporally located and called tigers.

I shall now say that the sign 'tiger', when used, *establishes* a category, and further that non-linguistic entities may be *assigned to* or *located in* a category. What Moore's meaningful interpretation of (1) implies in these terms is this:

> There are entities which are locatable in the category 'tiger', some of which are further locatable in space/time.

The point I am making can perhaps be better illustrated if we choose (2) as an example:

(2)   unicorns do not exist.

Employing the terminology just established, (2) states:

> There are entities which are locatable in the category 'unicorn', none of which are further locatable in space/time.

In other words, 'exist' can – at least in everyday language – be used to indicate that the entity denoted by the (lexeme underlying the) subject term in sentences like *x exists* is further locatable in space/time. Let us call this use of 'exist' the predicational use.

## 2.2 Existence and denotation

We are then left with the 'non-predicational' use. This is also embodied in (1)–(2) where it underlies the first half of the paraphrases provided. It is this usage which Sørensen (1959b) subjects to analysis. His conclusion is that 'A exists' is synonymous with '"A" denotes', and that is, as he points out, both a non-startling conclusion, a simple one, and one that has common sense on its side. It is also a conclusion that has nothing to do with determining what there is. If the linguist can rest content with stating that 'to be is to denote', the ontologist would have to begin from 'to be is to be denoted', and this statement gives him no clue as to what *is* denoted. Cf. Quine's slogan 'to be is to be the value of a variable', and in particular his reasons for discarding this slogan as a valid starting-point for determining what *is* a value of a variable (Quine 1953: 15).

Furthermore, Sørensen's catch-phrase has the awkward consequence that A in 'A exists' has to be changed into 'A' in '"A" denotes'. This change from use to mention may be innocuous as long as we are concerned with the relationship between the two sentences. But it certainly does not follow that 'exist' and 'denote' are synonyms. What 'exist' is 'synonymous' with is '"__" denotes', and that is altogether a different story.

'Denotes' in the preceding paragraph is – presumably – to be interpreted as 'denotes *actually*'. Signs may denote potentially. This is the case with 'unicorn'. So the distinction between existence and non-existence is reflected by the linguistic distinction between actual and potential denotation. In addition we can speak of essential and contingent non-denotation. It is an essential fact about (the sense of) 'a round square', 'a married bachelor', etc. that they cannot denote, even potentially. The same thing is expressed by saying that round squares and married bachelors do not have logical existence. On the other hand, it is a contingent fact (about English) that 'quasp' does not denote anything. It might denote, for it conforms to the rules that determine the phonological 'shape' of English signs.

The relevant consequence to be drawn from this is that there is a relationship between 'exist' and 'denote' which has nothing to do with spatio-temporal location and which can be exploited advantageously, provided due notice is given to the use/mention distinction. On the other hand, there is a relationship also between existence and location, in the sense that existence may be seen as *categorial* location.

## 2.3  Existence as categorial location

The easiest way to explain what I mean by saying that existence may be seen as categorial location is to consider an example. If I point to a particular animal in the Copenhagen Zoo and tell my daughter 'That is a tiger', (part of) what I do might be described as follows: (i) I direct her attention to a particular non-linguistic entity by means of my gesture and my use of the word *that*; (ii) I inform her that language offers the label 'tiger' by which that particular entity may be mentioned when she gets home; (iii) depending on my daughter's degree of linguistic sophistication, I may have informed her that language offers the label 'tiger' by which animals similar to the particular one she was shown may be mentioned.[2]

I should wish to capture (ii) in the following general formula:

(3)   To say of a non-linguistic entity, x, that it is a tiger is to assign x to the categorial location 'tiger'.

The validity of (3), however, depends on the validity of:

(4)   'tiger' denotes.

That this is so follows from the possibility of saying·

(5)   (a) To say of a non-linguistic entity, x, that it is a round square is to assign x to the categorial location 'round square';
(b) to say of a non-linguistic entity, x, that it is a quasp is to assign x to the categorial location 'quasp'.

(5) cannot be disqualified directly; they must be disqualified indirectly, by disqualifying:

(6)   (a) 'round square' denotes
(b) 'quasp' denotes.

[2]  This is the question of the relative status of individuals and universals, which it is not my aim to pursue further. I know from experience that it takes a number of showings to secure *stripes* (as opposed to *dots*) as criterial for tigers in a 3-year-old.

Since both of (6) are false – (a) necessarily (b) contingently – both of (5) are disqualified in the sense that no categories are established by 'round square' and 'quasp' to which x may be assigned.

It is now readily seen that what I did under (ii) above was to inform my daughter of the correct structure of a sign, plus something else that need not concern us here: the phonetic sequence /taigə/ establishes a particular categorial location in virtue of having a particular meaning. Generally, signs establish categorial locations in virtue of their meaning.

## 2.4 Categorial and spatio-temporal location

The term 'categorial location' is, of course, a metaphor derived from 'spatio-temporal location' which is supposed to make explicit the inter-relations between existence and location. These interrelations may be brought out in the following fashion:

(7)   Tigers exist $\begin{cases}$ (a) The phonological sequence /taigə/ establishes the categorial location 'tiger' to which non-linguistic entities may be legitimately assigned; \\ (b) Some entities (of C-location[3] 'tiger') may be assigned to spatio-temporal location y. $\end{cases}$

Here 'exist' is used in its everyday sense, which is spelled out in (b); (a) on the other hand, is the spelling out of the 'non-predicational' use of 'exist'.

The parallelism between (7)(a) and (b) is brought out further if (3) is compared to:

(8)   To say of a non-linguistic entity, x, that it is on the roof, is to assign x to the spatio-temporal location constituted by the referent of 'the roof'.

I shall now say that phrases like 'on the roof' establish ST-locations. In this way we posit a distinction between two types of sign, one that *denotes* and one that *indicates*:

(9)   (a) If '__' denotes then it establishes a categorial location;
      (b) If '__' indicates then it establishes a spatio-temporal location.

Indicating signs like 'on the roof' are subject to considerations of well-formedness in two respects. This one depends for its validity not only on the validity of 'roof denotes', but also on (grammatical) well-formedness; cf. *between the roof, *among the roof.

---

[3]   I shall avail myself, on occasion, of the abbreviations C-location ( = categorial location) and ST-location ( = spatio-temporal location).

## 2.5  Reference and referentiality

Philosophical discussions of reference often delimit the area of interest to the area of categorical, singular, definite reference (thus Searle (1969) and, implicitly, Linsky (1967)), thereby implying that other kinds of reference might be envisaged. Whatever the reasons for this delimitation might be, they are hardly good reasons for a linguistic treatment of reference, as we might expect there to be structural relationships between different types of referring expression which thus tend to be glossed over, but which might in fact yield insights into the nature of linguistic reference if they were considered together.

Instead of restricting the area of potential interest to a specific kind of reference at the outset, I shall adopt a rather different strategy (to be gone into in detail in chapter 4).

I propose to call the general area within which I am writing here the field of *referentiality*. This is a cover-term for any aspect of linguistic structure which may be related to the referential function of language. That is, referentiality is the set of properties of language in virtue of which we may employ language in a referential function.

The present study starts from the assumption that the referentiality of language has as its core those properties that ensure that signs establish locations, categorial and spatio-temporal. These properties are of a semantic nature, since signs establish locations in virtue of their meaning.

# PART II: THE THEORY

For, how can that be false, which every tongue
  Of every mortal man affirms for true?
SIR JOHN DAVIES *Nosce Teipsum*

# 3 Some fundamental notions

## 3.1 Referential function and referential potential

A number of points have been raised in a cursory fashion during the first two chapters which we need to take up in more detail. Prominent among these are the notions of the referential function of language and the distinction between different forms of semantic analysis.

It is universally accepted these days, I think, that there is no causal relationship between words and things. That which we call a rose by any other name would smell as sweet. Although this point may be held to be trivial now, one of the implications of it merits some attention. Since it is an important point, and since it has not been generally appreciated, if at all, I shall state it as concisely and as forcefully as I can:

(1)   There is no logical requirement on language, conceived of as a rule-governed system of signs, that it should correlate with things, events, states of affairs, etc. at all. Differently formulated: It does not necessarily follow from the fact that we can *speak* that we should be able also to speak *about* something.

The uninterpreted, formal languages of logicians give substance to (1). Since natural languages differ from formal languages at least in respect of being 'interpreted' we may say, in spite of (1), that there *are* correlations between signs and things, but that these correlations must be contingent rather than necessary.

The contingency of the inter-level relations of meaning is behind a number of important phenomena. It is the reason why we can speak meaningfully about a referential *function* of language, and it is behind two of the design features of language, namely, the design features of prevarication and of displacement (cf. Hockett 1958: 354, 579; and Lyons 1977: 80f, 83f). The latter sums up the fact that we can employ language to speak about things and events even if they are absent from the utterance-situation. It may or may not converge with the former, which I consider one of the most outstanding characteristics of natural language. It may be seen as a coin, the reverse of which makes language suitable as a vehicle of lies (cf. Weinrich 1966), the obverse of which equips language as the medium of literature ('afactual writing' – cf. in particular Frye 1957: 74ff).

It may, indeed, be difficult to accept (1). What use would language be, it might be said, if we could not employ it to speak about the things around us? I would, on the whole, agree with this objection, but it misses the point. What it does *not* miss, however, is the importance of the referential function of language, which it raises to a point where lack of it would reduce natural language to vacuity.

Quite obviously, the referential function of natural language, though not following logically from the notion of language, is of immense importance. It is inculcated in us from our first inception of language acquisition, indeed to such a degree that we must spend a few years (from 4–6) dissociating ourselves from the false idea that there *are* necessary relations between words and things which this inculcation gave rise to. My 4-year-old daughter Louise's realization that she does not have to be 'Louise' *all* the time, but may be 'Marie' for a while, and that a particular chair need not always be 'my chair' but may on occasion be 'the train' is part of this general process of stripping the world of individuals of the labels that it took so much work to attach to them.

I take the design feature of prevarication to be the defining characteristic of natural language which entails that the inter-level relation between entities of levels one and zero is a potential relation which may on occasion be actualized. It is our capacity for lying that constitutes the main argument for the potentiality of the relation – and it is the fact that we do not always lie which is behind the actualization of the relation.

In view of this dogma we may now refine the general concept of the referential function of language into a concept of referential functions of particular signs performed by them on specific occasions. Thus when a speaker performs a speech act of reference (in the sense of Searle 1969), he employs linguistic entities in a particular referential function.

This formulation is intended to establish a distinction between the properties of linguistic entities and the use a speaker may make of these properties. Such a distinction, it seems to me, is necessary. For example: a noun phrase of a given form, say, *the man in the brown jacket*, may on occasion be used by a speaker to refer to a particular man ('refer' in the sense of Searle). To say this is to say that this noun phrase may be used as a singular, definite, categorical referring expression. In contrast, a noun phrase like *some ten men in brown jackets* cannot be used to refer to a particular man on a given occasion, at least not without violation of one or more of Grice's (1975) principles for communicative interaction. A natural way in which to formulate these facts is to say that a noun phrase of a given form has a certain referential potential. It is incumbent on speakers to know at least part of the referential potential of the signs they employ for particular communicative purposes. (I return to this point in chapter 4.)

It is the task of the referential theory to account for the referential potential of linguistic entities. Since the referential potential of a linguistic entity is (or can be considered to be) a property of that entity, and since linguistics is the science that accounts for the properties of linguistic entities, it follows that the referential theory is a linguistic theory.

## 3.2 Syntactico-semantic and referential-semantic analyses

I shall now turn to the other point mentioned above, the distinction between different forms of semantic analyses, and I shall do so in connection with Frege's ontological terminology. Non-linguistic entities, it will be recalled, are held to be level-zero entities, whereas linguistic entities are entities of level one. Applying this distinction to the terms in Frege's overall ontological system – which comprises the term-pairs 'object'/'concept', 'argument'/'function', and 'proper name'/ 'predicate' – we find that objects, concepts, arguments, and functions are entities of level zero, whereas proper names and predicates are entities of level one (Frege 1891, 1892a, 1892b). What is of interest here is the difference (if any) between objects and arguments, and between concepts and functions. He does not give any explicit answer to this question himself, but by tracing his usage a precise distinction can be drawn.

This distinction is a functional one. In the three papers most central to the issue (referred to above), Frege invariably associates the pair 'object'/'concept' with reference (his *'Bedeutung'*), whereas arguments and functions are never spoken of as being references of anything. These two latter terms are rather used whenever he wishes to speak about the relations holding between different kinds of entities of level zero. Drawing on the distinction between inter- and intra-level relations, the situation can be formulated as follows:

> Whenever a level-zero entity is considered to be a term of an intra-relation, it is said to be either an argument or a function;
>
> whenever a level-zero entity is considered to be a term of an inter-relation, it is said to be either an object or a concept.

The asymmetry inherent in Frege's terminology – created by the fact that only one pair of terms denotes level-one entities against two pairs that denote level-zero entities – has no damaging consequences for his theories because, to Frege, signs of level one were mathematical symbols and because mathematical operations were incomprehensible if they were considered operations with signs dissociated from the objects symbolized by those signs (1891: 22). Therefore he could (and did) regard mathematical operations as performed with objects, and hence there was no need to introduce terms for level-one entities corresponding to 'argument' and 'function'.

When it comes to the analysis of language signs, however, such a pair of terms is called for, as recognized, for example, by Reichenbach (1947: 80–1), who speaks of 'argument-names' and 'function-names' in addition to 'subject' and 'predicate', if only for the following reason:

(2)  (a) Caesar Gallos vicit

(b) Galli a Caesare victi sunt.

Since there obtains a converse relationship between (a) and (b) in (2), the cognitive content in both sentences is the same: the same relation between the level-zero entities Caesar and the Gauls is expressed by both sentences. The same converse relationship obtains, for example, between multiplication and division:

(3)  (a)   $3 \times 6 = 18$

(b) $18 \div 6 = 3$

But whereas the converseness between the multiplication sign and the division sign is reflected by the active/passive relationship of the verb in (2), something 'more' has happened to the other signs in (2) as compared with (3) for which there is no non-linguistic reason.

To account for the relationships between the elements which constitute (a) and (b) separately, and for the relationship between them generally, is the traditional task of syntax and morphology, but two distinct aspects are involved:

(4)  (a) A cognitive aspect which is essentially concerned with the distribution of argument-names in relation to a function-name, in terms of which (2)(a) and (b) are identical;

(b) a formal aspect which is essentially concerned with the superficial appearance of the argument-names and function-name.

It is immediately clear from (2), however, that there is no simple one-to-one relationship between these two aspects of the linguistic analysis. In particular, the superficial form of the linguistic items does not follow from the cognitive aspect of the analysis since, in that case, (2)(a) and (b) should have been cognitively as well as formally identical (though not positionally identical).

Let us now return to Frege's terminology. So far I have disregarded the pair 'proper name'/'predicate'. These terms correlate with objects and concepts at level zero in much the same way as post-Fregean 'argument-name' and 'function-name' correlate with his arguments and functions. As is by now obvious, the main distinction between Frege's object and his argument is that whereas an object can be considered in splendid isolation (relative to other level-zero entities), an argument only acquires existence by being considered in relation to a function. Indeed, I believe we would represent Frege honestly by saying that an argument is an object seen in relation to a concept. In this way, what has hitherto been treated as two distinct entities (of level zero) becomes the *same* entity, only seen under two different viewpoints.

If we now apply this technique to entities of level one we see that, for example, 'Caesar' in (2)(a) performs a dual role. From one viewpoint the word 'Caesar' is an argument-name, partaking in the syntactic structure of (2)(a); from another it is a proper name – what Frege called an *actual* proper name (1892b: 58n), designating a particular object. On the basis of these considerations we can now add another aspect of linguistic analysis to those already listed in (4):

(4)   (c) A referential aspect which is essentially concerned with an analysis of those properties of linguistic entities which reflect the conditions under which a given linguistic entity can be said to correlate, actually or potentially, with a given non-linguistic entity.

I shall refer to a linguistic analysis which is concerned with aspect (4)(a) as a *syntactico-semantic* analysis (SS-analysis), and to a linguistic analysis which is concerned with aspect (4)(c) as a *referential–semantic* analysis (RS-analysis). Furthermore, I shall argue that, in order to deal satisfactorily with aspect (4)(b) – the formal aspect – one must in fact take account of the results of the SS-analysis as well as of the RS-analysis.

It would probably be fair to say that the main stream of current linguistic practice runs within the confines of SS-analysis, of which the salient points may be summed up roughly as follows. Heavy reliance is placed on a particular form of syntactic analysis in which predicational structure is taken as axiomatic. Insofar as a specific approach to meaning can be identified it is an intra-level ('syntagmatic') approach, manifest in the prominence of discussions of selectional restrictions and as the basis of synonymy which is the heuristic tool for the demonstration of transformational relationships. No uniform method of semantic representation is prevalent although feature-notations are often employed. These rough points are made even more clear by the fact that when linguists approach matters of a transparently referential nature, they tend to approach them through the framework designed to deal with SS-phenomena, or to exclude them from consideration altogether; thus for example McCawley (1971: 223): '... with perhaps some additional terms to cover the meaning of *the*, which I have ignored'.

My recognition of two equipollent, though distinct, types of linguistic analysis is due to the analysis of Frege's terminology outlined above, which leads to the conclusion drawn. It is therefore gratifying to see it supported by Jackendoff's (1971, 1972: §1.2) compartmentalization of the traditional Chomskyan semantic component into a four-layered hierarchical system. If we leave out of account his 'table of co-reference' – which, I shall hope to show, is redundant – we are left with two internally hierarchical structures, the *functional structure* and the *modal structure*, plus a (non-structured) compartment referred to as the *focus and presupposition*. His definitional explanations of these three compartments make it clear that they correspond quite closely to the three aspects set up in (4), or, respectively, to the SS-analysis, the RS-analysis and the formal aspect.

Latterly Fillmore (1977: 60) has drawn a distinction between the *Internal* and the *External* semantic system. This, too, I think reflects the essential distinction between SS-analysis and RS-analysis.

However, neither Jackendoff nor Fillmore appears to recognize the need for the development of a set of categories and other theoretical entities distinct from that employed in SS-analysis for use in RS-analysis. Since I happen to believe that it is a fallacy to suppose that one set of terms designed to account for one aspect of linguistic structure is also suitable for the account of a different aspect, I shall develop a set of terms designed to meet the requirements of RS-analysis.

# 4 *The basis of RS-analysis*

## 4.1 Form and function

The grammatical category with whose description I shall be concerned in the present work is the N(oun) P(hrase), or – to put it more precisely – I shall be concerned with an analysis of the linguistic material which is dominated by the label NP in a standard Chomskyan phrase-marker. I shall, however, disregard predicative NPs, i.e. NPs functioning as subject or object complements, which means that only NPs functioning as subject, object, indirect object or complement to a preposition will be taken into account.

I shall call every occurrence of a NP a *referential expression*, and I shall define a referential expression as an expression by the employment of which we may speak about objects, persons, substances, occurrences, emotions, places, etc. The italicized parts of (1) are referential expressions:

(1)  (a) *Charles* felt *a piercing pain* in *his head*

(b) *Many* are of *the opinion* that *the Concorde* should never have been built

(c) In *the recent Home Internationals Series*, *Scotland* beat *England*

(d) *Harry* was *a cab-driver*

(e) *Everything* was quiet in *the village*

(f) Have *you* sold *the green coat that was in that window yesterday*?[1]

(g) *She* could not explain *her feelings* to *anyone* for *all the gold in the world*

(h) There are *no unicorns*[2]

(i) *John's reckless driving* caused *the accident*.[3]

---

[1] In (f), *that window* is a referential expression in its own right, while at the same time serving as a constituent of a larger referential expression. The same may on occasion be true of *yesterday*, e.g. '*yesterday* was Sunday, so *today* must be Monday'.

[2] The status of *there* in (h) will be commented on in §9.1.2.

[3] We shall not generally be concerned with nominalizations, but the expression *John's reckless driving* in (i) would qualify as a referential expression on the definition adopted.

39

The term 'referential expression' is chosen deliberately in favour of the term 'referring expression', for the following reasons: Although 'referring expression' has a certain standing as a technical term in (philosophical) treatments of reference, it usually carries the implication, unfortunate for my concerns, that there is a referent for any referring expression. I would like, initially, to be able to say that an expression is a referential expression solely in virtue of its *form*, thus echoing Russell's dictum (1905: 103): 'Thus a phrase is denoting solely in virtue of its *form*.'

This means, for example, that the expression 'Smith's murderer' is *always* a referential expression although it is only sometimes a referring expression.[4] Other expressions, notably those introduced by an indefinite determiner or by a quantifier, may or may not be referring expressions, depending on one's definition of reference. To me they are invariably referential expressions, even when they occur as subject or object predicates. What differences there are between referring and predicative NPs should be accounted for in terms of *function* rather than form. Except for a very tentative suggestion (in §4.2.2, footnote 11), no attempt will be made in this work to account for these differences.

I want in this way to make it clear that a distinction should be drawn between *form*, on the basis of which an expression can be classified as a referential expression or not, and the *functions* that such expressions may perform. If we translate Donnellan's various points pertaining to *Smith's murderer* in these terms, we shall say that the (invariably) referential expression 'Smith's murderer' may perform (at least) two functions: referring and attributive. Indeed, this is precisely what Donnellan does himself. The only difference is that he speaks about definite descriptions where I, somewhat more broadly, speak about referential expressions: 'Definite descriptions, I shall argue, have two possible functions' (Donnellan 1966: 100).

This leads us to the question of what referential expressions there are. On formal/distributional grounds we can distinguish two main types, definite and indefinite. These two main types are further subdivided, each into four subclasses, as shown in (2).

Expressions such as these constitute the set of linguistic phenomena in the description of which we are interested. For a number of reasons,

---

[4]   Cf. Donnellan (1966), and Lyons' discussion of 'non-referring definite noun-phrases' (Lyons 1977: 185f).

however, the display in (2) can only be interesting in the sense of presenting various types of NP for further analysis. It cannot in itself serve as a basis for such an analysis, owing to its inherent negligence of functional (semantical) criteria. It is, for example, not entirely clear that both a class of definite and a class of indefinite pronouns can be

(2)

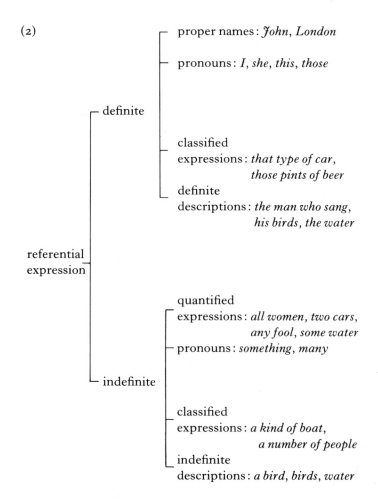

proper names: *John, London*

pronouns: *I, she, this, those*

classified
expressions: *that type of car,*
*those pints of beer*
definite
descriptions: *the man who sang,*
*his birds, the water*

— definite

referential
expression

quantified
expressions: *all women, two cars,*
*any fool, some water*
pronouns: *something, many*

— indefinite

classified
expressions: *a kind of boat,*
*a number of people*
indefinite
descriptions: *a bird, birds, water*

established on formal/distributional grounds *alone*. I may have anticipated matters somewhat by doing so.

The usual strategy for dealing with referential phenomena proceeds from observation of form to explicitation of referential function, as embodied in Russell's remark quoted above.[5] Such a strategy, it seems to me, is bound to lead to partial and/or fragmentary results, in that it calls for the analysis of a certain type of expression to the (partial) exclusion of others.

A different strategy can be envisaged on which we try to predict what referential functions there are, and then attempt to associate particular linguistic forms with these functions. Such a strategy would be in accord with Popper's general conception of empirical scientific enquiry (Popper 1963, 1972), the key notion of which is that progress in science is achieved through an interaction between two procedures: the establishment of hypotheses/theories (i.e. 'conjectures') and attempts to falsify the hypotheses/theories by confronting their predictions with observable data (i.e. 'refutations'). This is a conception which, among other things, rejects the view that theories are, or even may be, inferred directly from observable data, which latter view has characterized much writing in linguistics, and indeed still does.[6]

Acceptance of Popper's general strategy for scientific enquiry implies, in this case, that we must formulate a general-linguistic hypothesis of referential functions, that we must formulate a language-specific hypothesis for English (and others for other languages), based on the principles of the general-linguistic hypothesis, and that we must confront the predictions of the language-specific hypothesis(-es) with data from English (other languages). To the extent to which these data conflict with the predictions of the hypothesis(-es), the hypothesis(-es) is (are) discomfited if not necessarily falsified; to the extent to which the data conform to the predictions of the hypothesis(-es), the hypothesis(-es) is (are) confirmed, or supported, by the data; to the extent to which the predictions that can be formulated in terms of the hypothesis(-es) agree with observable linguistic data, these data are explained by the hypothesis(-es).[7]

---

[5] Such a strategy is implicit to Searle's (1969) and Strawson's (1950) theories of reference, as well as to the more linguistically biased analyses of Baker (1973); Givón (1972); Heringer (1969); Lyons (1977: 178ff); and Partee (1970).

[6] This is the case, for example, with much recent writing within the Continental 'school' of 'textlinguistics'; cf. Brinker (1971: 217) and Hartmann (1971: 12–15) for two general discussions of the fundamental doctrines of 'textlinguistics' which imply such a view.

[7] Readers familiar with Botha & Winckler (1973) will no doubt recognize these principles, which form the substance of chapter 2 of that work, and in particular with the principles of 'regressive reduction' (explanation) and 'progressive reduction' (confirmation) of non-demonstrative (inductive, non-conclusive) arguments (1973: 36).

What the present study purports to do in these terms is the following: Part II is concerned with the establishment of a general-linguistic hypothesis of referential functions (chapters 4 and 5), and with the establishment of a specific framework for describing such functions in English (chapter 6). Part III is devoted to an evaluation of the language-specific hypothesis for English on the basis of linguistic evidence pertaining to selected areas of English nominal composition.

## 4.2 Metatheoretical considerations

Let me, by way of introduction to this paragraph, return briefly to the discussion in §3.1. From there it emerged that I consider it necessary to distinguish between a referential *function* as a communicative function, or role, performed by a given linguistic expression of a specific form on a particular occasion, and the *use* that a speaker may make of a given linguistic expression of a specific form on a particular occasion for communicative purposes; that the sum of referential functions that a given linguistic expression may perform on different occasions is the referential *potential* of that expression; and that a speaker must *know* part of the referential potential of the expressions he employs on different occasions in order to use them correctly or appropriately. It was suggested that the design feature of prevarication is the principle which entails that there is no causal relation between words and things (together, perhaps, with such other design features as displacement of referent and the arbitrariness of the sign). I consider the substance of these various points evidently true and non-controversial although I concede that it may be expressed in different terms.

### 4.2.1 The metaphysical basis: 'mentioning things'. I want now to introduce three further points, all of which I also consider substantially true and non-controversial. It is these three points which together form the starting-point for our attempt to predict what referential functions there are.

(3)  (a) Although there is no causal relation between words (in a wide sense), and things (in a wide sense), it is a fact that we are capable of speaking about things if we want to;
     (b) it is a fact that we actually do speak about things on particular occasions;

(c) it is a fact that we are all capable of perceiving things as being spatio-temporally discrete or non-discrete; as being movable or immovable; as being one-, two-, or three-dimensional; as having shapes, sizes, colours, density, luminosity, etc., to mention but a few possibilities of perceptual discrimination.

Again, I do not claim these formulations are the only formulations capable of expressing the substance of each point. I am especially concerned that (c) may be considered controversial, owing to the formulation provided. Let me therefore point out what I do *not* consider to be covered by (c). I do not say that we all *agree* with respect to the classification of a given thing as movable/immovable, red/orange, etc. On the contrary, the very fact that we are able to *dis*agree over such matters follows from (c). If we were incapable of drawing a perceptual distinction with respect to movability, for example, then there would be no grounds for agreement or disagreement over the movability of a particular thing. The second, and perhaps more important, aspect of (c) is that it is neutral with respect to ontological commitment. In particular, it is neutral with respect to the question as to whether things are, or are not, movable/immovable, red/orange, etc., in some absolute sense, and it is neutral with respect to the different, though related question, as to whether things 'have' or do not 'have', properties that are denotata of words like *movable, immovable, red, orange*, etc. Nothing, it seems to me, of what I have to say about the referential structure of language hinges in any significant way upon one or the other of such ontological views. However, I shall quite often express myself as if things, and linguistic entities, 'have' certain properties. By this I mean that specific linguistic entities – a NP of a certain form, for example – can be characterized in a certain way on the basis of the various (syntactic and/or referential) functions performed by them, and that such a characterization amounts to a specification of inherent properties of these entities, the implication being that a particular linguistic item is capable of performing a particular function in virtue of having certain, specifiable, properties.

The three points under (3) may be expanded to the more explicit display (4) (cf. (5) for exemplification):

(4)    If on a particular occasion a person should want to, then he or she would be capable of mentioning, or saying something about, or telling someone about:

(a) all things, irrespectively of what kind of thing he or she considers them to be, and irrespectively of where they are;

(b) some things, irrespectively of what kind of thing he or she considers them to be, and irrespectively of where they are;

(c) some things, which he or she considers to be of a certain kind, irrespectively of where they are;

(d) some things, which he or she considers to belong to a certain subclass of a certain kind of thing, irrespectively of where they are;

(e) some things, which he or she considers to be individual things (belonging to a certain kind, or to a certain subclass of a certain kind), and irrespectively of where they are.

I shall refer to the five points under (4) as so many referential *modes* (i.e. ways of mentioning things); I shall also regard the list of referential modes in (4) as exhaustive. Thus the possibility of mentioning no, many (few), two (ten, a thousand . . .) things relies on the modes in (4) plus one or more secondary factors.

It might be objected that (4) does not allow for the possibility of mentioning *part* of a thing which is considered to be an individual, . . . : in other words, it might be objected that (4) does not make allowance for the part:whole relation. The relevance of the part:whole relation to *syntactico-semantic* analysis is clear (cf. Anderson 1971a: 114–15; Fillmore 1968: 61ff; Ivić 1970; Lyons 1977: 311ff), but it is not obvious that it is also relevant to referential–semantic analysis (cf. for some of the philosophical problems involved, Russell 1940: ch. 24). In particular, it is not obvious that the part:whole relationship does not in fact exploit mode (e) in (4), in the sense that eyes, arms, branches, roofs, etc., are considered to be individuals and consequently will generally be mentioned as such.[8] In view of these considerations I shall leave out of account the part:whole relationship; or more precisely, I shall implicitly assume that, from a referential point of view, there is no substantial difference between individuals and parts of wholes. Cf., however, chapter 7, footnote 1 for a pertinent comment on *half*.

Each of the five modes in (4) can be exemplified with reference to (5), where the blocks denoted by a specific letter correlate with the mode denoted by the equivalent letter in (4). If each of the sentences in (5) is considered as an utterance-product, produced by a speaker in, perhaps

---

[8] Cf. in this connection the treatment of the noun *member* in Webster's *Dictionary of Synonyms*: it is described as semantically related to words denoting *groups* of individuals (e.g. *part, portion, section*), *individuals* (e.g. *element, constituent*), and *parts of wholes* (e.g. *branch, limb*).

somewhat idealized, appropriate contextual conditions (of sincerity, topical relevance, etc.), then the italicized words reflect, in a fairly obvious way, his capacity for mentioning things in the five referential modes of (4).

(5)(a) (i)   *Everything* is created by God
    (ii)   *Nobody* knows *all*
    (iii)   There was *nothing* to be had
    (iv)   *Things* ain't what they used to be
  (b) (i)   *Something* is rotten in the state of Denmark
    (ii)   *Much* is still unaccounted for
    (iii)   *A great many things* still need explaining
  (c) (i)   *Boys* will be boys
    (ii)   *Whisky* is nice
    (iii)   He was taken to *hospital*
  (d) (i)   *Big boys* are a nuisance
    (ii)   *Scotch whisky* is better than *Canadian*
    (iii)   *Lions kept in a cage* will lose their killing instinct
  (e) (i)   *That boy* will always be troublesome
    (ii)   *We each* had *two whiskies* before dinner
    (iii)   He was taken to *the hospital*
    (iv)   *Our roof* leaks.

It is clear from some of these phrases (e.g. (5)(b)) that I am equivocating on the word *thing*, construing it to apply both to something perceived as spatio-temporally discrete (i.e. *objects*), and to something perceived as spatio-temporally non-discrete (i.e. *substance*). I am, in fact, using the word *thing* in the everyday sense according to which even 'love is a many-splendoured thing'. If disambiguation should be called for I shall use the terms *object* and (*abstract*) *substance*.

**4.2.2 'Referential function' defined.** It has been implicit to the discussion so far that there are such things as referential functions. Furthermore, it has been explicitly stated as the aim of this present section (4.2) that I want to show *what* referential functions there are. Obviously, in order to achieve this aim I must first answer the more basic question, 'What is a referential function?' In order to be able to do that I must return briefly to the discussion in §2.4, which resulted in my recognition of two types of location, categorial and spatio-temporal. It was said that signs *establish* locations for things to be assigned to, either categorial or spatio-temporal or both or neither, depending on whether they denote or indicate or both or neither.

A referential function may now be provisionally defined as a function through the performance of which a sign, S, establishes locations for the assignment of things.

Let us consider an example. If on a particular occasion someone were to utter (5)(e)(i) (i.e. *that boy will always be troublesome*), then, according to the definition of a referential function just given, *that boy* will establish a composite location for the assignment of things: BOY (the lexical noun, or lexeme; see below, §4.3.1) will establish a categorial location, *that* will establish a spatio-temporal location, while the singular morpheme will delimit the number of things to be assigned to this composite location to one.

However, recall now that the capacity of a sign to establish locations was said to be a capacity it has in virtue of having meaning. What the definition of a referential function provided above boils down to, then, is this: a sign performs the function of having meaning. This, at best, is not a very illuminating statement; clearly something else is required.

Although unilluminating, the above definition provides us with a clue as to what this might be, in that it contains recognition of an implicit agent for the activity of assigning things to locations. What is needed to make the notion of referential function non-vacuous is an explicitation of this implicit agent: *who* or *what* is it that assigns things to locations?

There are three possible answers to this question, namely, the speaker, the hearer,[9] or the sign itself. We can fairly easily and summarily dispose of the last of these possibilities: it would be strenuous to say that signs, apart from establishing locations, also assign things to these locations, even in a metaphorical sense. Let us therefore concentrate on the two other possibilities.

What a speaker does when uttering *that boy will always be troublesome*, can, I believe, fairly obviously be characterized as assigning one thing to the composite location established by the sign *that boy*. But there is one very important modification which has to be made in this connection: not only does the speaker assign things to locations, but he also – to a very large extent[10] – determines what locations are to be established

---

[9]  'The speaker' = 'the producer of the sign, written or spoken'; 'the hearer' = 'the recipient of the sign, whether by listening or by reading'. Though cf. §10.2.2.

[10]  The qualification should be taken to cover those aspects of linguistic structure on which obligations are imposed by language itself, for example concordial phenomena, anaphoric ties, etc.

through his choice of sign(s). It would therefore seem to be the case that the sign itself does not play any crucial role in the activity that might be termed speaker's assignment of things to locations.[11]

Where the sign plays a crucial role is with the *hearer's* assignment of things to locations, but here, too, a modification must be made. A hearer may hear a sign correctly, he may understand it perfectly well, and yet he may fail to be able to assign anything – i.e. any physical thing – to the location established by the sign, as would be the normal case when reading poetry or fictional prose, for example. But this is not to say that those signs that make up a poem or a crime novel do not perform the functions that signs in 'reality-bound' utterances do, which is this: to *invite* the hearer to assign things to the locations established by them.

We might sum up this discussion in the following way. We are interested in describing the speaker, the sign, and the hearer with respect to their capability of being agents of two activities, that of establishing locations and that of assigning things to locations. Whereas the sign and the hearer are the agents of only one of these activities each (respectively the establishment of locations and the assignment of things to locations), the speaker is the agent of both. Thus neither of these activities characterizes the speaker uniquely. But the sign and the hearer are uniquely characterized by one of them.

In the light of these various considerations I shall define a referential function as follows:

(6)   A referential function is a function through the performance of which a sign, S, invites the hearer, H, to assign things to the locations established by S.

I should now like to clarify one or two things of relevance to the suggestion that signs invite hearers to assign things to locations, beginning with an attempt to forestall an objection to the suggestion itself: Is it not *speakers* that do the inviting, by employing signs (of particular types)? No, it is not. It is true, as has indeed already been mentioned, that speakers are free up to a point to employ what signs they want for particular purposes. But if a speaker wants a particular communicative effect – say, if he wants to refer to a particular boy by

---

[11] It might perhaps be argued that speakers' assignment of things to locations is in fact equivalent to the speech act of predication (if it is a separate speech act; cf. Searle 1969: 122). By suggesting this I may be committing 'one of the most persistent mistakes in the history of Western philosophy', namely, 'the tendency to construe predication as a kind of, or analogous to, reference'. As already stated, no attempt will be made here to account for predicative NPs.

means of linguistic signs – then he is bound by the rules of language to employ a sign of type x rather than of type y. A speaker must know (part of) the referential potential of the signs he employs if he wants to be understood. What the speaker and hearer have in common is the knowledge of the referential potential of signs and particular sign-types. And this is as much as to say that it is signs that invite hearers to assign things to established locations. What speakers do is to produce signs of which they know that they (i.e. the signs) will have the proper authority to issue the right kind of invitation. The authority in question is provided by the meaning of the sign. (Cf. also §§4.2.3.1 and 9.2.)

I shall distinguish between *conditional* and *non-conditional* referential functions on the basis of whether a sign *invites* the hearer to accept the categorial location established by the sign, or just *presupposes* such acceptance.[12] This distinction has something to do with the well-formedness of signs or, if you will, with the existence of signs. What I mean by this can be made clear with reference to

(7)    (a) I was stung by *a quasp* in the water.

A native speaker of English who heard this would be likely to react by saying something like *You don't say. Incidentally, what is a quasp?*, rather than by saying outright, *No. There are no quasps, and there is no such word as 'quasp'.* This latter reaction is more likely to be provoked by

(7)    (b) A quasp is a small, blue insect that lives in or near water (preferably salt), and which stings.

I shall say that *a quasp* in (7)(a) performs a non-conditional referential function, whereas in (b) it performs a conditional referential function. The same applies, of course, to the pair in

(8)    (a) I was stung by a wasp this morning (non-conditional);

(b) A wasp is a black and yellow striped insect which stings (conditional).

The latter could reasonably be paraphrased 'if anything is a wasp, then it is typically a black and yellow striped insect which stings'. Hence the term 'conditional' (cf., however, Lyons 1977: 196–7).

In view of the supposition that signs establish locations in virtue of having meaning, what I mean by saying that a sign may *invite* the hearer to accept the categorial location(s) established by the sign, can be formulated as follows:

(9)    If the hearer accepts a certain location C as the C established by a

---

[12] Cf. Collinson (1937: 33) for a discussion of the intended distinction applied to various concrete 'indicaters'.

given sign, S, he has thereby committed himself to regarding the phonic (graphic) sequence P as the bearer of a meaning, M, such that $(P + M) = S$. In short, by accepting C as the C established by S, the hearer has accepted S *as a sign.*

A similar distinction applies to ST-locations. There are signs that *invite* H to assign things to places, and there are signs that *presuppose* H to accept a prior localization of things in space/time. In fact, this is the difference between traditionally indefinite and traditionally definite signs (determiners and pronouns). However, the relationship between these two kinds of sign is of a transformational nature, so I shall not regard this difference as the basis of two primitive types of referential function, as I did in the case of the conditional distinction above. These matters will be fully discussed at several junctures in Chapters 8 and 9.

One further point should be made clear in connection with the assignment of things to ST-locations. Utterances occur in space/time, and the function performed by signs by which they invite hearers to assign things to ST-locations must therefore be related to the time and place of utterance. What this means, in fact, is that H is not invited to assign things to any *absolute* ST-location, but to a ST-location related to the time and the place of the utterance act (cf. §§9.2.2–3 for details). Despite the fact that a similar modification is relevant to categorial locations, I shall in general disregard the implications of it. Suffice it to say that metaphorical usage relies on it. When having been given a description of a hand of an old man, for example, in terms which compare it to a gnarled root, we may produce or understand the utterance *he cupped the root to his ear*, and we may do so in reliance on the fact that categorial locations are established at the time of utterance. As I said, however, I shall restrict the notion of utterance-dependence to ST-locations, where it is inescapably necessary. The, counterfactual, assumption that I am hereby making, is that things are always to be assigned to the same categorial locations.[13]

Let me finally point out that my use of the word 'assign' in 'S invites H to *assign* things to . . . spatio-temporal locations' in no way should be taken to impute concrete action of 'placing things somewhere' to H if he complies with the invitation. This would be absurd. What is imputed to H is *recognition* of the fact that things of themselves occupy points in space/time.

---

[13] Cf. Thrane (1976: 370) for a discussion of 'same' bearing on this point.

**4.2.3 The set of referential functions. . . .** The outcome of the immediately preceding discussion is the general formula (10):

(10) There is a referential function, x, through the performance of which a sign, S, invites the hearer, H, to assign things, T, to categorial location C and/or to spatio-temporal location ST established by S at the time of utterance (TU).

Prediction of *what* referential functions there are is now clearly seen to be tantamount to showing in how many and in what ways the general formula (10) can, or should, be modified. The first major question that confronts us, consequently, is whether some principled basis can be given for a set of modifications of (10).

An advocate of the standard strategy for dealing with referential form vs. function might propose that a sign, S, invites H to assign things to the location(s) established by S in a different manner from that in which another sign, R, invites H to assign things to the locations established by R. Such a proposal would have to be based on a demonstration that, e.g. a quantified expression and an indefinite description differ with respect to the way(s) in which they invite hearers to assign things to the locations established by them. But such a demonstration would be circular, in that it would seem to presuppose knowledge of what referential functions there are.

Consider now a different approach. In (4) I established what I called five referential modes. What I want to argue with respect to these modes is that it is, in fact, they that determine what referential functions there are.

The argument needed to justify this proposal can be broken down to a number of minor arguments, which are all of them non-demonstrative in nature. This chain of minor arguments comprises (at least) the following four, all of which we shall be concerned with in greater or less detail:

(11) If the set of possible referential functions is restricted by the set of modes (4), then it must be shown why these modes should be able to restrict the possible set of referential functions.

This argument will be dealt with in §4.2.3.1.

(12) If the set of possible referential functions is restricted by the set of modes (4), then the restrictive mechanisms should be demonstrably derived from these modes, and they should be imposed on (10) in a principled manner.

This argument will be dealt with in §4.2.3.2.

(13) If the set of referential functions to be set up in §4.2.3.2 as a corollary to (12) is the maximal set of referential functions, then any (non-predicative) NP must be shown not to perform a referentional function not included in (15) below.

The demonstration of the support for this argument will not be undertaken directly. It will, however, be implicit throughout Part III, in that the analysis given there for any NP will be seen to rely only on the referential functions in (15).

(14) If the set of referential functions established as a corollary to (12) in §4.2.3.2 exhausts the referential potential of all (non-predicative) NPs, then it must be shown that (non-predicative) NPs have properties that will enable them to perform that set of referential functions.

This argument, which takes us into the more specifically linguistic area, will be the subject matter of §4.4, as indeed will be most of Part III.

**4.2.3.1** . . . *supported.* In this section we shall be concerned with the question asked in (11): why should the referential modes (4) be able to restrict the set of possible referential functions? In order to answer it we must look more closely at the determinants of each of the modes in (4) and of the general schema (10).

What are the factors that determine each of the modes in (4), exemplified by (4)(c)? There are two: (i) our ability to speak at all, and (ii) our ability to use language in such a way that it appears that we are mentioning some things, and that we consider these things to be of a certain kind. These two abilities are clearly not the same. We are not allowed to infer that, just because we are able to speak, we are also able to speak about things. Yet we could not speak about things if we could not speak. This characterization of the determinants of (4) is, however, not precise enough. It must be supplemented by an attempt to characterize the determinants of our ability to speak about things, since our ability to speak is not of itself sufficient to explain this ability. These supplementary determinants, I suggest, are our faculties of perception, in accordance with which we consider things to be movable/immovable, red/orange, similar/dissimilar, etc. It is our ability to speak in conjunction with our perceptual faculties which determine the modes in (4).

What factors determine the general schema (10)? Again, there are two: (i) the capacity of signs to establish locations, and (ii) the fact that signs, despite their arbitrariness (in a Saussurian sense), are not unprincipled with respect to what locations they establish. This latter point may need some clarification. What I mean by it is that if a sign, S, on a particular occasion establishes categorial location $a$ and spatio-temporal location $b$, then the same sign will, on another occasion, also establish *both* a categorial *and* a spatio-temporal location. The categorial location will typically be the same (i.e. $a$),[14] whereas the spatio-temporal location may differ from $b$ in an *absolute* sense, but not in a *relative* sense (owing to the egocentric structure of utterance situations: cf. Lyons 1977: 638).

Once again, the relation holding between (i) and (ii) is one of unilateral dependence. The precondition for signs to establish locations in a principled (as opposed to *arbitrary*) way is their capacity to establish locations at all. But this latter capacity is not of itself sufficient to explain why signs should do so in a principled way. And once again, I want to suggest that the ultimate determinants of the fact that signs establish locations in a principled way are our perceptual faculties. But this determination cannot occur in any direct way. I would say, rather, that the capacity of signs to establish locations in a principled manner is the linguistic embodiment of the principle that it is our perceptual faculties that determine the ways in which we mention things.

The essentials of this position seem to be in accord with the suggestions by O'Connor (1975: 130ff) which has come to my attention only recently. As a basis for a correspondence theory of truth O'Connor proposes a three-layered schema:

(A) *status rerum*
(B) things and their properties, situations, events
(C) empirical statements.

(A) is the layer of 'the raw unexperienced welter of objects and events' (O'Connor 1975: 130), (B) is 'a selectively processed and edited version of *status rerum*' (*ibid.*) and (C) is 'a selectively processed and edited version of B' (*ibid.*).

Between these layers there are certain links. Thus the links between (A) and (B) are 'the cognitive processes of sensation, perception, memory and concept formation', those between (B) and (C) are 'the semantic conventions (for a given language)', while 'the truth relation links A with C' (*ibid.*).

[14] Cf. p. 50 above for a brief discussion of the qualifications needed for this statement to be true.

Associated with this basic schema is the hypothesis – and this is where I feel myself in closest sympathy – that language (i.e. layer (C)) is structured in accordance with the limitations set on *status rerum* by our various capacities for perception, sensation, and conceptualization – and these limitations constitute precisely the impoverished (as compared to (A), *status rerum*) 'version' of the world, (B). I venture to draw from this hypothesis the implication that, since these limitations may presumably differ in points of detail from individual to individual and from group to group, we can explain differences in language structure in different languages on this schema. More importantly, however, the same hypothesis allows the implication that, if our powers of perception *always* ensure that we, *qua* humans, may distinguish spatio-temporally discrete things from non-discrete, etc., then this capacity is reflected in language structure.

We can now suggest an answer to the main question. The modes are able to restrict the possible set of referential functions, because the modes and the (actual) set of referential functions are in fact one and the same thing, only seen from different sides: the modes constitute guidelines for *speakers*, in that they specify the ways in which things may be mentioned whereas the referential functions constitute guidelines for *hearers*, in that they specify the ways in which things are to be assigned to the locations established by signs.

If it is true that the referential modes and the referential functions are one and the same thing, then why, it could be asked, do I complicate the issue by introducing referential modes as well as referential functions? The answer to this is quite simple. It is the referential functions which are our main concern. If therefore I restricted myself to establishing a set of referential functions, some kind of justification would have to be provided for my choice of this, rather than that, set of referential functions. The modes are considered to provide such justification, since they alone are directly accessible to observation.

**4.2.3.2 . . . *established*.** No one, I think, will argue with the principle expressed in (12), which was that it is incumbent on me to show a principled way in which the modes in (4) can be brought to bear on the general schema (10). There are, in fact, three such ways.

The first is derived from the difference in quantifier – *all* in (4)(a), *some* in (4)(b)–(c).

The second is derived from the difference with respect to explicitness of locations: in (4)(a)–(b), and sometimes (e) no explicit categorial location is required, in (4)(c)–(d), and sometimes (e) a specific categorial location is required. A similar distinction applies to spatio-temporal location. In each case of (4), an explicit spatio-temporal location may be present but it need not.

The third is derived from the difference with respect to the presupposition of previous assignment(s) to locations: (4)(d), and sometimes (e) presuppose an explicit, previous assignment of some things to C(x) – where C(x) may be either a particular C or no particular C – whereas (4)(a)–(c) and sometimes (e) do not.

These considerations lead to the following restrictive mechanisms for (10): In the general schema (10), T may be quantified by either *all* or by *some*, both C and ST may be qualified by either *a particular* or *no particular*, and *some T* may be qualified by *of C(x)*.

Applying these mechanisms to (10) we can identify twelve simple referential functions, as displayed in (15), where C(p) and ST(p) stand for 'a *particular* C' and 'a *particular* ST', whereas C(n) and ST(n) stand for '*no* particular C' and '*no* particular ST'.

(15)  
| | | | | |
|---|---|---|---|---|
| All things | a | b | c | d |
| Some things | e | f | g | h |
| Some things of C(x) | i | j | k | l |
| | C(p) | C(n) | ST(p) | ST(n) |

Each simple referential function should be read according to the following formula:

> There is a referential function, a, through the performance of which a sign, S, invites H to assign *all* things to a *particular* C.

The referential functions are allegedly the hearer-orientated variants of the speaker-orientated referential modes of (4). If this is correct we should now be able to demonstrate the similarity with reference to (15), but there is no immediate similarity between the functions of (15) and the modes of (4), at least not so far as numbers are concerned. It should be noticed, however, that whereas the set of functions consists of simple functions, the set of modes contains composite modes, in the sense that each mode involves reference to a categorial and a spatio-temporal location (at least). Thus the schema for the modes comparable to (15) should be rather (15)(a) – see next page – where ST(x) stands for either 'a particular ST' or for 'no particular ST', and where the letters refer to the letters in (4). Two points merit attention. First, the lack of a mode which permits a speaker to mention all things that he considers to

| (15)(a) | All things | | a |
|---|---|---|---|
| | Some things | c,e | b,e |
| | Some things of C(x) | c,e | d,e |
| | | C(p)/ST(x) | C(n)/ST(x). |

belong to a particular category is only apparent. It is provided for by
(4)(c), which, through its incorporation of a non-restrictive relative
clause, permits a speaker to mention some things, *all* of which he
considers to be of a certain kind. This formulation is, I think, quite
precise. By mentioning all things *of a given kind* we in fact only mention
*some things*: there is always a complement class of things, the members
of which are considered *not* to belong to the kind in question.

Secondly, the appearance of (e) and (d) at more than one point in the
schema is due to the fact that the variables C(x) and ST(x) are not
spelled out, and – in the case of (e) – to certain affinities between
definiteness, individuation, and space/time location which will be gone
into in some detail later. To the extent to which these affinities cannot be
brought out by (15)(a) the schema is insufficient. Barring these potential
difficulties we could easily 'expand' (15)(a) to display simple referential
modes along the lines of (15) by spelling out all the variables, but this
would hardly be very interesting. What is of far greater interest is the
empirical fact that there is no one-to-one correlation between particular
types of NP and the simple referential functions of (15). NPs do not
perform simple referential functions, they perform composite functions
of a kind comparable to the composite modes of (4) and (15)(a).

In connection with this point I shall take it as an axiom of RS-analysis
that all NPs perform a referential function by which the hearer is invited
to assign things to a space/time location. There is then a clearly defined
group of NPs that do not establish a categorial location, but even these
contain elements that make it necessary to incorporate both *all* and *some*
in a statement of their meaning, so even these perform composite
functions.[15] All other NPs establish both at least a spatio-temporal and
a categorial location, so they clearly perform composite functions.

It is a matter of arguable fact that the actual number of such
composite referential functions can be reduced to just three (in English,
at least), all of which may then be either conditional or non-conditional
in the sense explained above (pp. 49–50).

---

[15] The NPs in question are some pronouns and all proper names. They will be discussed
in detail in chapter 10.

(16) (a) There is a referential function, *sortal*, which is performed by S
    if S invites H to assign some T (of C(z)) to C(x) and all T of C(x(z))
    to ST(y) at TU.

    (b) There is a referential function, *selective*, which is performed by
    S if S invites H to assign some T (of C(z)) to C(x) and some T of
    C(x(z)) to ST(y) at TU.

    (c) There is a referential function, *identitive*, which is performed
    by S if S invites H to assign some T (of C(z)), located at ST(y) at
    TU, to C(x).

In these formulae, C(x) and C(z) stand for either 'a particular C' or for
'no particular C' and (C(x(z)) stands for the intersection of the classes
denoted by the categories C(x) and C(z); ST(y) stands for either 'a
particular ST' or for 'no particular ST'; T stands for either 'object(s)'
or for 'substance'; and TU stands for 'time of utterance'.

A number of comments relative to (16) are in order, but let me first
quote a few paradigm examples of NPs performing these composite
functions (disregarding for the moment the conditional-distinction):

(17)(a) (i)  *All cats* hear well

      (ii)  I like *grey cats* better than *black*

  (b) (i)  *Some cats* are grey

      (ii)  I have *some grey cats*

      (iii)  There is *something* I don't understand

  (c) (i)  *My cats* are grey

      (ii)  *That grey cat* isn't *mine*

      (iii)  *I* told *you* so.

Even if it had not transpired from the formulations (16), the examples
in (17) will probably highlight the possibility of relating the three
composite functions to the universal, the existential, and the iota-
operators, respectively, of predicate-calculus analysis. I think, however,
that this possibility should not be pressed too far, owing mainly to the
central involvement of the partitive relationship in (16). It would be
more appropriate to relate the functions with class-calculus analysis if
we wanted to look for a parallel framework outside linguistics.

The choice of terminology is influenced by this consideration. Instead
of 'universal' for (a) and 'existential' for (b), the terms 'sortal' and
'selective' are considered to be neutral with respect to implications of
logical analysis. 'Sortal' is borrowed from Strawson (1959: 168). There
a sortal universal is defined as a term that 'supplies a principle for
distinguishing and counting individual particulars which it collects'.

However, I want to play down the stress on 'individual particular', promoting rather the stress on 'kind of thing' immanent to Lyons' use of 'sortal' in the combination 'sortal classifier': 'A sortal classifier is one which individuates whatever it refers to *in terms of the kind of entity that it is*' (Lyons 1977: 463; my italics). Thus the characteristic of a sign performing a sortal referential function is that it emphasizes what *kind* of thing is being talked about.

The notion of 'kind' is also pertinent to the composite function *selective*, but the characteristic feature of this function is rather that it emphasizes that a selection, or part, of things of a certain kind is being talked about.

The term 'identitive' may be an unfortunate coinage. It is meant to suggest that a sign performing this function *enables* a hearer to identify what thing(s) is (are) being mentioned. It is chosen in preference to 'identifying' since it is hearers, rather than signs, that identify things.

A comment is needed concerning the appropriate interpretation of 'at/to ST(y) at TU' in all of (16). ST(y), it was said, may stand for either 'a particular ST' or for 'no particular ST', but what, more precisely, is meant by saying that a sign may invite a hearer to assign things to no particular ST at the time of utterance? We can answer this question with reference to two principles already introduced, namely, the utterance-dependence of ST locations, and the fact that things are located (in a concrete sense) in space/time independently of what signs may invite hearers to do. These two principles are mutually inconsistent. But the inconsistency is only apparent, and the qualification needed to resolve the inconsistency at the same time provides the answer to our question.

It has already been pointed out that the instruction by a sign to the hearer to *assign* things to ST at TU is a metaphorical expression for the hearer's recognition, or awareness, of the concrete location of things at TU. On this background the utterance-dependence of ST may be seen as the *relevance* of the concrete (actual) location of things at TU to the utterance act. Interpreted in this way, what a sign does in inviting the hearer to assign things to no particular ST at TU is to signal *lack of relevance* to the utterance act of the concrete (actual) location at the time of utterance of the things being talked about. See §§9.2.2–3 for further details.

One final point should be raised explicitly in connection with (16), namely, the question of whether the three functions are in fact the only functions in English, and, if so, how I know? The answers to these questions cannot be stated here, nor can they be stated briefly. In fact, all of Part III *is* the answer. But it is possible, at this stage, to maintain that, judging by the analyses in Part III, these functions are probably the only 'productive' functions, but that it may be necessary to allow for one or two others in order to account for such expressions as 'there he stood, gumboots *and all*', and perhaps also '*it* is raining' (see §§8.4; 10.3.4).

## 4.3 The elements of NP

The main issue that confronts us after the discussion in §4.2 is a demonstration of the properties of NP that ensure that NP can perform the referential functions of (16). Before I can begin this demonstration, however, a number of terminological and methodological matters have to be cleared out of the way. Three such points will be dealt with in the present section, namely, my terminology pertaining to NP, nominal, and (lexical) noun (§4.3.1), an evaluation of the capabilities of two general linguistic models, a phrase-structure model and a dependency model, to accommodate our needs (§4.3.2), and my use of the terms 'class', 'category' and 'feature' (§4.3.3).

**4.3.1 Noun phrases, nominals, and nouns.** NP is generally seen as a category which is capable of performing certain grammatical functions (as subject, object, etc.), certain semantical functions (as agentive, instrumental, etc.), and/or certain rhetorical functions (as topic or theme, etc.). These functions all belong to the syntactico-semantic structure of language and should be accounted for in terms of SS-analysis. From the discussion in §4.2 it emerges that I consider NPs capable, in addition, of performing certain referential functions (sortal, selective, and identitive). These belong to the referential–semantic aspect of language structure, and should be accounted for in terms of RS-analysis. What is of immediate interest to us here, however, is the fact that NP on considerations such as these is a category the definition of which is no simple matter, since such a definition must incorporate criteria gleaned from different aspects of linguistic analysis (and the situation may be even more complex than the above outline suggests, mainly in that a certain amount of departmentalization can be envisaged within the SS-component).

Most likely we need to be able to refer to such a complex category in the (integrated) linguistic analysis, so I shall reserve the term 'NP' for this purpose. But then we need a term for that 'part' of a NP that will serve as the initial symbol for the RS-analysis, and the term 'N(ominal)' immediately offers itself: it is well established as a technical term in linguistics, and it is often redundant in that it is used inter-changeably with NP. Thus N is a 'narrower' category than NP in that it belongs exclusively to RS-analysis, where it is the initial symbol. A NP, in contrast, may now be defined as a N which is specified for SS-function(s). A graphic representation of the situation I envisage is presented in:

(18)

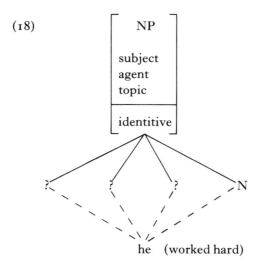

he   (worked hard)

The question-marks indicate that I am not certain whether all, or indeed any, of the syntactico-semantic functions in the complex symbol on NP require a separate category. This is a question which I shall not go into.[16] However, I might suggest, on the strength of the analyses to be provided in Part III, that N is the crucial category for the semantic interpretation of NP.

There remains to be given an account of my use of the term 'noun', or, more precisely '*lexical* noun'. A noun is a lexeme (in the sense of Lyons

---

[16] Li (1976) is a volume dedicated to explorations of the relationships between the various (SS and RS, in my terms) functions of NP. See especially the papers in that volume by S. Anderson, Chafe, Keenan, Kuno, Li & Thompson, and Schachter.

(1968: 197; 1977: 19), and Matthews (1972: 161; 1974: 11)), i.e. a word considered as an abstract semantic unit, but specified with respect to its distributional potential. In the framework to be developed, a noun is distributionally defined with reference to its occurrence under a particular node in the structure generating N.

**4.3.2 Constituency vs. dependency.** For the purposes of the present section I shall discuss some general properties of phrase-structure grammars (PSG) and dependency grammars (DG) in relation to NP, rather than single out some specific treatment for attention. The basic differences between PSG and DG were gone into in §1.2. Seen in relation to NP, these differences are the following:

(19)  (a) PSG specifies NP with respect to constituency structure. That is, whatever elements are contained in a NP are co-constituents of NP and no direct relations obtain among these constituents. The basic relation in PSG being the part:whole relation, the PS-rule NP→Det N specifies that Det + N, taken together, *is a* NP.

(b) DG specifies NP with respect to the relations of dependency reputedly holding among the elements of NP. One of these is the governor, the rest are dependents. The governor is itself a dependent (on V or S (CL), or on some other element), but not on an element of (that same) NP. The notion of Noun *Phrase*, however, is upheld only indirectly in DG since only terminal (lexical) category symbols occur in dependency rules, e.g. N(D*).

A general rule for rewriting NP in PSG is:

(20)  NP→(Det) N (Comp)

where N is the symbol for lexical noun (in my terms). According to this rule, N is the only obligatory constituent of NP, and some NPs may be rewritten simply as N (proper names and pronouns; possibly uncountables and countable plurals, the latter depending on whether or not a zero-article is reckoned with). Otherwise (20) will ensure that Det and N are independently bracketed elements, so that for example *the girl in the sweetshop* will be given a constituency reading like:

(21)  [$_{NP}$($_{Det}$the)$_{Det}$ ($_N$girl)$_N$ ($_{Comp}$in the sweetshop)$_{Comp}$]$_{NP}$

where possibly the complement prepositional phrase derives from an underlying S. This point need not detain us here. The status of Comp presents special problems for an attempt to integrate RS-analysis with a purely PSG-model which we shall not go into. We concentrate on Det and N.

Essentially the same constituency reading will be given to any NP containing a determiner, but various suggestions have been published for further expansion of Det so as to allow phrase-structure analysis of expressions like *all those five brown bottles in the fridge*. The principle, however, is always that behind (20).

Nowhere in this scheme do we find properties of Det and N that will account for the capability of NP to perform the referential functions we have established, and it is clear why not. The rule (20) is a purely distributional rule that involves no reference to the meaning of the constituents. If we want to account for the referential functions in terms of PSG, we must do so with reference to the meaning of the constituents identified by the PS-rules for NP.

Initially, this would appear to be not too difficult. There is, in (20), embodied a duality that quite conceivably could be related to our dichotomy of categorial and spatio-temporal locations, such that the meaning of Det established ST locations, whereas the meaning of N established categorial locations:

(22)

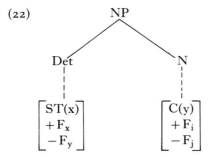

where $ST(x)$ and $C(y)$ are lexically initial symbols, each to be subcategorized in terms of semantic features, F. The complex symbols created in this way are the input for the lexical rules.

However, problems appear when we consider the axiom of RS-analysis – that any NP establishes *at least* a ST-location – in relation to (20), for according to this rule the obligatory element will be C, rather than ST. Other problems appear where NP is rewritten only as N, realized by *I, you, John*, etc. As already intimated, such NPs are considered here to be 'non-categorial', i.e. they do not establish a C. On the PSG-analysis they *only* establish a C. And still other problems appear when we consider the inability of PSG to even allow the postulation of direct relations between Det and N.

The notions of selectional rule and strict subcategorization rule have been introduced in PSG in order to solve some of the problems of the latter sort, which are pertinent to the constituents of any construction, not just to the constituents of NP. Selectional rules and strict subcategorization rules are, essentially, rules that specify syntagmatic relations between lexical items in construction. Whether selectional restrictions are basically syntactic or semantic does not affect the point that the rules expressing them must refer to complex symbols of features, as must also strict subcategorization rules. It is then noteworthy that a grammar that permits its rewrite rules to refer to complex symbols is no longer a PSG, but rather a kind of transformational grammar (Chomsky 1965: 89–90, 98–9).

Despite Chomsky's defence of the role of PSG in the base component of a transformational grammar, which is said to be 'that of defining the grammatical relations that are expressed in the deep structure and that therefore determine the semantic interpretation of a sentence' (Chomsky 1965: 99), I am inclined to believe that PSG does not have the exclusive place in the grammar which it is said to have, precisely because it provides no way of accounting for the relations that hold between lexical items in construction without necessitating a fairly radical departure from its basic principles. The fact that the deep structure status of such functional relations as 'subject-of', 'object-of', etc., has been challenged by Fillmore (1968) and many others – although Fillmore (1977) appears to be less insistent on this issue nowadays – leaves the central role of PSG significantly reduced, in general. More specifically, with regard to NP, the only 'relations' that are defined in configurational terms are 'Det is the determiner-of NP' and 'N is the noun-of NP'. These relations are neither revealing nor interesting, and they may be among the reasons for Chomsky's development of the double-bar notation (Chomsky 1970), which defines the relations 'x is the specifier-of NP' and 'y is the specified-of NP'.[17] The head of NP – previously indeterminable in PSG – can then be defined as the specified member of NP (cf. Akmajian & Lehrer 1976: 400).

In contrast to PSG, DG provides the necessary framework for dealing with the relations obtaining between lexical items in construction. However, problems adhere to what might be called the standard DG

---

[17] I here disregard the fact that Chomsky in this paper eliminates NP as a *category*, in favour of (a node specified as) as complex symbol of *features*. The two proposals (concerning specifiers and the elimination of categories) are mutually independent.

analysis of NP. It is, I believe, generally held by proponents of DG (thus, for example, Robinson (1970b: 260), and Anderson (1971a: 32)) that the noun is the head of NP, i.e. that N (here = noun) is the governor while D(eterminer) is a dependent:

(23)  N(D*)

This is a dependency rule which states that the governor (N) occurs with a dependent (D) to its left (cf. especially Hays (1964) for discussion of the three types of dependency rule, of which (23) is one) and it generates structures like

(24)

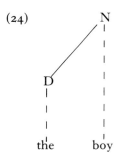

Quite obviously, the same remarks as were made above of (22) about the capacity of the overall grammatical model to accommodate RS-analysis also pertain to (24). Here, too, we have a dichotomy which could reflect ST and C, but C would still be the obligatory element. Recently Lyons (1977: 430, 464) has suggested that something might be said for regarding D as the governor and N as dependent, and if assignment of headship is made on the basis of distributional equivalence, this might indeed seem to be the case with such expressions as *this* vs. *this book*. It would, however, not be possible in general to establish D as the head in distributional terms, and in many instances (uncountables, countable plurals, proper names) there is no determiner present to be reckoned with as head at all (unless the zero-article is given a rather heavy load to bear).

The problem is stateable in these terms: DG systematically exploits the notions of head (governor) and dependent to account for the relations holding between the members of a particular construction. In one construction (NP), however, the notion of head is hazy, in that both members in a two-member construction on occasion show distributional features that normally characterize the head.

I shall provide a solution to this confusing state of affairs, and I shall do so by initially suggesting that the question 'which member of NP, the determiner or the noun, is the head of NP?' is a spurious question that admits of no answer other than 'both and neither'. I shall take the view that a NP like *the boy* is the superficial realization of a composite dependency structure consisting of what I shall call *referential phrases*, and that the question of headship should be asked about such phrases rather than directly about NP. It will appear that in some respects the abstract material underlying *boy* is 'head' relative to the material underlying *the*, but that in others it is the other way round. Hence the contradictory answer to the question above.

There is one more aspect of DG that merits attention. Robinson (1970b: 260) states that DG only employs terminal category symbols (like N, V, D, A, etc.), and no non-terminal ones (like S, NP, VP, PP, etc.). That is, the category symbols that DG operates with are all of them symbols of lexical categories (in Chomsky's (1965: 74) sense), in that they all appear to the left of some lexical rule. This is a basic principle of DG, and it means that we cannot adopt a purely DG-framework for the description of NPs, for the following reason:

> The initial symbol of RS-analysis was said to be N(ominal). This symbol, consequently, would have to be the symbol of the governor in a number of D-rules, and this, in turn, would mean that N would have to be construed as a terminal (lexical) category. This we cannot do if we wish to develop the notion of referential phrase. It is the categories that constitute these that are the terminal categories.

Neither PSG nor DG alone can accommodate RS-analysis without adjustments of various sorts, as we have just seen. It is then interesting that the adjustments needed for each of the two models can be gleaned from among the basic principles of the other: the notions of head and dependent, lack of which disqualifies PSG as a viable framework for RS-analysis, are the two basic notions of DG; and the notion of non-terminal category, and its implication of an 'abstract' level of representation, lack of which hampers DG for RS-purposes, is crucial to PSG.

There are neither theoretical nor empirical considerations that prevent us from adopting a 'mixed' format of grammatical description in which both constituency and dependency find a natural place. I shall adopt this practice.

**4.3.3 Class, category and feature.** The term 'category' is used in a variety of senses in linguistic theory, and I myself use it in both a linguistic and an ontological sense (the latter in 'categorial location', which we may disregard in the present context).

The traditional use of the term in linguistics is in collocation with either 'inflectional' or 'grammatical'. This is inspired by the Aristotelian notion of the categories as a set of accidental properties that may characterize (primary) substances. The primary substances in grammar are the word-classes – that are sometimes regarded as 'primary' categories themselves (cf. Lyons 1968: 270ff) – and the (secondary) categories are then the 'accidentia' of the various word-classes: case, gender, number, person, tense, mood, aspect, and comparison. These are the traditional inflectional categories or simply grammatical categories.

In more recent linguistic theory the term has been used also more or less synonymously with 'class of construction', and distinctions are made between lexical and non-lexical (grammatical), terminal and non-terminal (or preterminal), major and minor categories (see esp. Chomsky 1965: 44, 212 fn 9).

Still more recently, Chomsky has proposed to discard categories altogether, replacing them by complex symbols of *features* (Chomsky 1970: 48–9). In Anderson's (1971a) framework both categories and features play a major role, but as noted by Bauer & Boagey in their sympathetic review of Anderson's book, it is not particularly clear what difference there is between, say, a category like erg and a feature like [+ergative] (Bauer & Boagey 1977: 138). Since I, too, shall be working with both categories and features, I need to make my terminology clear. The present section should be read, therefore, as an attempt to clarify my use of the terms 'class', 'category', and 'feature' rather than as a critical or polemical account of others'.[18]

A feature is a semantic primitive. It consists of two variables, one indicating a *value*, and one indicating a *name* [$\alpha$F]. The values of $\alpha$ may be one, two, three, four, ... n, and of these, 'two' may be of especial interest. This is the traditionally binary feature, which is normally

---

[18] For general discussion of the traditional grammatical categories, see Hockett (1958: 211ff); Hjelmslev (1941, 1972); Jespersen (1924); Kuryłowicz (1964); Lyons (1968: ch. 7). For discussion of one or more nominal categories, see Anderson (1971a: good bibl.), Fillmore (1968, 1977), Hjelmslev (1935/7) (case); Hjelmslev (1956), Ibrahim (1973), Royen (1929), Wienold (1967; good bibl.) (gender); Havers (1926), Hjelmslev (1956), Mey (1960), Sten (1949) (number).

symbolized by ' $\pm$ '. Perhaps higher-valued features may all be reducible to binary features, but, following Bierwisch (1967), I shall assume that some 'scalar' features are needed. Another problem with values on features is that of the 'Boolean condition' on binarism: Given a binary feature, $\pm$F, a positive value signals 'positive relevance' of F only, whereas a negative value may signify either 'negative relevance' or 'irrelevance' of F. Associated with, in the sense of being apparently directly explained by, this asymmetry is the general linguistic theory of 'markedness': a 'marked' member of an opposition is positively specified for some property P, whereas an 'unmarked' member may be regarded as either negatively specified or as neutral with respect to P. It will be convenient later to be able to speak of the value of a feature as being neutralized. For this reason I shall adopt a system of value-constants that include ' $+$ ' ( $=$ positive relevance of F) ' $-$ ' ( $=$ negative relevance of F) and 'o' ( $=$ unspecified relevance of F), whereas irrelevance of F will be indicated by the absence of the feature in question from a given complex system of features.

The name-variable F may be substituted by anything likely to convey the contribution to the meaning of a sign specified by [$\alpha$F]. In a 'natural' type of semantic representation this will mean that we have to substitute F by (what in other circumstances would count as) a sign in its own right. We still need to develop a viable 'semantic transcription' capable of presenting the content-side of signs, comparable to phonetic transcriptions designed to present the expression-side (in a Glossematic sense) of signs.

With respect to the notion of category, we note first that it is a *semantic* notion. As such it is closely related to features. I shall then define a category as a complex of features in which the *name*-variables have been substituted by constants. Consider gender. If this is a category, then it must be a complex of features, and I suggest that it is a complex of two features, at least in the Indo-European and the Semitic languages [$\alpha F_a$] and [$\alpha F_b$].

Instead of the constant-symbols $F_a$ and $F_b$, we may introduce the mnemonic symbols *male*, and *female*, and we may construct a formula that displays the intended points in the following fashion:
(25) gender ([$\alpha$male] & [$\alpha$female])
This formula can be read in two directions: gender is a category that consists of the features [$\alpha$male] and [$\alpha$female] or the complex symbol ([$\alpha$male] & [$\alpha$female]) is the category gender.

Traditionally, categories may also be viewed as classes with at least two members. From this angle, and provided that we still consider the notion of category a semantic notion, a category may be defined as a closed class the members of which are in paradigmatic contrast, and which is obligatory in the sense that a syntagm requires the presence of one and only one member of each category relevant to the syntagm (cf. §5.1 below). I shall define a member of a category as a complex of features in which not only the *name*-variables but also the *value*-variables have been substituted by constants.[19] Consider neuter. If this is a member of a category then it must be a complex of features with constants introduced for both name- and value-variables. The relevant formula is

(26)   neuter ([−male] & [−female])

The category that neuter is a member of is determined by the name-constants, which are the same as those entering into the defining formula for gender.

Consider lastly the sense of 'category' in which it is (more or less) equivalent to 'class *of construction*'. Implicit to this use is the notion of 'rank' (cf. esp. Halliday 1961). So far, I have referred to N (=nominal) and NP, etc., as categories without further modification. Such usage belongs to this last sense of 'category'. The question now is, is N a category on the definition adopted above? If it were it would have to be a complex of features in which the name-variables had been substituted by constants. For a number of reasons such a view would be untenable, especially since it would gloss over the notion of 'rank'. What a nominal is a complex of is *categories*, rather than *features*, and an ordered one at that. Anticipating matters somewhat, N consists of an ordered sequence of four functional categories and four lexical categories, or of three functional categories and three lexical categories. I shall henceforth call N a *class*. Thus a class has categories (or other classes) as members.

We can now relate the present discussion to the decision made at the end of the previous section to adopt a mixed format of grammatical description, making allowance for characteristics of both dependency and constituency. We shall say that the relationship holding between a class and another class, or between a class and a category, is one of

---

[19] I have deliberately simplified this point. A more precise formulation would be: in which the name-variables have been substituted by constants, and in which one and only one value is substituted for the value-variable, such that a selection has been made among the values of binary or multi-valued features.

constituency, such that, in the former instance, one class is a constituent of another class; in the latter, the category is a constituent of the class. If the same class has two or more categories as constituents, then these categories are internally ordered in a dependency system. This means, in configurational terms, that the only constituent to be connected to the dominating node is the (absolute) head of the associated dependency structure. Let C be a class, and let x, y, z, w, all be co-constituent categories of C. A mixed configuration will display one of the relevant situations as follows:

(27)

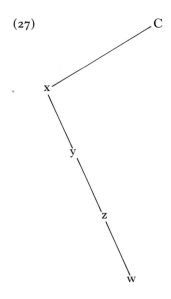

In this configuration, x is defined as the (absolute) head of the dependency structure x–y–z–w, but note that, relative to z, y is also 'head'. All four elements xyzw are co-constituents of C. Other configurations could, of course, be envisaged, for example one that involved y and z as co-dependents of x. However, unless we want to maintain that surface serialization is a direct reflection of underlying dependency structure – which seems to me to be unwise – we will meet with no linguistic phenomena in the present work that require representation by configurations differing from (27). But, as implied, this uniformity is bought at the price of introducing a transformational component that will handle natural serialization. In this respect the mixed format does not differ from simple PSG-models (nor from simple

DG-models either, I suspect, although this point may well be disputed; cf. Dahl (1971) for discussion of some pertinent points).

As should be clear from (27), all categories are terminal in the sense that lexical items may be inserted directly under them. In contrast, no class is terminal.

## 4.4  Referential phrases

In this section I shall develop the notion of referential phrase, which is crucial to RS-analysis. Following the implication stated (p. 44 above), I regard the system of referential phrases as a formalization of those semantic properties of NP that ensure that NP may perform the referential functions established in (16). I shall begin, therefore, with a discussion of just what those properties are.

### 4.4.1  Functional and lexical categories: FC and L. Consider the italicized NPs in

(28)  (a)  *the children* came out early
      (b)  *a child* is not always a blessing
      (c)  we heard *some children* playing in the yard
      (d)  I don't know what to do about *the children*
      (e)  *any child* could do that.

There is a naive sense in which we could say that all of these are the 'same'. This could only mean that we considered the presence of the lexeme CHILD a valid criterion on 'sameness'. More obviously, none of these NPs are the 'same' as any other in the list. Our criterion of 'sameness' is then no longer lexeme identity, but what we could call, loosely, *functional* identity, subsuming under this head a variety of oppositions.

Now it is an essential fact about English (and language in general, I suppose) that a lexeme (like CHILD) cannot occur in discourse – excepting metalinguistic discourse – without a number of functions being associated with it, not even in superficially deceptive cases like *I like child* (in appropriate cannibalistic circumstances). On the other hand, I shall suggest that some of the functional oppositions may be directly 'lexicalized' without requiring the presence of a lexeme, either necessarily (as in the case of proper names and certain pronouns) or contingently (as in the case of *some, this, it*, etc.).

The distinction that I am making in these terms is the traditional one between 'lexical' and 'functional' (or 'grammatical') meaning (cf. Lyons 1968: 435ff). Although this is hardly a distinction that is clear in every detail – how can we recognize different 'kinds' of meaning when we hardly know what meaning is – I believe that it is clear enough in outline for me to exploit it in more formal terms. I shall do so by recognizing two distinct types of category, *lexical* categories (L), and *functional* categories (FC). It is these two kinds of category that are associated with our doctrine of hearer's assignment of things to locations, in the following manner: L establish locations, categorial as well as spatio-temporal, whereas FC reflect the number and nature of the things to be assigned to the locations established by L.

**4.4.2 The referential phrase.** Consideration of two points discussed above – namely, that FC and L are *categories*, and that L presupposes FC whereas FC does not presuppose L – leads us to the recognition of a configuration such as:

(29)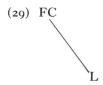

This is what I call a *referential phrase*. A referential phrase is a dependency structure consisting of two categories: a functional category which is governor, and a lexical category that is dependent. The referential phrase is the analytical tool with which we shall give an account of the ability of NP to perform the referential functions in (16). Any NP can be analyzed as the surface realization of a number of referential phrases.

The most pressing question that confronts us now, then, is the question of how many referential phrases to recognize. Taking the set of referential functions (16) as our starting-point, I assume that there is one referential phrase to account for each salient feature of (16). There are four salient features of the set of functions and consequently, there are four referential phrases:

(30)  (a)  one whose central concern is C;
      (b)  one whose central concern is ST;
      (c)  one whose central concern is 'all';
      (d)  one whose central concern is 'some'.

The four referential phrases we shall recognize are:

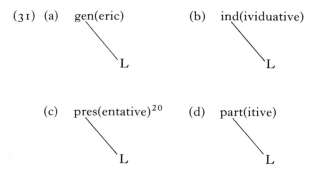

(31)   (a)   gen(eric)              (b)   ind(ividuative)

                    L                              L

       (c)   pres(entative)[20]     (d)   part(itive)

                    L                              L

That is, gen(eric), ind(ividuative), pres(entative), and part(itive) are the names of four functional RS-categories. There are also four lexical RS-categories, and when the need arises I shall distinguish between them by subscribing to L the name of the functional category that governs them, thus: $L_{gen}$, $L_{ind}$, $L_{pres}$, and $L_{part}$. If I want to speak about a particular referential phrase in the body of the text I shall symbolize it in this way: gen-L, ind-L, pres-L and part-L.

Judging the four referential phrases by the saliency feature of (30) that each is centrally concerned with in connection with the distinct functions of FC and L within the phrase, it is clear that FC is the 'salient' category in (c) and (d), whereas L is the 'salient' category in (a) and (b). This difference in 'saliency', however, does not affect the status of FC and L as governor and dependent, respectively. It does, however, reflect a difference in the 'ease' with which the categories are lexicalized. Salient categories are 'easily' lexicalized, and when they are the NP in which they occur is semantically unmarked, or neutral. When a non-salient category is lexicalized, however, the resultant NP is semantically marked.

### 4.5 Summary of main points

Before I continue with, in particular, the ordering of the four referential

---

[20] 'Presentative' has a certain standing as a more or less clearly defined term in discussions of referentiality. It is one of the terms used by Carnoy (1927) in his discussion of the psychological functions of the Greek articles. Collinson (1937: 37) reports on Kalepky's distinction between 'apperceptive' and 'presentative' expressions, of which the latter type is said to be expressions of 'indication' (Collinson's term for deixis), more 'objective' than mere zero-indication, which is a characteristic of 'apperceptive' expressions.

phrases in a dependency system and lexical insertion which is closely related to that ordering, it might be helpful if I briefly summarized the main points of chapter 4.

Any NP performs one or more referential functions in addition to one or more syntactic functions. Any NP is therefore a referential expression.

Only those referential functions are covered here that are performed by NPs functioning as subject, object, or complement to a preposition. This means that the referential function(s) performed by NPs functioning as (subject or object) predicates is (are) left unaccounted for.

A referential function is a function performed by a sign by which it invites the hearer to assign things to locations, both categorial and spatio-temporal.

On the basis of various considerations pertaining to our ability to speak in conjunction with our faculties for perceptual discrimination, twelve simple referential functions can be identified.

Since no one-to-one correlation between these simple referential functions and NPs can be found, the simple functions are considered to be constituents in a number of composite referential functions.

We can identify three composite referential functions, *sortal*, *selective*, and *identitive*. These may all be either *conditional* or *non-conditional*.

The capability of NP to perform these referential functions is due to the fact that NPs have certain (referential–semantic) properties.

These properties are conceived of as *categories*.

There are two distinct kinds of RS-category: functional and lexical. Lexical categories establish locations, both categorial and spatio-temporal. Functional categories reflect the number and nature of the things to be assigned to the locations established by the lexical categories.

The analytical unit central to RS-analysis is the referential phrase. Such a phrase consists of one functional category and one lexical category.

All RS-categories are co-constituents of the same class, N. As such they are ordered in an internal dependency relationship. In particular, within the referential phrase the functional category is the governor of the lexical category.

There are four different referential phrases, gen-L, ind-L, pres-L, and part-L. These are derived from the salient features of the three referential functions.

# 5 Referential–semantic features

## 5.1 Features on FC

It is assumed that FC dominates linguistic material that would be interpreted as having grammatical or functional meaning, such as the articles, (other) determiners, quantifiers, and classifiers, whereas the denotative categories (L) dominate material that would be interpreted as having lexical meaning. The present section will be devoted to an account of the – functional – features on FC. The – lexical – features on L will be dealt with in §5.3. Cf. Bierwisch (1971) for detailed arguments in favour of a similar distinction between two comparable types of semantic features.

Central to the present account are the traditional grammatical categories – case, gender, tense, mood, etc. – among which standard descriptions of the (classical) Indo-European languages usually recognize as the indispensable nominal categories the following: case, gender, number, and person. Views differ as to whether definiteness should be accorded categorial status (possibly subsumed under the label 'article') on a par with these four, and the status of person as a purely nominal category is sometimes disputed.

There are good reasons not to regard either definiteness or person as being of the same primitive status as case, gender, and number (see §§8.1, 10.2.2 for details), and there are further good reasons to suppose that these three primitive categories must be supplemented with yet a fourth which is not normally given independent categorial status, namely, countability (cf. §5.1.3).

Before embarking on a more detailed discussion of these four categories a general point should be made. At several junctures in Lyons (1968: ch. 7), comments are made on various interdependencies between two or more of the categories we are interested in. Thus number and gender are discussed in the same paragraph (7.3), number and countability are discussed together (7.3.1), and case and gender are

74

seen as interdependent in the Indo-European languages (7.4.3). Reflection upon these points would appear to sanction a general characterization at a fairly high level of abstraction, something like this: Although various, particularly inflectional, characteristics of the Indo-European languages permit us to distinguish (at least) four nominal categories, these categories are interrelated in ways that suggest a common background to them all. This, I take it, is sufficiently general to arouse no serious objection. I want now to supplement this general formulation with a more specific, and potentially controversial, suggestion, a suggestion that was already foreshadowed in chapter 4. The common ground of the grammatical categories is meaning. It is that area of meaning in which the *perceptual* characteristics of the things we mention are given linguistic embodiment, such as the number of them, what we take to be their essential and contingent properties, where they are, what they do or have done to them, etc. The fact that no semantic basis can yield an exhaustive explanation of, for example, gender (Ibrahim 1973; but cf. also Wienold 1967) need not surprise us. The grammaticalization of the 'genus' distinctions in the Indo-European and Semitic languages – as opposed, apparently, to the lexicalization of them characteristic of many classifier languages – demands that appropriate morphemic distinctions be made even in those cases where the semantic motivation is absent.

The consequence of adopting a semantic view of the traditional grammatical categories is to take the following characteristics as defining for a grammatical category: (a) a grammatical category is a closed semantic system; (b) the members of the same category must be paradigmatically contrasted; (c) membership of a grammatical category must be limited to a finite, relatively small, set of members (in virtue of (a)); (d) no grammatical category can have only one member (in virtue of (b)); (e) any syntagm, for which a given grammatical category is relevant, must receive obligatory, systematic marking for one, and only one, member of the category. Notice that this last point does not commit me to the traditional view that members of grammatical categories must be realized by inflectional morphemes.

With respect to (c) I doubt that any specific number can be set up as a limit to how many members a given category may have. What is involved, it seems to me, is a scope sufficiently small for a speech-community to *know*, without reflection, precisely what other members are *excluded* by the employment of a given member. Studies of the highly intricate problems connected with diachronic reductions (and, rarely, additions) among the members of a given category are likely to shed light on this question (cf. Kuryłowicz 1964, and especially, Hjelmslev 1972).

I shall now turn to a more specific discussion of the four grammatical categories: case, gender, number and countability, paying especial attention to the questions of how they should be specified in terms of semantic features and what the relationship is between them and the four functional RS-categories gen, pres, part, and ind.

The grammatical categories (case, gender, etc.) are not identical with the referential–semantic categories (gen, part, etc.). They are, however, contained in them, or subsumed by them. That is, a given RS-category contains the features of one grammatical category, plus something more. We can therefore divide the discussion into two rough parts: (a) which RS-category is specified for which grammatical category; and (b) what is the nature of the 'surplus' which turns a grammatical category into a RS-category. The first part will be the topic of §§5.1.1–4, whereas the second part will be taken up in §5.1.5.

**5.1.1 . . . on gen.** By way of introduction to the present topic I shall make explicit an assumption that lies behind much of the discussion in chapter 4, namely that it is the primary referential function of lexical nouns to denote *kinds* of things.

I want now to relate this assumption to the well-known fact that gender is idiosyncratically characterized against the other nominal categories by the fact that it is invariant for a given noun. Whereas any noun in Latin, for example, inflects for five (six) cases and two numbers, it has no gender inflection. This distinguishes nouns from adjectives in Latin. (Cf. §5.1.3 for discussion of countability in relation to this characteristic.)

These two points together invite the suggestion that gender is subsumed by gen(eric), i.e. the head of that referential phrase whose central concern is the establishment of categorial locations ('kinds').

I have already suggested one reduction of gender to semantic features by way of illustration (§4.3.3). However, since our main stock of data will be drawn from modern English we might consider incorporating a feature that was redundant at earlier stages of the language, namely, [αanimate]. Gender, in modern English, is then equal to ([αanimate] & [αmasc] & [αfem]), where a choice of [−animate] in normal circumstances renders the choice of [±male] and [±fem] superfluous. This feature-specification at the same time is an integral part of the specification of gen.

**5.1.2 . . . on ind.** Individuative is the head in the referential phrase whose central concern is the establishment of ST-locations. The point that interests us here is the relationship between individuation, conceived as our capability of distinguishing between particulars, and the notion of ST-location, with a view to showing how this relationship can serve as the basis of the notional content of one of the three remaining grammatical categories.

The fundamental issues are discussed by Strawson (1959: ch. 1), whose conclusion is that identification of particulars ultimately relies on a unified framework of spatio-temporal co-ordination imputed to all of us.

Accepting this relationship between individuation and ST-location we may now pursue our issue by saying that individuation is the precondition for our capacity to distinguish between two or more *identical* particulars, and hence that our unified framework of spatio-temporal co-ordination is the basis of the notional content of the grammatical category of number. This is sufficient for our present purposes, but some pertinent points will be raised in the next section.

Number, in modern English, is apparently a category that consists of just one feature, say [$\alpha$singular]. However, there are good reasons to suppose that the singular form of an English noun is unmarked *vis à vis* the plural form. I shall therefore take [$\alpha$plural] to be more appropriate.

I shall now explore a possibility of giving a more precise feature specification for number, for it is not quite as simple as it appears. First of all, the number category has undergone a historical change from Old English to Modern English: Old English still had remnants of a dual. Secondly, certain quantifiers (notably *some*) may occur in construction with a noun in plural as well as in singular form. This fact could no doubt be captured by the employment of just the one feature [$\alpha$plural], but it would lead to a 'lopsided' account of the relationship between, on the one hand, *some* and numerals like *two*, *three*, *four*, etc. (which cannot, of course, appear with a noun in singular form), and, on the other, between *some* and *one*, *a(n)*. What is needed, it seems to me, to solve this potential lopsidedness is a feature that states whether a *specific* number of things is being mentioned, say [$\alpha$specified].

The number category in Modern English is then taken to consist of the feature complex ([αplural] & [αspecified]). The members of the category are:

(1)  (a)  specified plural ([+plur] & [+spec])
     (b)  plural ([+plur] & [−spec])
     (c)  specified singular ([−plur] & [+spec])
     (d)  singular ([−plur] & [−spec]).

These members are systematically distinguished morphologically and syntagmatically: (a) and (b) by /-s/ vs. (c) and (d) by /-∅/; (a) by co-occurrence with *two*, *three*, etc., vs. (b) by co-occurrence with zero and *some*;[1] (c) by co-occurrence with *one*, *a(n)*, vs. (d) by co-occurrence with zero and *some*.

**5.1.3 . . . on part.** Partitive is the head in the referential phrase whose central concern is 'some'. It is also, for reasons that will become clear during the following discussion and the discussion in §5.1.4, the RS-category which subsumes countability. Since countability is in many respects a tricky notion, and since it is rarely, if at all, seen as a separate category – separate from number, that is – I shall discuss it in fairly great detail, taking my point of departure from a short article by Hjelmslev (1956) which has only appeared in Danish and which therefore cannot be assumed to be widely known.

Hjelmslev's main objective in that article is to point out the inter-relations between gender and number, as indeed the title suggests. What emerges, however, is implicit recognition of an intermediate area between the two categories, in some sense shared by them but not identical with either of them. It is this area which I propose to raise to categorial status in its own right, and which I propose to call the category of countability.

Hjelmslev discusses a distinction between what is perceived as being unlimited, spreading, diffuse, suggesting for this the term *expansive*, and what is perceived as being limited, formed or shaped, firmly confined in space and time, suggesting for this the term *concentrated*. These two terms may fairly easily be seen as two values of the same semantic feature, say [±concentrated]. This is the area shared by gender since

---

[1] Note the syncretism between the two plural members brought about by co-occurrence with numerals like 100, 1000, etc. It is noteworthy, also, that different languages adopt a different (large) numeral as the sign of unspecified number of large quantity, English *101*, Danish *117*, French *trente six*, etc.

the distinction is sometimes brought out in terms of the gender distinction in Danish between /-*n*/ (common gender; [+conc]) and /-*t*/ (neuter; [−conc]). Cf.:

(2)(a) *den* øl    de    brygger er god
        the beer they brew    is good
   (b) *det* øl    de    brygger er god*t*
        the beer they brew    is good.

The difference between (a) and (b) which interests us here (and there are others) can be stated roughly as follows: (a) would be used to indicate that, among several competing types or labels of beer, the actual one that 'they' brew is good; (b), on the other hand, would rather be used to indicate that, whichever sample of 'their' beer production you were to try, it is sure to be good.

A similar distinction applies to an area shared by number. Hjelmslev considers the singular as conveying the notion of something firmly joined, undivided. His term for this is *compact*. The plural, on the other hand, is said to convey the notion of something spread out, distributed. This he calls *discrete*. Once again, these two terms are easily seen as opposites, and I shall conflate them in the feature [±discrete]. One of the examples that he discusses on the compact/discrete axis is the French distinction between *la neige* (of the snow on the ground) vs. *les neiges* (of the snow(-flakes) in the air).

Now the metaphorical language that Hjelmslev employs in order to describe the content of these two 'features', as we have seen, is quite similar in both instances – except for one thing. What he calls *discrete* is clearly a collection of individuals regarded *en bloc*, as opposed to what he calls *expansive*, which is something amorphous, unindividualized. Because of this, and despite the great number of metaphors shared by *compact* and *concentrated* on the one hand, and by *discrete* and *expansive* on the other, I venture to regard the area defined by these terms as the area of countability, constituting a 'linking' category between gender and number, rather than an area in which gender and number lose their respective identities, as suggested by Hjelmslev (1956: 180).

However, Hjelmslev is clearly right in suggesting a *close* semantic affinity between gender and number. And in consequence of what I have just said, I should be inclined to include countability in a group of three grammatical categories between which close semantic affinities can be found. These semantic affinities seem to me to converge on the notion of *individuation*: gender is a systematic linguistic means of individuation in terms of inherent properties, or *kind*; countability is a systematic linguistic means of individuation in terms of contingent properties; and number is a systematic linguistic means of individuation in terms of spatio-temporal co-ordination.

Let me now comment on the affinities between, on the one hand, gender and countability, on the other number and countability. It was said above that gender was characteristic in being invariant for a given noun. Furthermore, the class of nouns in a gender language (like Danish or German) must be exhaustively subclassified in gender-classes. Now it is often said of English that a given noun 'is' either countable or uncountable, which would seem to mean that we could subclassify the class of nouns in English exhaustively as either countable or uncountable. If we could, then the countability-system of English would be directly comparable to the gender system of Danish. But we cannot. Except for a relatively small number of noun-pairs, the members of which are lexicalizations of the countability distinction (*laugh* vs. *laughter*, *sheep* vs. *mutton*, *shadow* vs. *shade* etc.), we cannot say of a given noun that it 'is' either countable or uncountable 'in itself'. It is always possible to 'recategorize' a (so-called) countable noun as uncountable, and vice versa. In contrast, it is never possible to 'recategorize' a German masculine noun as feminine or neuter. In cases where the 'same' noun appears in two genders (e.g. *der See* and *die See*), *two* nouns are recognized, not one which may be 'recategorized'.

The distinction between the two categories of gender and countability is now clear: if a language has gender distinctions then it has a systematic means of subcategorizing its nouns in such a manner that the subclassification is absolute and allows no recategorization; if a language has countability-distinctions then it has a systematic means of subcategorizing its nouns in such a manner that the subcategorization is relative and allows recategorization. On this distinction, English is a countability language, German a gender language and Danish is both a gender and a countability language.

The very term 'countability' invokes consideration of numbers; and it is indeed common, for pedagogical purposes, to describe uncountable nouns as nouns that cannot occur in the plural. It would not be true to say, however, that uncountable nouns are nouns that denote entities (substance) that cannot be counted. This would mean that nouns in different languages which have the same denotatum would have to be identical in terms of countability, which they are not always. Cf. Danish and English:

(3)(a) et  stykke legetøj = a toy
       a   piece (of) toy
   (b) et  møbel = a piece of furniture
   (c) en  ukrudsplante = a weed
       a   weed  plant
   (d) ukrudt = weeds

If there is a semantic relationship between countability and number, the logical, or perhaps just common-sense, view of it would be that countability is a precondition on plurality; if a noun is countable, then and only then it can be plural. But what is not always appreciated is that countability is of necessity also a precondition on *singularity*. This lack of appreciation is due to the fact (in English) that any noun must occur in either singular or plural *form*. Since the singular form is commonly the form of uncountable nouns, uncountables are held to be 'singular'. This is nonsense from a semantic viewpoint. For a noun to be *semantically* either singular or plural, it *must* be countable; if a noun is uncountable, the question does not arise whether it is *semantically* either singular or plural. It is a separate, and fairly uninteresting, question what *form* is used to express the various semantic distinctions. It is also a question that admits no general and exhaustive answers, since both plural and singular form may be used to express all the semantic distinctions, thus necessitating a fairly extensive list of 'irregular' nouns in descriptions of Modern English.

Having in this way opted squarely for a semantic conception of number and countability, we may now specify the members of the category of countability. In fact they are well known:

(4)    (a)  count ([+concentrated] & [+discrete])
       (b)  mass ([+concentrated] & [−discrete])
       (c)  collective ([−concentrated] & [+discrete])
       (d)  abstract ([−concentrated] & [−discrete]).

**5.1.4 . . . and on pres.** Presentative is the head in the referential phrase whose central concern is 'all'. It will also by now be clear that I consider pres to subsume the last of the four traditional categories, case. Like many other traditional terms, 'case' is ambiguous. It may be taken to cover the syntagmatic relations between a verb and its arguments, or it may be taken to cover the inflectional morphemes that in some languages express syntagmatic relations between verb and arguments. Case, in the former sense, is a syntactico-semantic term, and it is this sense that is prevalent in modern theories of case like Fillmore's and J. Anderson's. In the latter sense, 'case' is a morphological term of some importance for the establishment of language typologies. I shall take 'case' in the former sense, contrasting it with 'case-form' whenever the need for a distinction arises.

Case is radically different from the other three categories we have been looking at in being a *relational* category. It might, indeed, be argued that it plays no role in a referential–semantic analysis, but belongs exclusively to syntactico-semantic analysis. It is, however, a fact of some significance in this connection that case-forms, wherever they occur, are morphemes on *nouns*. Indeed, case is the category in terms of which Hjelmslev (1928: 316) *defines* the class of verbs, by the negative demonstration that the verb is the only class *incapable* of case-marking. There are, however, languages (Hungarian, Amerindian, Eskimo, and perhaps even (proto-)classical languages (Kretschmer 1947)), which have so-called 'objective' (or 'definite') conjugations which might be regarded as morphological case-inflections of verbs. In so far as the distinction is apposite, such instances seem to me to be rather pronominal reflexes than merely case-inflection.

The interpretation that I shall propose of this is that, although case is basically a category which 'mediates' between verbs and nouns,[2] it is also a category the presence of which is required *within* a nominal in the form of a replica of the semantic content of the relational category.

The search for appropriate specifications of the semantic content of the case-systems of various languages is as old as linguistics. The issues have been raised in modern times by a number of scholars; and some of these, e.g. Anderson (1971a, 1977), Hjelmslev (1935/7), and Nilsen (1972, 1973), have attempted to give such specifications in terms of semantic features.

Of these proposals that by Anderson (1977: 115ff) is the simplest. What is more, its localist foundation makes it particularly attractive to RS-analysis.

---

[2]  Case-relations may be viewed as dependency-relations between a verb and its arguments, as in Andersonian case-grammar (and, indeed, in most traditional grammatical theory). Then the distinction posited here between *classes* and *categories* (cf. §4.3.3), and the concomitant distinction between constituency and dependency, may create some problems. Since they would be problems for SS-analysis, however, I shall leave them on one side, assuming that they can be solved in a satisfactory manner.

Anderson's main thesis is that the case-system of any language may be explained and described on the basis of just two semantic components, [αplace] and [αsource].[3] These combine into four different cases ( = case-relations):

(5)  absolutive ([ −place] & [ −source])
     ergative ([ −place] & [ +source])
     locative ([ +place] & [ −source])
     ablative ([ +place] & [ +source]).

Each of the four cases abs, erg, loc, and abl does not always stand in a one-to-one correlation with a given case-form (or other form of expression); they may combine in various ways to give composite 'cases'. A tentative set of rules is provided for the delimitation of such composite cases (Anderson 1977: 109).

Whether this set of simple cases and the set of composite cases allowed by the rule-schemata are precise enough for an exhaustive SS-analysis is not my concern here. I shall simply adopt the specifications (5) as a viable notation for my purposes, assuming that they constitute a reasonable basis for SS-analysis.

**5.1.5 Lexical reflexes of FC.** The formal reflexes of the four grammatical categories in inflectional languages like Latin and in agglutinating languages like Turkish are typically what are variously known as grammatical morphemes, grammatical formatives, structural items, flexives, etc. I shall employ the term *flexive*. Thus a flexive is a bound morpheme which expresses the meaning of a member of a *grammatical* category.

However, as already intimated, the grammatical categories are subsumed by the functional RS-categories. Differently formulated, a functional category is a grammatical category plus 'something more'. It is the nature of the 'something more' that shall occupy us now.

Initially we shall say that the functional RS-categories, possibly in addition to reflexes by flexives, have language-specific *lexical* reflexes which are associated with their metaphysical origin: pres contains the meaning expressed in English by *all*, gen that expressed by *kind*, part that expressed by *some*, and ind that expressed by *one* (*two, three,* ...). I take these to be the semantic primitives of English in terms of which all referential functives (see §7.1) are to be analyzed.

---

[3] Anderson's (1977: 115) features are unary, SOURCE and PLACE. I have modified them in accordance with the notation for semantic features proposed in §4.3.3.

Consider gen. It is held to contain the meaning expressed by English *kind*, plus the meaning of the grammatical category of gender. Suppose we indicate this in the following fashion:

(6)   gen ([αkind] & [αanim] & [αmasc] & [αfem]).

The morphological material employed in various languages to express the members of this category is not only highly diversified owing to language-specific rules, but it may also be discriminated more generally in terms of the distinction between lexicalization and grammaticalization.

Assuming all members relevant to the present discussion to be marked [+kind], English is fairly simple in this connection. Disregarding pronouns for the moment, the most important morphological reflex of the category is the noun *kind* itself. This would be treated as an instance of lexicalization.

Consider next German. Here the (singular) definite articles indicate the gender of the associated noun (among other things irrelevant to the present topic), and they may therefore be seen as reflexes of the features ([αanim] & [αmasc] & [αfem]) only. These are flexives and would, as such, be instances of grammaticalization.

Latin is more complex. Still assuming the presence of [+kind], morphological expression differs according to the values chosen for the remaining features in the category. The morphemes in question are, of course, the 'thematic' elements on the basis of which Latin nouns are divided into gender-classes. These are bound morphemes, but they are not flexives. They are a systematic means of indicating what form an associated flexive should have, operating in conjunction with case-distinctions and number-distinctions. The three situations may be illustrated as follows:

(7)   (English) *kind*        : $\left\{ \begin{array}{l} [+\text{kind}] \\ \begin{bmatrix} [\alpha\text{anim}] \\ [\alpha\text{masc}] \\ [\alpha\text{fem}] \end{bmatrix} \end{array} \right\}$  $\left. \begin{bmatrix} -a- \\ -o- \\ -e- \\ -i- \\ -u- \\ -C- \end{bmatrix} \right\}$: (Latin)

(German) *der, die, das*:

Morphemes, like the Latin thematic elements, which neutralize the distinction between lexicalization and grammaticalization will be called *formatives* (e.g. German *-chen, -lein*; English *-ess, -hood*).

The English signs for which a specification as [−kind] is feasible are first and second person personal pronouns, some indefinite pronouns, and proper names (see § 10.2).

In analogy with (6) we can now give the specifications of the other three functional RS-categories:

(8) (a) part ([αsome] & [αconc] & [αdisc])
    (b) ind ([αitem] & [αplur] & [αspec])
    (c) pres ([αall] & [αquest] & [αplace] & [αsource]).

English is typologically characteristic in having a relatively low number of flexives. It is, in fact, only in (8)(b) we find a clear instance of a flexive, namely /-s/ for the plural members. The so-called genitive in /-s/ – which is a special kind of determiner – will be commented on in § 10.4.1. In all other instances English lexicalizes these categories, if not always directly; cf. § 8.4 for further clarification. The feature [αquestion] is lexicalized in Danish (*mon*) and Latin (*num*, *(non)ne*), but no material morphological status can be given to it in English. As already indicated, Danish grammaticalizes the countability distinction in (8)(a) in connection with certain quantifiers. Consider the four Danish nouns in (9) in connection with the quantifier *nogen/noget* ( = *some* or *any*):

(9)(a) *en* bil  – bil*en* (common gender; typically [ + count])
       a car  car-the
   (b) *et* hus  – hus*et* (neuter gender; typically [ + count])
       a house  house-the
   (c)      kaff*en* (common gender; typically [ − count])
            coffee-the
   (d)      smørr*et* (neuter gender; typically [ − count])
            butter-the

| (10) | | [ + count] | | [ − count] |
|---|---|---|---|---|
|  |  | [ − plur] | [ + plur] |  |
| common |  | nogen bil | nogen biler | noget kaffe |
| neuter |  | noget hus | nogen huse | noget smør |

The gender distinction between -*n* and -*t* seen in countable singulars is neutralized in favour of a countability distinction, also brought about (in the spoken language)[4] by -*n* and -*t*, between countable plurals and uncountables.

---

[4] In the written language, and sometimes in careful speech, the form *nogle* is used as a plural form common to both genders.

## 5.2 The hierarchy of referential phrases

A nominal was defined (§4.3.1) as a class constituted by a number of referential categories ordered in referential phrases. Since the head of a referential phrase was said to be the functional category (FC), not only is the number of referential phrases dictated by the number of FCs in a nominal, it is also FC that determines the dependency hierarchy said to obtain among the referential phrases. Two possibilities offer themselves for a formal characterization:

(11)  (a)

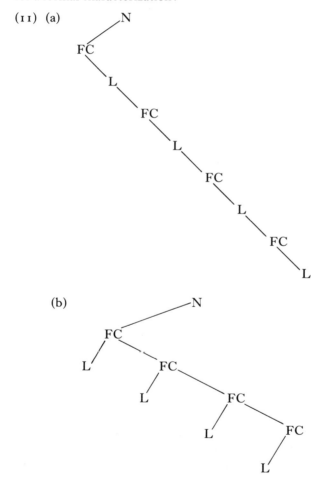

(b)

That is, (a) although $L_y$ is a dependent of $FC_y$, it is head relative to $FC_x$ immediately below it; or (b) a given L is always only a dependent, never a head relative to any other category. The reasons for preferring

(a) to (b) were given above (p. 65). It is the object of the present section to discuss more fully the principles behind (11)(a) and to establish what labels should be inserted for the variable FCs in it.

The classical dependency relation, as formalized by Hjelmslev (1939; 1943: 23, 33 under the name 'determination'), relies on a notion of presupposition. If y depends on x, then the occurrence of y presupposes the occurrence of x, or, equivalently, the occurrence of x is a necessary condition on the occurrence of y. The conditioning term, x, is then a constant, the conditioned one, y, a variable, so determination is a relation of dependency between a constant and a variable. Hjelmslev's two other dependency relations, interdependence and constellation, are defined to hold between two constants and between two variables, respectively, so the two terms in an interdependency presuppose each other, whereas those in a constellation do not.

It is now important to notice that, in a determination, it is the variable that determines the constant, and further (Hjelmslev 1939: 143) that the statement 'y determines x' is equivalent to the statement 'x governs y'. In relation to a referential phrase of the form

(12)  FC

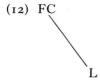

      L

FC is the cover-term for a constant and L for a variable, and the following equation would appear to be valid:

(13)  L depends on FC = FC governs L = L determines FC = L presupposes FC.

It is explicitly allowed for by Hjelmslev (1943: 31) that a 'function' (i.e. a relation plus its terms) may be a 'functive' (i.e. a term of a relation). We therefore also speak about dependencies among referential phrases.

Among the difficulties raised by Hjelmslev's characterization of dependency, the gravest is the unclarity of the notion of presupposition in connection with the notion of occurrence. Hjelmslev's favourite example concerns the Latin preposition *sine*. Traditionally, *sine* is said to govern the ablative. By the criterion of presupposed occurrence, however, it is clear that the ablative must govern *sine*: the occurrence of an ablative (*any* ablative) is a necessary condition on the occurrence of *sine*, whereas the occurrence of any ablative does not presuppose the occurrence of *sine*. We get the configuration:

(14)  ablative

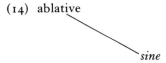

*sine*

Yet the occurrence of a *particular* ablative may be due to the occurrence of *sine*, as in *vitiis nemo sine nascitur* ('no one is born without vices'). Here *vitiis* is 'necessarily called forth' by the occurrence of *sine*, so we get the configuration:

(15)  *sine*

*vitiis*

One way of resolving this seeming incongruity is to relate the configuration (14) to the language system (*la langue*) and (15) to the language process (*la parole*) but this would hardly be satisfactory – and it is not what Hjelmslev does – unless a reasonable account is provided why variables in the system may become constants in the process, and vice versa. Such an account is implicit in the very organization of the dependency structure (11)(a).

Like all other formal systems designed to generate linguistic structures, (11)(a) may be regarded from a dynamic as well as from a static viewpoint. From a dynamic angle (11)(a) represents the working of an ordered sequence of dependency rules of the general form:

(16)  (a)  $FC_x (*L_x)$
      (b)  $L_x (*FC_y)$

which apply after relevant rewrite rules have produced an unordered sequence of symbols from N:

(17)  $N \rightarrow FC + L$.

From a static angle, (11)(a) represents the result of the application of (rewrite and) dependency rules. Quite clearly, for all categories except the 'highest' (and the 'lowest', unless recursion is allowed – which it will be; cf. below, §6.5), each category whether lexical or functional, can be described alternately under the dynamic viewpoint as governor (head) and dependent (or constant and variable), depending on the stage of derivation reached at any one time. Under the static viewpoint, all categories (except, again, the 'highest') can be described as either constant or variable, depending on whether it is seen in relation to 'lower' or 'higher' categories. This changing nature of the categories has an important consequence connected with the dynamic viewpoint of (11)(a). The movement in which the 'nature' of the categories changes is invariably from variable to constant, not vice versa (since we start from a constant). This means that (11)(a) may in fact be viewed both as a hierarchy of determinations, or, as I shall say henceforth, *unilateral dependencies*, and as a hierarchy of interdependencies, but *not* as a hierarchy of constellations. And this is in keeping with Hjelmslev's remarks (1943: 25) that, from a 'universal' point of view, the relation between *sine* and its regimen may 'on occasion' be interdependence.

Recall now that the lexical reflexes (in English) of the categories gen, part, ind, and pres are, respectively, *kind, some, one,* and *all*, which I regard as primitives. These primitives arrange themselves in an implicational hierarchy:

(18)  all x are f ⊃ there is a kind of x, all of which are f ⊃ some x are f ⊃ one x is f.

I should perhaps point out, since *kind* is not an operator of logical systems, that the only implicational direction between *kind* and *some* is the one given; we are not allowed to infer that, just because some houses are red, there is a kind of house which is red.

The implicational hierarchy (18) provides us with a basis for the hierarchy of referential phrases, as displayed in (19):

(19)

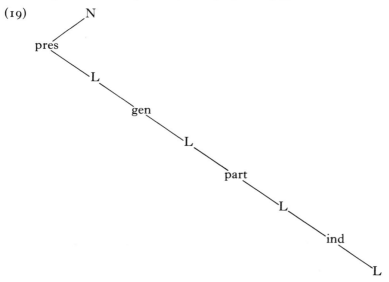

We are now in a position to recast the terminology of (13), aligning it with two concrete situations: one in which each FC in (19) is a constant and each L a variable (i.e. one of the possible 'static' situations in which (19) is a hierarchy of unilateral dependencies), and one in which every category of (19) is a constant (i.e. the 'static' situation when (19) is a hierarchy of interdependencies).

I shall adopt the term 'presupposes' as a term characterizing the structure as a hierarchy of unilateral dependencies, so that $L_{pres}$ is said to presuppose pres, $L_{gen}$ to presuppose gen, etc., and gen-L is said to presuppose pres-L, part-L to presuppose gen-L, etc. Presupposition, taken in this way, is still a relation between two terms, x and y, such that, if y presupposes x, y presupposes the occurrence, or presence, of x; but what this means should be explained in notional terms. Let x be pres-L and y gen-L. To say that gen-L presupposes pres-L is to say that we cannot mention a given kind of thing without implicit recognition of a class of things which do *not* belong to that kind. These two classes, the class of the particular kind of thing plus its complement class, constitute the class of all things. Thus pres-L, with its notional content of 'all things', serves as a background against which gen-L with its notional content of 'a kind of things', may be set off.

In contrast, the term 'determines' characterizes the structure (19) as a hierarchy of interdependencies. Thus gen-L is said to determine pres-L, part-L to determine gen-L, etc. The explanation of this term is again notional. To say that gen-L determines pres-L is to say that the feature specification on gen-L delimits, or specifies, or narrows down, the feature specification on pres-L. Determination, in this sense, becomes the basis of what is generally known as selectional restrictions; see especially §5.3.2 for further details.

Finally, the term 'governs', as in 'x governs y', will be used indiscriminately as between unilateral dependency and inter-dependency. All it says is that x is immediately above y in the hierarchy.

## 5.3  Features on L

The features on L, or the denotative features, are, I suppose, the nearest equivalent in the present framework to the 'classical' semantic features like [±human], [±abstract], etc.

Among the host of methodological and theoretical objections levied against componential analysis, one is that semantic analysis by means of components is circular because (a) the status of the relationship between 'words' and components is unclear, and (b) because no component offers itself as a 'natural' starting-point for componential analysis. I attempted to meet the first half of this objection above (§2.1).

The second half of the objection must be met on the ground of a particular form of semantic analysis. Taking meaning as a set of conditions on non-linguistic entities, as we do here, *components* of meaning must be abbreviations, or specifications, of single conditions on non-linguistic entities. A componential specification of a lexeme is therefore a formula indicating the set of necessary and sufficient conditions to be satisfied by a non-linguistic entity for that entity to be properly denoted by the lexeme. It is possible, on these grounds, to enquire after a 'natural' starting-point for componential analysis; and such a starting-point must be of a metaphysical nature, in that it must yield a semantic component which specifies the most general condition on non-linguistic entities. I shall call this component [$\alpha$entity]. This feature establishes the basic metaphysical distinction between *things* ([+entity]) and *locations* ([−entity]). Beginning from this feature we can – in principle and by definition – derive all other denotative specifications by a process of systematically choosing one of the values of whatever subsequent features we introduce.

**5.3.1 ... on L$_{pres}$.** The feature [$\alpha$entity] is presupposed – in the sense of §5.2 – by all other denotative features. It is therefore a feature on the lexical category which is presupposed by all the other lexical categories, namely, L$_{pres}$. There is, in English at least, only one other feature on L$_{pres}$, which I shall call [$\alpha$person], in terms of which things are distinguished from people. It is introduced by [+entity].

(20)  L$_{pres}$ ([$\alpha$entity] & [$\alpha$person])

The members of lexical categories are lexemes, or, more precisely, abstract items that may on occasion be substituted directly by a lexeme (see further §5.5). The members of (20) are (in English):

(21)  (a) 'place' ([−entity])
      (b) 'thing' ([+entity] & [−person])
      (c) 'people' ([+entity] & [+person]).

What I am saying here is that L$_{pres}$, insofar as it is lexicalized at all – which it rarely is in English and, generally, Indo-European – can only be lexicalized by either *place*, *thing*, or *people*. I hereby imply a special status for just these three lexemes in English, a special status which is in accord with the availability of these three against all other lexemes for the register of angry and surprised English in expressions like

(22)  (a)  Charles gave me a spanner of all things!

(b)  I heard that joke from a priest of all people!

(c)  The teapot was in the catbox of all places!

Expressions like *today of all days, king of (all) kings*, etc. are reduplications which are not relevant in the present respect.

The special status of *thing* is further brought out by expressions like *that pencil-thing you gave me*, which are explicable on the assumption that ([+entity] & [−person]) on $L_{pres}$ may on occasion be lexicalized optionally, yielding a semantically 'marked' NP; cf. §4.4.2.

It might be held, also, that (21) are involved in the pronominal forms *somewhere, something*, and *somebody*. Some substance to this suggestion will be given in §10.2.4.

Notice finally that possible lexicalizations of $L_{pres}$ occur in French (*tout-le-monde*), and Danish (*allandsens*: a slightly archaic phrase found almost exclusively in the fixed collocation *maa allandsens ulykker ramme dig* (='may all possible misfortunes befall thee'); a transliteration would be 'all-the-country's misfortunes'; and *alverdens*: less archaic and more productive, it may be transliterated as 'all-the-world's__').

The noteworthy thing about these expressions is their obvious correlation with 'place', and their setting of bounds, as it were, for the occurrence of the things denoted by the head noun. They may quite easily be seen as establishing a spatial universe of discourse (cf. (23) below). *Tout-le-monde* has the peculiarity that it 'refers' to people although it 'lexicalizes' [−entity].

All the English, the French, and the Danish expressions are idiomatic. This correlates well with the suggestion (mentioned in passing and to be gone into more specifically in chapter 6) that pres-L, though an integral part of the referential structure of language, is not systematically exploited in Indo-European to the extent to which it is exploited by languages with numeral classifiers.

**5.3.2 ... on $L_{gen}$ and $L_{part}$.** $L_{pres}$, it was just said, is rarely lexicalized in English. Yet its notional content, as specified by the features ([αentity] & [αperson]), is determined – in the sense of §5.2 – by the content of $L_{gen}$. This latter category has already been mentioned as the node under which lexical nouns are generated, i.e. the category the members of which typically denote kinds of things. The category whose members determine lexical nouns is the category of adjectives, and that determining adjectives is the category of adverbs. Thus I consider $L_{part}$ as the node under which adjectives are generated and $L_{ind}$ as the node which generates adverbs, notably those of place, time, and degree (see further below, §5.3.3). The relationship between $L_{gen}$, $L_{part}$, and $L_{ind}$, as conceived here, can in fact be explained in terms of Jespersen's ladder:

The method of attaining a high degree of specialization is analogous to that of reaching the roof of a building by means of ladders: if one ladder will not do, you first take the tallest ladder you have and tie the second tallest to the top of it, and if that is not enough, you tie on the next in length, etc. In the same way, if *widow* is not special enough, you add *poor*, which is less special than *widow*, and yet, if it is added, enables you to reach farther in specialization; if that does not suffice you add the subjunct *very*, which in itself is much more general than *poor*. *Widow* is special, *poor widow* more special and *very poor widow* still more special, but *very* is less special than *poor*, and that again than *widow*. (Jespersen 1924: 108)

Although Jespersen is supposedly concerned with giving a grammatical account of the mechanisms of subordination, junction and adjuncts, he is in fact quite clearly giving a referential account in the quoted passage. The appeal to 'specialization' is only intelligible if he is thinking of the relative sizes of the classes whose members constitute the extension of the words 'widow', 'poor widow', and 'very poor widow'.

Such a progressive specialization is essentially what is expressed in the hierarchical structure which we can interpret in the following way:

(23)  the extension of pres-L = the universe of discourse;
      the extension of gen-L = the class of things whose members belong
      to the kind of thing spoken about in the universe of discourse;
      the extension of part-L = the class of things whose members
      belong to a given subclass of the class whose members belong to
      the kind of thing spoken about in the universe of discourse;
      the extension of ind-L = the class of things whose members are the
      individuals belonging to (a particular subclass of) the kind of thing
      spoken about in the universe of discourse.

Anderson (1973: 75) provides a feature-notation in terms of which nouns, adjectives and verbs may be distinguished:

| (24) | noun | adjective | verb |
|------|------|-----------|------|
| subst(antive) | + | − | − |
| stat(ive) | + | + | − |

Applying this notation to our lexical categories, I shall say that $L_{gen}$ (and $L_{pres}$) is inherently specified as ([+subst] & [+stat]), and $L_{part}$ as ([−subst] & [+stat]). Normally, however, the features on $L_{pres}$ are carried downwards in the hierarchy to be lexicalized by $L_{gen}$.

Apart from the features [αsubst] and [αstat], $L_{gen}$ and $L_{part}$ are both specified by denotative features, the precise nature of which need not concern us. Suffice it to say that they all denote various qualitative properties of things, either essential ($L_{gen}$) or contingent ($L_{part}$), such as size, shape, colour, age, sex, social status, etc. I shall therefore simply employ the term [αQUAL] as a variable for any complex symbol of denotative features.

As mentioned briefly above, we can now define selectional restrictions between adjective and noun in terms of determination by a particular complex symbol of denotative features of another particular complex symbol of features. Quite clearly, from a purely syntactic viewpoint – if such there is – the relationship between an attributive adjective and a noun may be described as unilateral dependency. We capture this view by saying that $L_{part}$ presupposes $L_{gen}$, or, in the absence of this – cf. §10.1 – $L_{pres}$. But equally clearly, from a semantic viewpoint, the relationship between a particular noun and a particular adjective is such that the question of compatibility is irresoluble in a non-arbitrary fashion on the basis of unilateral dependency alone. Should we say, for example, that *rancid* presupposes *butter*, or that *butter* presupposes *rancid*? Even in cases like this, involving an adjective with a very restricted range of co-occurrence possibilities, it takes but little reflection to see that both alternatives could be argued for. It is in this light that Hjelmslev's (1943: 23) footnote should be read, to the effect that the relation between adjective and noun in the language system is one of interdependence. And consequently I shall say that the question of compatibility between concrete feature specifications on $L_{gen}$ and $L_{part}$ should be settled with reference to the notion of interdependence, such that the specification on $L_{part}$ is said to *determine* the specification on $L_{gen}$.

It could perhaps be argued that not only the denotative features, but also the functional features were involved in this determination, and so it could well be for gender and countability. However, it cannot be so for case. Cf.:

(25)   (a)   the little house was quiet
      (b)   the little boy was quiet.

Apart from the actual denotative features, the underlying representation of (25)(a) differs from (b) only on one point. Instead of $L_{pres}$ being specified as ([+entity] & [+person]) as in (b), it is specified as [−entity] in the structure underlying (a). It is this difference that is behind their different ranges of paraphrasability:

(26)  (a)  it was quiet in the little house

(b)  *it was quiet in the little boy.

Unless some radical reorganization of the SS-component is contemplated, both *the little boy* and *the little house* in (25) are governed by abs, abs being the only obligatory case. In order to account for the asymmetric paraphrases in (26) we cannot, therefore, simply let *the little house* be governed by loc in the SS-component. Anderson's solution (1971a: 96–7) is to consider a (tentative) notion of 'reflexive locative clause' where loc is imposed on nom ( =abs, in Anderson 1971a).

The two different specifications for $L_{pres}$ suggested here, however, not only account neatly for the paraphrases in (26) but also highlight an important point in the distinction between entities and places.

If the choice between [+entity] and [−entity] determined the case on pres, so that [−entity] depended on loc (and perhaps abl), whereas [+entity] depended on abs (and erg), we could not account for the fact that language exploits the possibility of regarding entities as locations (and perhaps vice versa: cf. *Scotland beat England*). What is needed, and what the present analysis supplies, is a distinction between an 'extra-nominal' and an 'intra-nominal' source for locative. The former is characterized by the presence of loc in the SS-structure; the latter by [−entity] on $L_{pres}$ in the RS-structure.

Let me finally point out that not all nominals in which $L_{gen}$ is lexicalized by HOUSE have $L_{pres}$ specified as [−entity]. It would be specified as ([+entity] & [−person]) in e.g. *the little house collapsed*.

**5.3.3 . . . and on $L_{ind}$.** So far we have been concerned with denotative features on $L_{pres}$, $L_{gen}$, and $L_{part}$, or, in line with the suggestions towards the end of chapter 2, with features which establish categorial locations. We shall now look into the features on $L_{ind}$, which establish spatio-temporal locations.

However, since the justification for the position adopted presupposes a number of points not yet raised, I shall only give a general outline here and postpone the more detailed discussion to the chapter on determiners, with which $L_{ind}$ is intimately connected (see §9.1.1).

The two central features on $L_{ind}$ are $[\pm space]$ and $[\pm time]$. In addition to these, a feature, $[\alpha degree]$, is required, which, however, may possibly be a scalar variant of $[\pm space]$. At least a case could be made for regarding degree as some sort of abstract spatial ordering along a vertical axis. For the time being, I leave $[\alpha degree]$ out of account.

These two features are supposed to subsume the semantic properties which equip language with a deictic function. As such they are presumably universal. However, different languages superimpose a variety of further distinctions on these fundamental deictic features ('visible' vs. 'not-visible', 'approaching' vs. 'receding', and, most commonly in the Indo-European languages, various degrees of 'nearness' to one or more necessary components of the utterance situation). For the description of modern English just one such superimposed distinction is relevant, which I – following Lyons (1973) – shall call $[\alpha proximate]$. It is introduced by previous selection of either $[+space]$ or $[+time]$.

The members of $L_{ind}$ are then the well-known deictic adverbs *here*, *there*, *now*, and *then*, but with a distinction drawn between two functions of *there* and *then*:

(27)(a) 'here'    ($[+space]$ & $[+prox]$)
  (b) 'there$_2$' ($[+space]$ & $[-prox]$)
  (c) 'there$_1$' ($[-space]$)
  (d) 'now'    ($[+time]$ & $[+prox]$)
  (e) 'then$_2$' ($[+time]$ & $[-prox]$)
  (f) 'then$_1$' ($[-time]$)

Due to the co-presence of $[\alpha space]$ and $[\alpha time]$ on $L_{ind}$, each of (a)–(c) may combine with each of (d)–(f), yielding in all nine complex 'members' of the form 'here-now', etc.

The numerals subscripted to *there* and *then* are employed by Lyons (1973) (though for *there* only; he does not consider the temporal adverbs) – following Allan (1971) who in turn interprets Jespersen's (1949: §3.1) distinction between existential *there* and local *there* in these terms – to distinguish a weak (1) from a strong (2) non-proximate deictic adverb. I interpret Lyons' distinction as a synchronic parallel to the diachronic distinction established by Pilch (1968: 176; 1970: 22 and §29) in the Old English deictic system between 'swache Deixis' and 'starke Deixis' over and above the proximity system 'Jenerdeixis' and 'Dieserdeixis'. Lyons' and Pilch's analyses thus support each other – in a manner similar to that in which Christophersen's (1939)/Jespersen's

(1949) diachronic analysis of *a* is supported by, and supports, Perlmutter's (1969) synchronic analysis of *a* – so as to highlight the appropriateness of working with two deictic axes in the description of (modern) English.

I shall exploit the possibility which in this way offers itself as a basis for my account of the two ways in which individuation may take place (Searle 1969: 86): by description or by ostension. Since in both cases *individuation* takes place, ind-L must be present in the underlying structure of both kinds of individuating phrase. The difference between them – as yet stated only in barest outline – is that purely descriptive identifying phrases involve specifications of $L_{ind}$ which are not realized as strong (i.e. [$\alpha$prox]) deictics (spatial or temporal). In effect this means that only ([$-$space] & [$-$time]) is involved in purely descriptive identifying phrases, whereas the rest of the possible complex members of (27) are involved either in the derivation of purely ostensive identifying phrases, or in 'mixed' (i.e. subsuming both descriptive and ostensive elements) identifying phrases.

It is clear that purely descriptive identifying phrases rely exclusively on categorial location, whereas ostensive phrases rely also on spatio-temporal location. And since categorial locations are established by $L_{gen}$ and $L_{part}$ (and, sometimes, $L_{pres}$), it follows that the weak deictics indicate that the entity being talked about 'exists' in the sense that they guarantee that the categorial locations established under $L_{gen}$ and $L_{part}$ may have entities of level zero assigned to them. The weak deictics indicate that the feature-specifications which they determine are 'correct', i.e. that they specify a meaning that can be lexicalized.

This function is also inherent in the strong deictics. The strong deictics may therefore be interpreted as encapsulating the weak deictics plus an element of proximity.

## 5.4 Summarizing rules and sample derivation

The various points discussed in the course of the preceding sections can be summed up in terms of the following system of rules:

(28)  (A)  Rewrite rules:

     (1)  N → FC + L

$$(2)\quad FC \rightarrow \begin{pmatrix} pres \\ gen \\ part \\ ind \end{pmatrix}$$

where the parenthesis represents an inclusive disjunction.

   (B)  Dependency rules:
       (1)(a)  pres (*L)
          (b)  gen (*L)
          (c)  part (*L)
          (d)  ind (*L)
       (2)(a)  pres-L (*gen-L)
          (b)  gen-L (*part-L)
          (c)  part-L (*ind-L)
   (C)  Subcategorization rules:
       (1)(a)  pres ([$\alpha$all] & [$\alpha$quest] & [$\alpha$place] & [$\alpha$source])
          (b)  gen ([$\alpha$kind] & [$\alpha$anim] & [$\alpha$male] & [$\alpha$female])
          (c)  part ([$\alpha$some] & [$\alpha$conc] & [$\alpha$disc])
          (d)  ind ([$\alpha$item] & [$\alpha$plur] & [$\alpha$spec])
       (2)(a)  $L_{pres}$ ([$\alpha$entity] & [$\alpha$person])
          (b)  $L_{gen}$ ([+subst] & [+stat] & [$\alpha$QUAL])
          (c)  $L_{part}$ ([−subst] & [+stat] & [$\alpha$QUAL])
          (d)  $L_{ind}$ ([$\alpha$space] & [$\alpha$prox] & [$\alpha$time] & [$\alpha$prox])

If we wanted to attribute explicit generative capacity to these rules, some of them would have to be given a more precise formulation. For example, it would have to be specified as a contextual condition on (C)(2)(d) that [$\alpha$prox] is only introduced after [+space] and [+time]. These details are considered not to detract from the substance of the rules as a means of a formal characterization of a particular analytical strategy.

We can now proceed to give a sample derivation (see (30)) of:
(29)  all those five pretty girls (jilted John).


## 5.5  Lexical insertion: initial statement

It was mentioned above (§4.3.3) that categories are terminal symbols, which means that lexical material may be inserted directly below them in configurations like (30). But what is meant by 'lexical material'?

One of the basic assumptions of the present work is the validity of the Saussuro–Hjelmslevian biplane sign: a sign consists of an expression (form) and a content (meaning) between which interdependence holds. It is therefore clear that what is displayed by the configuration (30) is the *content* of the sign *all those five pretty girls*, and it is equally clear that what must be inserted under the category-symbols in (30) is graphic or

(30)

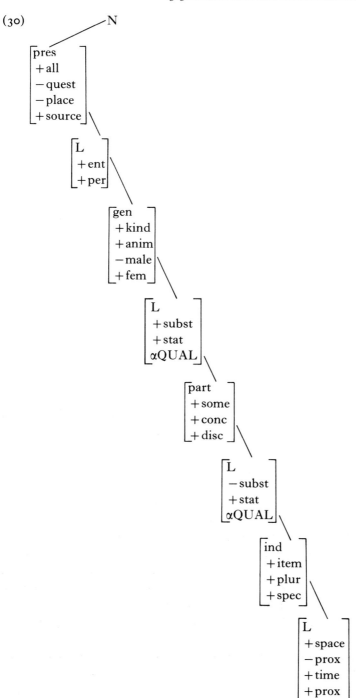

phonological expressions which carry the meaning of the category above them. The configuration (31) is thus equivalent to (30), in that it displays the formal expression of the appropriate category-members.

(31)

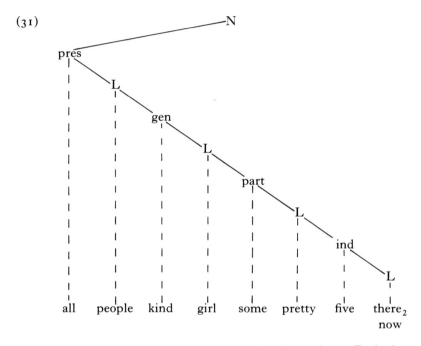

Both (30) and (31) are incomplete in themselves. Each is a representation of only one 'half' of the sign *all those five pretty girls*. A complete representation of a sign must therefore combine (30) and (31), since only such a composite representation will capture both the content and the expression of a sign.

(30) and (31) are similar in one respect, however. They both represent deep structure properties of the sign in question. It is obvious, particularly with respect to (31), that a number of processes must reorganize the relative order of categories, and delete or conflate others, in order for an acceptable surface string to be produced from (30)–(31). These processes are transformational in nature, and they will be described in detail in the following chapter. Before we come to that, however, I want to be explicit about the nature of lexical insertion as understood here.

Due to the semantic orientation of the framework, configurations like (30) will be taken to generate a string of 'dummy' symbols à la Chomsky

(1965), which may be interpreted as 'place-holders' or 'slots' in which appropriate graphic/phonological forms may be inserted. The substitution of these dummy symbols by graphic forms does not take place until appropriate transformations have produced a final derived string of categories. In 'traditional' terminology, then, lexical insertion is here understood to be a process of post-cyclic transformation.

# 6 *Subjunction and adjunction*

## 6.1 Serialization

If $(5:30)^1$ is a reasonable means for determining the deep structure properties of *all those five pretty girls*, we obviously need a set of rules that will ensure that the items constituting the terminal string appear in correct surface order. Whereas conventional transformational rules may not only change the order of the categories referred to in the structural index of a given T-rule, but may also add and delete material (not) generated by the phrase structure rules, the question of sequence for our purposes seems to have top priority, although obviously some form of deletion is required to account for e.g. *kind* and *some* in $(5:31)$. This matter, however, is linked with the question of serialization.

The surface order of the elements in an English NP allows a certain amount of fluctuation within a stable, basic scheme, a fluctuation which to a large extent is due to the possibility of a number of adjectival modifiers occurring with the same noun (cf. e.g. Goyvaerts 1968; Sussex 1974), and also to a number of idiosyncratic properties of certain quantifiers, notably *all*.

However, the rules we need to transform a terminal string like that in $(5:30)$ into an acceptable surface string all conform to the basic principle of *subjunction*.

## 6.2 Subjunction

The term 'subjunction' – and its ally, 'adjunction' – in the sense in which it is to be taken here, is introduced by Anderson (1971c) and further developed by him in subsequent works, notably (1977: ch. 2). Lyons (1973: 71) feels the need for a similar process, which he introduces under the name 'amalgamation', while at the same time

---

[1] This is the first instance of the convention adopted for reference to 'chapter-external' examples: $(5:30)$ refers to example (30) in chapter 5.

pointing out that this process is difficult to formalize in standard Chomskyan transformational grammar. The reason for this is not hard to find: subjunction (and adjunction) is intrinsically bound up with dependency.

The notion of subjunction trades on what Porzig (1934) calls 'wesenhafte bedeutungsbeziehungen' (*sic*), i.e. syntagmatic sense-relations between lexemes. These relations are explained by Porzig as relations of presupposition: '*greifen* kann man nur mit der hand, aber die *hand* kann noch manches andere tun als greifen' (Porzig 1934: 76). This means, with a parallel English example, that *kick* presupposes *foot*, but that *foot* does not presuppose *kick*. We might perhaps say that the meaning of *kick* 'encapsulates' the meaning of *foot*, but not vice versa. Apart from the meaning of *foot*, *kick* may also be said to 'encapsulate' the meaning of *hit*, which does not presuppose *foot*, plus some kind of 'instrumental' meaning. We can therefore decompose the meaning of *kick* into the three meaning-elements [hit] + [with] + [foot], which may be organized in the dependency structure:

(1)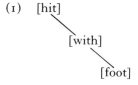

where [hit] etc. are abbreviations for appropriate feature-specifications. It is such structures which are said to undergo subjunction, by which (1) becomes:

(2)  [hit]
      |
     [with]
      |
     [foot]
      |
     KICK

Subjunction is now seen to be part of the process of lexicalization. Indeed, Anderson (1977: 138) suggests that lexicalization comprises two steps: subjunction of a dependent to a governor, and lexical insertion.

It is clear that the categories that partake of a subjunction must be specified semantically – if not necessarily by means of features. The term 'amalgamation' adopted by Lyons may then be illuminating:

subjunction is a process by which the complex symbol of features on a dependent category is amalgamated with the complex symbol of features on the governing category. It is this new complex symbol created by amalgamation that is lexicalized (Lyons 1973 : 77).

Consider now (5 : 30) again. This is a dependency structure in which each category is specified by semantic features. But, in virtue of various points discussed in chapter 5, (5 : 30) may be analyzed in two ways: each FC is governor relative to L, or each referential phrase (i.e. FC–L) is governor relative to the referential phrase immediately below it. Since subjunction is a process by which a dependent is amalgamated with its governor, we can distinguish two types of subjunction: (a) L is subjoined to the FC that governs it; and (b) a given referential phrase is subjoined to the referential phrase that governs it. I shall call the former type L-subjunction, the latter R(eferential) P(hrase)-subjunction. In both types the subjoined category carries its dependents with it (if any).

**6.2.1 L-subjunction.** L-subjunction may be formalized in a general fashion as shown in:

(3)

where '$\triangle$' identifies a 'slot' into which a phonological form may be inserted.

One of the conditions on the general theory of subjunction is that the categorial status of the complex category created by subjunction is identical with the categorial status of the term serving as governor in the pre-subjoined structure (Anderson 1977: 137). The consequence of L-subjunction, therefore, is that an originally lexical category 'comes out' as a functional category. This is a happy consequence in view of the fact that a number of signs (e.g. pronouns, some determiners, and, from a different sphere, modal verbs (cf. Chomsky 1965: 212, fn 9) are not amenable to a simple classification in terms of the distinction between 'lexical' meaning and 'functional' meaning.

**6.2.2 RP-subjunction.** The subjunction of one referential phrase to another may be thought of as occurring in a number of different ways which we could formalize in each of the fashions (4)(a)–(d) (see p. 106).

Of these, (b) represents a variety of L-subjunction, in that it amalgamates a functional and a lexical category, but in this case the two categories involved belong to different referential phrases. Although such a situation cannot be absolutely excluded on theoretical grounds[2] I want here to exclude it by decision, imposing the requirement on L-subjunction that it must involve the two categories in the same referential phrase. Whether (4)(b) represents a permissible subjunction is an empirical question that must be decided on the basis of RS-analyses of various languages. For English I believe it can be dispensed with, despite footnote 2.

The same holds for (4)(c), the result of which is the amalgamation of two (or more) functional categories *and* two (or more) lexical categories. Again, this possibility cannot be excluded on theoretical grounds, but it is not required in a RS-analysis of English. It might, however, be required for the analysis of so-called polysynthetic languages like Greenlandic Eskimo (cf. Rischel (1972) for a survey of some of the problems posed by the productive derivational morphology of Greenlandic for syntactic theory as currently enforced).

(4)(d) represents a situation which also is not impossible from a theoretical point of view. I shall exclude it, however, with reference to the formal representation of subjunction. I shall say, in general, that dependency relations (here represented by unbroken lines) may not be crossed by relations of dominance (represented by broken, vertical lines).

We are then left with (4)(a), which represents the only form of RP-subjunction apparently required in a description of English. Its effects are to amalgamate two (or more) functional categories and to reverse the deep structure order of lexical categories. The latter effect is a consequence of the general requirement that subjoined categories carry

---

[2] It might even be considered a satisfactory explanation why it is *nouns* that are regarded as (un)countable, namely, where $L_i = L_{gen}$ and $FC_j = $ part in (4)(b). Part is the category that contains the countability-features, and by (4)(b) it is amalgamated with $L_{gen}$, the category which dominates nouns.

(4)

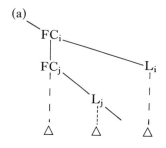

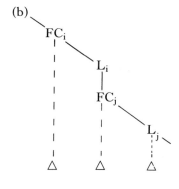

$\Rightarrow$

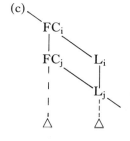

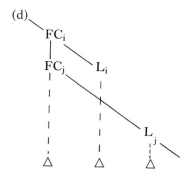

their dependents with them under subjunction and the specific restriction on 'crossing' relations just established.

### 6.2.3 The relationship between L-subjunction and RP-subjunction. The two kinds of subjunction introduced above are both transformational processes; and although I consider both kinds of subjunction to be universal – in the sense of being generally justified in the description of any language – particular instances of them are held to be language-specific. I wish to discuss three separate, though related, issues in this connection: (a) the relative order of L-subjunction and RP-subjunction; (b) whether one or both types of subjunction is (are) optional or obligatory in general; and (c) the possibility of explaining morphological language-types with reference to different subjunctional conventions.

The question of the relative order of L-subjunction and RP-subjunction raises a complex of problems concerning the definition of the term 'transformation' itself. The suggestion that transformations may be *ordered* implies that they are concrete phenomena which may be submitted to arrangement in space and time. The definition that captures such concrete properties of transformations is, for example, 'a grammatical transformation [is] a structure-dependent mapping of phrase-marker into phrase-marker that is independent of the gram-matical relations or meanings expressed in these grammatical relations' (Chomsky 1972: 1–2). Another favoured definition, however, has a transformation as a kind of 'filter' to prevent the generation of ungrammatical surface strings from permissible deep structures (Chomsky 1965: 139). This is a far more abstract definition which implies a mental or psychological reality of transformations, but which at the same time makes the concept of ordering extremely difficult to attach substance to (cf. Huddleston (1972) and Miller (1975) for further discussion).

On the whole I favour a definition of 'transformation' which makes it even more concrete than the first one above and certainly far less mysterious than the second. To me, a transformation is simply a descriptional procedure. Given a structure, $S_1$, we may, *qua* analysts, rearrange $S_1$ as another structure, $S_2$, provided $S_1$ meets the conditions (of analyzability and perhaps other kinds) specified in transformational rule $T_x$. The implication of this view subjects a transformation to various limitations generally considered irrelevant, such as conditions of

two-dimensional representation (but cf. Chafe 1970: 5), interpretation
of $S_2$ as the explicit, static result of a dynamic descriptive process
whereby the analyst has rearranged $S_1$ in an explicit sequence of
analytical steps, etc. It makes practical sense, then, to ask which of the

(5)

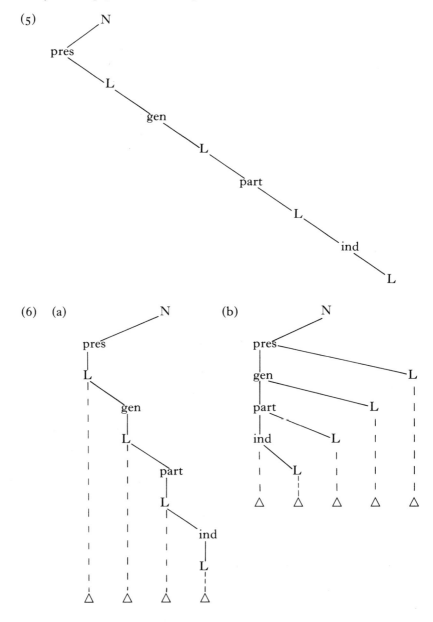

(6)   (a)                          (b)

two types of subjunction we should apply first. Given a 'deep structure' of form (5) (disregarding irrelevant material), we may rearrange it in two ways, in both instances beginning at the bottom (6).

Here (6)(a) is the static, two-dimensional representation of the result of a series of L-subjunctions, whereas (b) represents the static, two-dimensional result of a similar sequence of RP-subjunctions.

Now if L-subjunction precedes RP-subjunction, the latter must apply to structures like (6)(a), whereas, if RP-subjunction precedes L-subjunction, the latter must apply to structures like (6)(b).

Disregarding for the moment what empirical considerations there might be, it seems obvious that at least some consideration of concrete phenomena of representation must be brought to bear on the question. It is clear, for example, that two general and highly similar T-rules can be formulated if L-subjunction is held to precede RP-subjunction:

$$(7)(a) \quad \text{X} \quad \text{FC} \quad \text{L} \quad \text{Y}$$
$$\phantom{(7)(a)} \quad 1 \quad\quad 2 \quad\quad 3 \quad\quad 4 \Rightarrow 1 \quad 2 \quad 4$$
$$\phantom{(7)(a)(b) XX FC FC Y 1 2 } 3$$

$$(b) \quad \text{X} \quad \text{FC} \quad \text{FC} \quad \text{Y}$$
$$\phantom{(b) \text{X FC}} | \quad\quad |$$
$$\phantom{(b) \text{X F}} \text{L} \quad\quad \text{L}$$
$$\phantom{(b)} \quad 1 \quad\quad 2 \quad\quad 3 \quad\quad 4 \Rightarrow 1 \quad 2 \quad 4$$
$$\phantom{(b)(a)(b) XX FC FC Y 1 2 } 3$$

If (7)(a) – the L-subjunction rule – applies first, it creates a sequence of formal, complex entities, each of which consists of an L-subjoined referential phrase, which then occur in the structural description of (7)(b), the RP-subjunction rule. Except for the nature of the formal entities mentioned in the two rules they are exactly the same.

If RP-subjunction is held to apply before L-subjunction, however, it would be extremely difficult to formulate a *general* T-rule that would L-subjoin structures like (6)(b). In fact the structural descriptions would have to refer explicitly to each of pres, gen, part, and ind in order to secure that the various lexical categories were subjoined to their respective governors. But this, also very clearly, is a problem created by the two-dimensional format of the representation. Subject to falsification by empirical evidence we shall therefore work under the assumption that L-subjunction precedes – i.e. is applied before – RP-subjunction in the descriptive procedure.

The two rules in (7) were presented as if they were both obligatory. If they were, all structures would end up in the same way (8), which would hardly be an encouraging result. In contrast to the point discussed

(8)

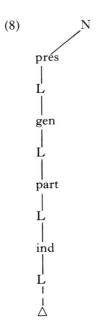

above, however, the question of optionality is purely empirical. For English, the assumption we shall work under is that L-subjunction is optional, whereas RP-subjunction is obligatory (see further below).

This assumption has repercussions on the interpretation of rule (7)(b), which states that only already L-subjoined referential phrases undergo RP-subjunction. Obviously, if L-subjunction is optional and RP-subjunction obligatory, a modification must be made which ensures that referential phrases that have *not* undergone L-subjunction can undergo RP-subjunction. I propose the following reformulation of (7)(b):

(7)(b′) X   FC   Y   FC–L   Z
         1    2    3     4      5 ⇒ 1   2   5   3
                                          4

where the dash between FC and L represents the dependency relation.

The essence that I want this reformulation to capture is that the dependency relation is neutral with respect to subjunction. Dependency holds between the categories in both of the following configurations:

(9)   (a)   FC                    (b)   FC

with FC as the governor in both instances.

The implication of taking L-subjunction as optional and RP-subjunction as obligatory is that we allow for both (6)(b) and (8) as possible final derived strings: (6)(b) is the result when no referential phrase is L-subjoined, (8) is the result when every referential phrase is L-subjoined. In contrast, (6)(a) is not a possible final derived string (in English), because it is not RP-subjoined. Apart from (6)(b) and (8), a number of other final derived strings are allowed for, namely, when only some phrases are L-subjoined.

In a tentative footnote, Postal (1966: 210 fn 16) suggests that the process which he calls *segmentalization* is connected with what is known as inflection in traditional grammatical theory. Segmentalization is a process which has not been explored further in the transformational literature. It is explained by Postal as a process whereby a subset of a given set of syntactic features is 'segmented out' and given morphological expression. The articles, and, in Postal's treatment also the personal pronouns, are segments that are inserted transformationally on the basis of the complex symbol of syntactic features in terms of which a given NP node is subcategorized in the deep structure. The footnote deserves quoting in full:

It is my feeling, however, that such [segmentalization] rules characterize whatever is really common in those features of language which have been referred to as *inflection*. That is, inflectional elements are those segments added by SEGMENTALIZATION provided these segments are added in such a way that they become part of the same *word* as does that element whose features they mark.

This quotation contains an implicit reference to different types of morphemes and, hence, to different morphological types of language. The traditional division of the languages of the world into analytic and synthetic, and the latter into agglutinating, polysynthetic, and inflectional types, is based on morphological considerations.

It seems to me eminently possible to revive this traditional classification within a framework equipped – if only contingently – with properties for a description of morphological types.

Consider, by way of example of a 'pure' analytic type, a Vietnamese NP like

(10) cái    cŏng gỗ        lón kia   (Emeneau 1951 : 84)
     'thing' gate  wooden big  that = that big wooden gate

*Cái* is a so-called numeral classifier, in this instance the general classifier for 'things'. On the assumption that the Vietnamese NP meaning just 'that wooden gate' would be (10) minus the attributive element *lón* ('big', 'to be big'), we may insert (10) in a referential structure along the lines of (11), i.e. in a structure in which every

(11)

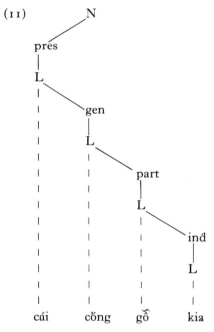

referential phrase is L-subjoined but in which no instance of RP-subjunction has occurred, in fact a structure similar to (6)(a). Notice also the important occurrence of a lexical item under pres-L. Languages with numeral classifiers (and these are many – cf. Allan (1977), Friedrich (1970: 400ff), Greenberg (1972: 2 fn 5) for valuable surveys) provide immensely gratifying empirical support for the presence within the referential structure of pres-L in which – as already mentioned – $L_{pres}$ is rarely lexicalized in Indo-European.

The neatness of the Vietnamese example (11) should not be overemphasized. It is only in connection with demonstratives like *kia* we get a serialization that exactly fits the referential structure in this way. In fact, Greenberg (1972) suggests that only four surface orders are realized among the three elements C(lassifier), H(ead) N(oun) and Num(eral) in classifier languages: HN C Num, HN Num C, Num C HN, and C Num HN. The order predicted by the referential structure (C HN Num) – though realized on occasion in Vietnamese, as we have just seen – is one of the two serializations excluded by Greenberg, the other being Num HN C. Okell (1969: 209) suggests by way of explanation of this that C and Num are in fact a 'numeral compound' the members of which cannot be separated.

Contrast (11) with the structure assumed to be the final derived string underlying the German NP *der grosse Hund* (German being a predominantly inflecting language) (12) with just one occurrence of L-subjunction (to account for definiteness – see below, §§8.1 and 9.1 for details) but obligatory occurrence of RP-subjunction. The defining characteristic of inflecting languages is that flexives are realizations of clusters of grammatical properties. Thus *der*, in German, traditionally signals case, gender, number and definiteness. These properties are all contained in the complex category symbol realized by *der* in (12).

(12)

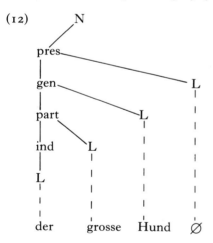

On the basis of analyses such as these we might now provisionally suggest that isolating (analytic) languages have obligatory L-subjunction and optional (or a low proportion of obligatory – cf. above on Vietnamese) RP-subjunctions, while synthetic languages have obligatory RP-subjunctions and optional (or a low proportion of obligatory) L-subjunctions.

**6.2.4 The Mirror-Image convention.** I return to one or two additional points connected with morphology types below, but first we have to explore further some consequences of subjunction.

Subjunction is closely related to, if not identical with, the traditional concept of *syncretism*, which Bloomfield simply defines as 'the merging of inflectional categories' (Bloomfield 1933: 388). I am unable to attach more than two substantial interpretations to this definition:

(a) Given two categories, $C_x$ and $C_y$, and given two members of these, ($[+F_i]$ & $[-F_j]$), morphologically realized by *-pa-*, and ($[-E_k]$ & $[+E_m]$), morphologically realized by *-lu-*, we might expect to find a syntagm, for which $C_x$ and $C_y$ are both relevant, with the morphological marking *-palu-* or *-lupa-*. In that case the language would be described as an agglutinating language (with respect to $C_x$ and $C_y$). However, if it can be made clear, from distributional analysis, that the feature-specification ($[+F_i]$ & $[-F_j]$ & $[-E_k]$ & $[+E_m]$) is morphologically realized as *-mi-*, then the language would be described as an inflecting language (with respect to $C_x$ and $C_y$).

(b) Given a category, $C_x$, and two members of $C_x$, ($[+F_i]$ & $[-F_j]$), morphologically realized by *-pa-*, and ($[-F_i]$ & $[+F_j]$), morphologically realized by *-pu-*, *-pa-* and *-pu-* being identified as different members of $C_x$ by commutation, we may find contexts or situations in which *-pa-* occurs although *-pu-* was to be expected. In such cases the opposition between *-pa-* and *-pu-* is suspended, and we have an instance of what is traditionally called *neutralization*.

With respect to (b) we note that neutralization can only occur between two members of the *same* category, so it is only by a stretch of the terminology that we can here speak about a merging of *categories*. With respect to the two situations in (a) I believe, but I am not sure, that traditional grammar would recognize only the situation involving *-mi-* as an instance of syncretism.

Since both types of subjunction lead to 'merging' of categories, we need to clarify these matters. I recognize three distinct types of 'merging':

(13)(a) The morphological reflex of the complex category member created by subjunction is identical to both (all) of the morphological reflexes of the simple category members involved in the subjunction. This type of 'merging' will be called *explici-*

*tation.* (Cf. *-palu-* and *-lupa-* above.)

(b) The morphological reflex of the complex category member created by subjunction is identical to one or the other of the morphological reflexes of the simple category members involved in the subjunction. This type will be called *absorption*.

(c) The morphological reflex of the complex category member created by subjunction is identical to neither (none) of the morphological reflexes of the simple category members involved in the subjunction. This situation will be known as *conflation*. (Cf. *-mi-* above.)

There is a tendency towards what we might call – following Pilch (1968: 166) – *monomorphemic structure* of the expression (in a Glossematic sense), particularly of functional signs. That is, meaning-elements often and consistently merged will, diachronically, be expressed by morphologically less and less complex forms, the limiting case being a form consisting of just one morpheme. Consider, as a case in point, the diachronic development of Modern English *each* and *every*.

The usual etymology for these is, for *each*, a West Germanic phrase, *\*aiwō ȝalīkaz*, meaning 'ever alike' (Onions, *Etym.*; *NED*, art. *each*). This phrase became Old English (West Saxon) *ǣlc* by a number of historical phonological changes. Then, in Old English, the process repeated itself. $\overline{Ælc}$ was modified by *ǣfre* ('ever') and the resultant phrase *ǣfre ǣlc* developed phonologically into Modern English *every*. From a diachronic point of view, *each* and *every* would therefore be instances of conflations in the terminology of (13).

Explicitations raise a particular problem not shared by the two other types of merging. Since two (or more) otherwise independent morphological reflexes appear as the realization of a complex node, the question

(14)  (a)                                     (b)

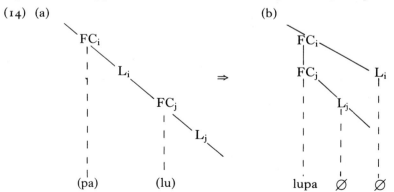

of natural serialization crops up. Subject to further discussion in the light of empirical evidence I shall suggest, for such cases, a working hypothesis according to which the morphological reflexes of the categories involved change places under subjunction (14).

Here RP-subjunction merges two functional categories, each of which may be considered to have a potential morphological expression. If the morphological expression of the complex FC-category in (b) is an explicitation, both these reflexes will occur, but in reverse order. This convention will be known as the Mirror-Image convention with a term borrowed from Leech (1969), or simply the MI-convention.

## 6.3 The morphophonemic component

One of the grammatical facts about inflecting languages is that certain syntagmatic relationships are marked morphologically. If both (all) members of a syntagm receive morphological marking for the same category, we speak traditionally about *concord*, whereas, if only one (some) member(s) of a syntagm receives such marking, the traditional term is *rection*, or *government*. If it is true that gender is a category on nouns, for example, then the descriptive framework must contain a mechanism to secure that adjectives receive appropriate morphological marking by which its modification can be read off. For Latin, French, and Danish such a mechanism must be able to handle both attributive and predicative adjectives, whereas, for German, it need account for only attributive ones; cf.:

(15)(a) (i)　*en* stor dreng – dreng*en* er stor
　　　　　　a big boy　　　boy-the is big
　　　(ii) *et* stor*t* hus　– hus*et*　　er stor*t*
　　　　　　a big house　house-the is big
　　(b) (i)　ein gross*er* Knabe – der Knabe ist gross
　　　　(ii) ein gross*es* Haus – das Haus ist gross

Matters such as these belong to the morphophonemic stratum of language, and I shall call the mechanism which deals with them the morphophonemic component.

Consider a Ciceronean NP like that italicized in (16) (I disregard *ciuitatum* for the present):

(16)　Primum enim numero definieram *genera* ciuitatum *tria probabilia*,
　　　... (*De Re Publica* II xxxix 65)
　　　('For I began by defining the three good forms of government')

Immediately underlying this NP is the derived structure (17).

$L_{ind}$ is L-subjoined (the NP being contextually specifiable as definite). Recall now that each category, lexical as well as functional, is held to be subcategorized by a particular feature-specification which indicates which member of the category is relevant to the derivation in question, at a stage prior to that represented by (17). Nevertheless only the non-subjoined lexical categories are endowed with such specifications in (17). Notice also the orthographical forms of the expressions

(17)

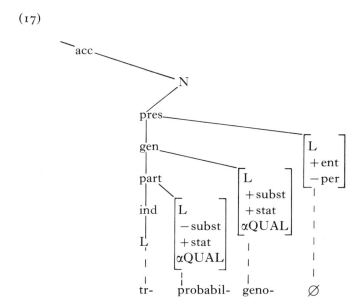

inserted below the categories, which are intended to capture their neutrality, at this stage, with respect to flexives. It is the fate of the features on the subjoined categories and the insertion of flexives which are our present concern.

Due to the facts of concord, it seems to me not unreasonable to propose that all the functional features relevant to a given derivation are merged, or amalgamated, and that it is this amalgamation which decides the form of the flexives to be inserted. In order to formalize this proposal I shall now adopt the convention that, associated with a referential structure, there is a compartment into which the features of functional and L-subjoined lexical categories are inserted during RP-subjunction. These features thus come to form one complex symbol.

These proposals are captured by (18).

(18)

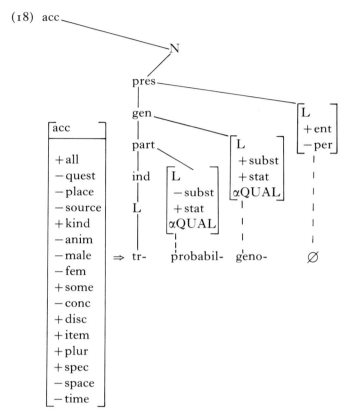

A number of points should be made in relation to (18). First of all, (18) displays a convention of descriptive procedure. I am not imputing any other status or reality to (18) than that of convenience for the sake of exposition of the facts of concord mentioned above. Secondly, the complex symbol of features and the complex category symbol are related, in that each category symbol is represented, or 'realized', by the relevant subset of features in the complex symbol, which indicates which member of the category is involved in the derivation. Thirdly, it will have been noticed that the complex symbol of features is bipartite, and that it contains *two* entries for case, one given in the traditional case-labels for latin (acc(usative)), and one in terms of the Andersonian features. This is because the structure is assumed actually to *contain* two case-labels, one (the syntactico-semantic relation between verb and argument) 'outside' the nominal structure proper, and a replica of this[3] (the referential–semantic occurrence) 'within' the nominal, on pres. Arguments will be given later (§7.5.2) why both occurrences are considered necessary in the complex symbol.

The important point about (18), however, is that it provides a reasonable basis for the explanation of concord phenomena. The complex symbol of features contains information relevant to *all* of the lexical items inserted into the referential structure. The complex symbol can, in somewhat mechanistic terms, be seen as a carriage that 'moves through' the string of lexical reflexes, leaving on each a replica of itself in the form of appropriate flexives.

## 6.4 Adjunction

Consider once again the two configurations (9), repeated for convenience here:

(19) display the only two configurations possible of a referential phrase. With respect to these we have said of (b) that it represents an L-subjoined phrase, but we have no comparable term by which to describe (a). I shall say that (a) represents a referential phrase in which L is *adjoined* to FC. In general, the referential (deep) structure is a representation of a number of referential phrases in which each category is adjoined to the one above it.

Given the notion of adjunction, we can now describe L-subjunction as a process by which a lexical category is moved from adjunct position to subjunct position.

There are indications, moreover, that adjunction may provide a basis for the proper analysis of a large variety of phenomena if we incorporate it also in the account of RP-subjunction. We might do this by regarding RP-subjunction as a two-step process where the first step is the

---

[3]  If I had 'translated' this occurrence of the Latin accusative into Andersonian features, it would have been as ([ −place] & [ −source]), the semantically neutral case.

adjunction of a lower referential phrase to a higher FC, along the lines of:

(20)  (a)                                        (b)

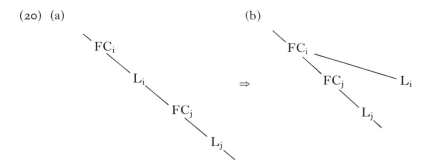

The second step is the subjunction of a lower FC to its (new) governing FC. The T-rules which embody these steps – and which replace (7)(b') – are:

(21)(a) X   FC   Y    FC–L   Z
        1    2   3      4     5 ⇒ 1   2   4   5   3

   (b) X   FC   FC   Y
       1    2   3    4        ⇒ 1   2   4
                                      3

Let me at this stage briefly sum up the tentative points made over the preceding pages concerning morphological typology. The major distinction between analytic (isolating) and synthetic morphology is attributed to a difference in priority given to L-subjunction and RP-subjunction. Polysynthetic structure might be regarded as the result of different forms of merging, not only of functional but also of lexical categories. Inflectional structure is characterized by adjunction *and* subjunction of the functional categories, the result being a high proportion of absorptions and conflations (in the terminology of (13)).

Consider now the third synthetic type, commonly known as the agglutinating type (Turkish, Armenian), in the light of the configurations (20)(a) and – particularly – (b). The main characteristic of agglutination is a one-to-one correlation between a member of a grammatical category and a particular flexive. If (20)(b) were to be 'lexicalized', such a one-to-one correlation would be the result. Agglutination might therefore tentatively be described as arising from application of (21)(a) without the subsequent step of subjunction, formalized as (21)(b).

These various observations are clearly far too general and far too tentative to be of any immediate use. However, they place in their proper perspective two well-known facts about morphological typology, namely, that languages may change types diachronically (English, Armenian), and that there are very few, if any, 'pure' languages as far as morpheme structure is concerned. If morphological type is a function of (language-specific) applications of (universal) transformational processes, then the general theory of subjunction, with its various interlocking processes, may provide a reasonably precise framework for the description of these processes. Also, if no language is absolutely 'pure', the general theory of subjunction may account for this, since both L-subjunction and (the two steps of) RP-subjunction are universal processes which particular languages may exploit to various degrees and in various ways.

Modern English presents a rather confusing picture in terms of morphology type. It derives historically from a predominantly inflecting language (Old English), and there are quite a few remnants of inflection left. There are also a few isolated, non-productive instances of agglutination (*oxen's*). However, from a productive point of view it might perhaps be described as an isolating language. The description of the English NP to be given below will nevertheless be based on the assumption that the 'isolating' nature of modern English is a 'secondary' development which presupposes a 'synthetic' background. That is, obligatory RP-subjunction is assumed to be a synchronic fact of modern English which reflects its typological origin. In addition, a fairly high frequency of L-subjunctions accounts for its 'isolating' nature.

## 6.5 Preliminary comments on recursion

The Ciceronian NP employed to illustrate the operations of subjunction and the associated morphophonemic rules in (18) contains an adnominal case-phrase, superficially realized as *ciuitatum*. That is to say, *ciuitatum* realizes a N which is subordinate to another N. The whole NP in (16) is the realization of a referential structure with two 'branches'. These are what I shall call complex structures. The derivation of a complex structure involves recursion of the rules established throughout Part II.

The basic, schematic representation of a complex structure is shown in (22).

(22)

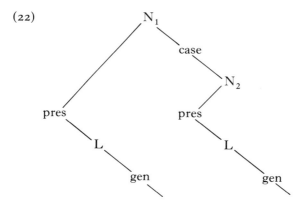

Both types of subjunction apply to (22), recursively and from the bottom up. However, a number of niceties are involved in the derivation of complex structures in English, associated with the supposition that the subordinate case-phrase (case + $N_2$) may be adjoined and subjoined to various categories in $N_1$. I return to this throughout Part III.

# PART III: THE APPLICATION

Party is Nature too, and you shall see
By force of Logic how they both agree;
The Many in the One, the One in Many;
All is not Some, nor Some the same as Any;
Genus holds species, both are great and small;
One genus highest, one not high at all;
Each species has its differentia too,
This is not That, and He was never You,
Though this and that are AYES, and you and he
Are like as one to one, or three to three.
GEORGE ELIOT *Middlemarch*

# 7 Referential functives

## 7.1 'Referential functive' defined

In this the final part I shall apply the theoretical framework developed in Part II to selected areas of English nominal composition.

From the very first inception of the research reported on in the present work my focus of attention was on pronouns, and it was my original plan 'simply' to account for pronominalization in English, essentially on the basis of a substitution model à la Harweg (1968) and Crymes (1968); several – abortive – attempts were made to come to grips with what Hjelmslev calls 'la nature du pronom' in this way. The present work may be read as the testament of my disillusionment with such an approach. From being traditionally a comparatively clearly delimited, closed class with a rather small membership, the class soon became invaded from all sides, by modal verbs (Crymes), by definite NPs (Harweg) and by determiners (Lyons 1973; Sommerstein 1972; Sørensen 1958). The result was that 'the pronoun' gradually receded to the point of vanishing (Postal 1966), hiding behind all manner of phenomena which all seemed to have one thing in common: referentiality. From being a major class within – apparently – easy access for investigation, it became a minor class virtually inaccessible.

The shift in viewpoint from 'pronouns' to 'referentiality' as the basic notion thus shifted the approach in the direction of Collinson (1937) with its basic appeal to 'indicaters'. Although this is in many respects an interesting work I think it is fair to say that it is somewhat impressionistic and too intuitive to constitute a principled basis for a general theory of linguistic reference. The framework developed in Part II of the present work purports to provide such a basis.

This framework restores autonomy to the class of pronouns – or rather to *a* class of pronouns; but it does not restore it as a major class. The class of pronouns constitutes itself naturally within the major class of referential functives.

125

This term is the name of a class of functional items the defining characteristic of which is that at the last stage in their derivation they are dominated ultimately by a FC. The class of referential functives is a large, heterogenous, but closed class (though for a qualification of this latter claim, cf. §7.3.3). *A priori* I submit that the traditional classes of determiners, quantifiers (indefinite pronouns), and pronouns (demonstrative, personal, possessive, interrogative, relative) are referential functives in the present sense, and that we further have to incorporate a class not generally considered in this connection – at least in descriptions of English – namely, the class of what I shall call E-classifiers.

## 7.2 Delimitative and juxtapositive serialization

English NPs can be classified on the basis of a great many different characteristics, like definiteness, quantification, restrictiveness, etc. The characteristic I shall employ has to do with the way in which the elements of NP are connected, or, as I shall say, serialized. Consider:

(1)  (a) the best friends
     (b) the best of friends.

(1)(a) is an instance of what I shall call *juxtapositive serialization*, whereas (b) is an instance of *delimitative serialization*. In general, a NP which overtly displays a preposition (most often *of*, but frequently also locative prepositions like *at*, *in*, *on*, etc., less frequently 'directional' prepositions like *for*, *towards*, *against*, etc.) will be considered an instance of delimitative serialization, whereas NPs without a preposition in their internal structure will be regarded as instances of juxtapositive serialization.

This is a simple criterion which relies entirely on observational data. Consequently, a NP like *the boy's mother* will be considered an instance of juxtapositive serialization despite the obvious possibility of relating the genitive with the preposition *of*.

The distinction between juxtapositive and delimitative serialization provides an important heuristic principle for the referential theory. Accepting the view that prepositions are – or at least may be considered to be – superficial realizations of underlying case-relations, it turns out that the presence of a preposition in the surface structure of a NP is an indication of recursive derivation of that NP. The reverse inference does not hold, however. We cannot conclude from the fact that a given surface NP displays juxtapositive serialization that it derives from a non-recursive structure.

Apart from this, heuristic, importance, the distinction between the two serialization-types provides a basis for the subclassification of referential functives.

## 7.3 The classes of referential functives

Consider:

(2)  (a)  some men
     (b)  some of these men.

These are manifestations of the juxtapositive and delimitative seriali-zation-type, respectively. In general we can set up the following two formulae:

(3)  (a)  x Noun

(b) $\text{x of} \begin{cases} \text{these} \\ \text{this} \\ \emptyset \end{cases} \text{Noun}$

where x is a referential functive, and where Noun may be either singular or plural in form.

These two environments are referentially diagnostic, and on the basis of them we define:

(4)  (a) 'a quantifier' = 'a referential functive that may occur in place of x in both (3)(a) and (b)';
     (b) 'a determiner' = 'a referential functive that may occur in place of x in (3)(a) but not in (b)';
     (c) 'an E-classifier' = 'a referential functive that may occur in place of x in (3)(b) but not in (a)';
     (d) 'a pronoun' = 'a referential functive that may occur in place of x in neither (3)(a) nor (b)'.

A brief glance at these definitions is sufficient to show that terminological distinctions will now separate items usually considered to belong to the same class. For example, *each* will be a quantifier, *every* a determiner; interrogative *which?* will be a quantifier, *what?* a de-terminer; *I* a pronoun, *we* a determiner, etc.

This may at first look rather unattractive, but in fact it is not. First of all, these phenomena stress the high degree of interrelation that there is between the subclasses, an interrelation which is due to the fact that the important class-membership for these items is membership of the major class of referential functives. We highlight the debate between Postal (1966) and Sommerstein (1972) as to whether personal pronouns are articles (Postal) or vice versa (Sommerstein) as essentially vacuous. They are similar in that they both belong to the major class of referential functives. Furthermore there are quite good reasons for these anisomorphisms, which are explicable on the basis of the general principle of suppletion. This principle is of some importance to the class of referential functives. Thus, the subclass constituted by E-classifiers is the suppletive counterpart to the class of quantifiers. They fill the gap which is created by the inability of quantifiers to occur in delimitative serializations unless the head noun is definite. Quantifiers conform to the pattern *x of these Noun*, E-classifiers conform to the pattern *x of Noun*, with some of them (the partitive E-classifiers) also conforming to *x of these Noun*.

In this way we could – at least in principle – claim that the 'word-class' of referential functives is constituted by abstract, underlying entities which are often realized superficially by a suppletive pair, as suggested in (5).

(5)

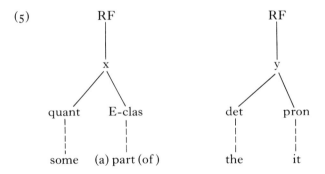

However, the meaning of these abstract entities (RF) would largely correlate with (the inherent meaning of) the functional categories, so to establish an abstract class would only complicate matters without yielding any great profit in return in terms of descriptive adequacy.

**7.3.1 The class of quantifiers.** Application of the distribution test established in the preceding section to the items which I have *a priori* singled out for attention yields the following list of quantifiers in English:

(6)  | all | (n)either | more | one | first |
     |-----|-----------|------|-----|-------|
     | any | (a) little | less | two | second |
     | some | (a) few | most | three | ... |
     | each | much | least | four | last |
     | both | many | half | ... | next |
     | which? | | | ... | (an)other |

However, although all of these conform to (3) in the same way, they do not behave alike in all respects. In particular, they are sensitive to a preceding definite article. Thus, on the basis of the pattern (7) we can establish two subclasses within the class of quantifiers:

(7)    the x of these Noun.

I shall say that quantifiers which are incompatible with (7) are the *central* quantifiers, whereas those that are compatible with it are the *peripheral* quantifiers:

(8)  | *central* | *peripheral* |
     |-----------|--------------|
     | all | (a) little |
     | any | (a) few |
     | some | more |
     | each | less |
     | both | most |
     | much | least |
     | (n)either | (an)other |
     | many | half[1] |
     | which? | last |
     | one | next |
     | two | first |
     | three | second |
     | ... | ... |

I shall (arbitrarily) restrict the discussion to the central quantifiers. As for the peripheral quantifiers, the most important point seems to be that they involve a number of diachronic lexical subjunctions in combination with the synchronic subjunctions on which the central quantifiers

---

[1] 'Half' is a special case. Its applicability is certainly greater than that of most other quantifiers, but it is quite possible that it is in fact incompatible with (7). However, due to its availability for noun-status – which suggests affinity with E-classifiers – I have decided to leave it out from the group of central quantifiers. Moreover, if we included it, we would have to go into a more detailed discussion of the part:whole relation than we have.

depend. The diachronic subjunctions all appear as fossilized representations within the synchronic representations.

**7.3.2 The class of determiners.** The class of determiners that can be
established on the basis of the distribution test in (3) comprises the
following items:

(9)    (a)              (b)            (c)            (d)
       that             the            a              no
       this                            what?          such
       those            my             every
       these            your
                        her
       we               our
       us               their
       you
       them             which(R)
       his
       its


       same

   The layout of the determiners in this manner is meant to suggest that
I consider a certain amount of subclassification relevant within the class.
The subclassifications are related to what I have called the suppletive
nature of the referential functives.

   In one sense the determiners form a hybrid class. That is, each
determiner has a suppletive counterpart in one of the other subclasses of
referential functives, whereas not all quantifiers, E-classifiers, and
pronouns have a suppletive counterpart in one of the other subclasses.
This viewpoint is behind the organization of (9), which is based purely
on formal and distributional criteria. In this way (a) and (b) are
suppletive with pronouns, (c) with quantifiers, and (d) with E-
classifiers. The distinction between (a) and (b) is of a formal nature: the
members of (a) are suppletive with formally identical pronouns, the
members of (b) with formally non-identical pronouns. This view, of
course, depends on multiplication of entities. It recognizes two kinds of
*this*, *that*, etc. on the basis of a pattern like

(10)  (a) her:hers::his:x; x = his
      (b) the:it::that:x; x = that.

Although such a view is stringently in accord with distributional analysis it gives rise to a certain uneasiness. First, and not very seriously, it cuts across traditional classifications. Secondly, it multiplies entities apparently beyond necessity. Thirdly, and most seriously, it is not even clear that it is semantically (or referentially) tenable. In particular, whereas determinative *we* (etc.) – at least intuitively – is parasitic upon pronominal *we*, pronominal *that* (etc.) conversely encroaches on determinative *that*. A formal/distributional analysis cannot account for this intuition. Furthermore, it cannot account for the fact that only the plural forms *we* and *them* are suppletive, not the singular forms *I, he, she*. *One*-deletion along the lines of Postal (1966) accounts for it – superficially, at least. Yet Postal neglects to explore the possibilities of *one-insertion* instead, which, as Sommerstein (1972: 198ff) points out, is not only more economical but also far more plausible.

If we want to take heed of this intuition about group (a) and at the same time do not want to reduplicate from one class to the other, *that, this*, etc. come out as determiners with no suppletive counterparts, but with occasional pronominal function. The same applies, *mutatis mutandis*, to *we, you*, etc., whereas the question is indeterminable for *his* and *its*. We have ended up in a deadlock.

This discussion might appear rather whimsical. Yet the issue lurking behind it is a real and important one. I believe it is fair to say that when linguists have spoken about determiners it has on the whole been tacitly assumed that *the* and *a* in some sense are the basic determiners on the behaviour of which all other determiners had to be explained or described. This view, as will have appeared, is a natural and justifiable one as long as the determiners are considered in isolation. These two can *only* behave like determiners, as can the other members of groups (b), (c) and (d) with the exception of relative *which*(R) (which is suppletive with itself as a pronoun, and with *who*(R) and *that*(R)). However, when the immanent suppletive structure in the system of referential functives is taken into consideration, it emerges that *this, that, these, those*, and *same* – the latter not generally taken to be a determiner because it co-occurs with *the*[2] – have an equal, if not greater claim on being taken as basic, since it can be argued that they have no suppletive counterparts except themselves. To this might be added the historical evidence of the

[2] Just as a verb may have two tenses, in the sense of two time-references – cf. *John has been here* with reference to both past and present – a noun might be thought capable of having a composite determiners. *The same* and *such a* are such composite determiners.

development both of *a* and *the* (cf. Christophersen 1939: ch. v; Heltveit 1953: 99ff) from a numeral and a demonstrative, respectively.

Thus, Lyons (1973) takes *that* as basic with *this*, deriving *the* from the weak non-proximate deictic (i.e. *that*₁) in the synchronic description. Although he only discusses a limited number of determiners, the implication is that they should all be dealt with in terms of the system which generates *that* and *this* as basic.

The difficulty of deciding in a principled way which determiner is basic is a consequence of the fact that none of the determiners are basic *qua* referential functives. They all derive from (various combinations of) the functional categories and the deictic adverbials by different transformational processes, notably lexical subjunction and the MI-convention. Whether or not a given determiner can be established as basic relative to the other determiners is a question on which I suspend judgement.

**7.3.3 The class of E-classifiers.** The class of referential functives was said above to be a closed class, with one modification. The modification concerns the class of E-classifiers.[3]

E-classifiers are defined by their inability to occur in juxtapositive serialization with their head noun, and among them we find such typical examples as *kind, sort, pair, group*, etc. Yet we also find a great many 'normal' nouns which have this characteristic, e.g. *cup, school, bag*, etc. It could also be taken to imply that a number of nouns are capable of a duplicity of function, and that specific selection restrictions apply to the function which the noun performs on a given occasion. Whichever of the two views we take, however, we are forced to recognize that some nouns display syntactic peculiarities which can be explained on the assumption that they may function as E-classifiers. Consider in this connection the noun *hop* ('can') in Vietnamese, which occurs at least in the following two environments:

(11)(a) hai cai   hop sua
          two thing can milk = 'two milk cans'
     (b) hai  hop sua
          two can milk = 'two cans of milk'

(exx. from Thompson (1965: 198) – though without tone-indications).

---

[3]   I disregard the question as to whether the natural numbers actually form a closed class. I avoid this question by simply noting that a *new* number cannot be introduced, only a *further* number. The numerals constitute an open-ended class, not an open class.

In (a), *hop* is the head noun, classified by the general classifier, *cai*, and with *sua* as an attributive noun. In (b), *hop* is itself a classifier, classifying the head noun *sua*. It is a situation which is precisely comparable to the situation for which I am arguing in English with respect to e.g. *bag*.

Relative to the distinction between closed and open sets I suggest that the class of E-classifiers is an open set with a fairly large but restricted membership. Sparkes (1975) lists a little over a thousand 'collective nouns and group terms', but he does not include a number of quite ordinary ones, like *cup*, *bottle* and *basket*. The actual number of E-classifiers is therefore somewhat larger. The open nature of the set is manifest in the fact that innovations may occur. Thus the following are all fairly recent, according to Sparkes:

(12)   a column of accountants
       a leap of banderilleros
       an aroma of bakers
       a crash of rhinoceros.

The restriction imposed on the productiveness of the class is seen from these examples to be largely punning in nature. I shall suggest below (§7.6) an overall notional content of the class of E-classifiers which explains this restriction.

**7.3.4 The class of pronouns.** The last class of referential functives is the class of pronouns. These are defined by their inability to occur in either of the two diagnostic frames in (3). The pronouns in English comprise the following:

(13)

|        |        | (a)        | (b)     |         |
|--------|--------|------------|---------|---------|
|        |        | I, me      | he, him |         |
|        |        |            | she     |         |
| (I)    |        | -thing     | it      |         |
|        |        | -body      | they    |         |
|        |        | -one       |         |         |
|        | mine   | myself     | who(R)  |         |
|        | yours  | yourself   | that(R) |         |
|        | hers   | herself    |         |         |
| (II)   | ours   | himself    |         |         |
|        | theirs | itself     |         |         |
|        |        | ourselves  |         |         |
|        |        | yourselves |         |         |
|        |        | themselves |         |         |

The subclassification of these is made on the basis of the minimal referential structure they require for their proper analysis: (I)(a) a simple referential structure in which gen-L does not appear, (I)(b) a simple referential structure in which gen-L appears; and (II) a complex referential structure.

A number of traditional pronouns are left out of account here, most evidently *you, we* and *them*. These may be considered pronouns with occasional determiner function. An attempt to explain their determinative function will be made in §§ 10.2.2, 10.3.

It should be made clear that the subclassification in (13) is based on the *minimal* structure which is capable of generating the pronoun(s) in question. I do not hereby commit myself to deriving all instances of a particular pronoun from the minimal structure.

## 7.4 Ill-formed, well-formed, and deviant strings

There is one more area in which the distinction between the two serialization-types will have repercussions, namely, the area of acceptability judgements. Since natural serialization plays a major part in accounting for the syntax of referential functives I shall employ the terms 'ill-formed' and 'well-formed string' solely in relation to judgements of natural serialization. Consider once more (2)(a) and (b), and compare them to

(14)   (a)  $^{if}$ some these men

     (b)  $^{if}$ some of men.

These are both ill-formed strings, a fact indicated by means of the raised $^{if}$. A well-formed string, like those in (2), will appear without diacritics of any kind.

However, a string may be well-formed, and yet be unacceptable. Consider

(15)   (a)  *some of these man

     (b)  *each men

     (c)  *this kind of roses.

Such strings will be deemed *deviant* rather than ill-formed, and their deviancy may stem from a variety of factors, grammatical as well as semantic. Deviancy is indicated by an asterisk.

This raises a general question about the nature of the data that I shall adduce in support of the analyses to be provided.

I shall avail myself of a fairly small set of data of which each example in the majority of cases clearly belongs to either the set of well-formed or the set of ill-formed strings of English. Within each set, some examples may be considered deviant, others not. I have constructed the majority of the examples myself, but rely in those cases on acceptability judgements passed on the more dubious examples by native speakers of (British) English. I have not felt it necessary to consult native speakers on such strings as *the horse, all the horses, every one of the horses,* and many more. I have, however, felt it necessary to consult native speakers over strings like *We cannot take responsibility for any statements made by our agents.* Could *any statement* (singular form) occur instead? If so, what would the difference be? What influence, if any, would different stress assignments to *any* and *statements* from the one you would choose have on the choice of singular/plural form? I make no consistent attempt to collate the various answers to such questions in the present study. I take them, rather, as pointers to what I should (not) claim about a particular string. That is, I do not take them as a body of incontrovertible truths.

I should want to be explicit about two things in this connection. First, it is quite deliberate that I draw on what some would no doubt find an unrepresentationally small body of data. This is because I am convinced that what I have to say about the referential structure of English can be judged 'true' or 'false' on the basis of the evidence provided. Qualifications to what I have to say are naturally to be expected but they will probably be found on closer inspection to be token-relative, rather than type-relative. Secondly, and connected with the first point, doubts have been raised about the theoretical feasibility of the 'clear-case approach' to linguistics (most explicitly by Householder (1973), and Botha & Winckler (1973: 204ff). I share their concern, and I would welcome a fixed set of criteria by which, for example, 'genuine intuitions' about language structure could be distinguished from 'spurious intuitions' based on such alleged irrelevancies as perceptual limitations, contextual limitations, etc. (cf. Botha & Winckler 1973: 194ff). Until such a set of criteria is found, however, I find myself in sympathy with Haas (1973: 82) who takes it as a definite possibility for establishing 'clear cases' that recourse should be had to a consistent procedure of contextualization, or 'contextuability'.

## 7.5 Derivational characteristics of the referential functives

The class of quantifiers was defined distributionally as a class of referential functives the members of which may enter both delimitative and juxtapositive serializations. Since all of the quantifiers listed in (6) above may also on occasion have what is traditionally known as pronominal function – which, in my terms, is a statement to the effect that a given occurrence of a quantifier *need* not appear in construction with a head noun – it follows that we can in fact illustrate the main derivational characteristics of determiners, E-classifiers and pronouns by examining the derivational characteristics of quantifiers in, respectively, juxtapositive and delimitative serialization and in pronominal function.

### 7.5.1 Juxtapositive serializations: quantifiers and determiners.
It was mentioned above that, whereas delimitative serializations are considered invariably to derive from complex structures, juxtapositive serializations may derive from either simple or complex ones. My initial presentation will be concerned with such juxtapositions as are held to derive from simple structures. Examples are:

(16)  (a)  some dogs
      (b)  one dog
      (c)  a dog.

Except for the feature-specification on ind, (16) derive from the same structure, and the same subjunctional processes apply to all of them. The common underlying structure is given in (17).

The specification given is that relevant to the derivation of *some dogs*. That relevant to *one/a dog* would be ([ −plur] & [ +spec]); see further §8.5. The specifications [ɔmale] and [ɔfem] are in accord with the notational suggestions above (p. 67) to the effect that [ɔF] signals neutralization of [ ±F].

No lexical subjunctions apply, and full application of RP-subjunction yields a final derived string like (18).

The derivational history (17)–(18) is the simplest one allowed for in the present framework, so indefinite determiners, and the 'determinative' side of indefinite quantifiers, are the least complex referential functives in derivational terms. Definite determiners like *the*, *that*, etc. and the definite quantifier *both* involve lexical subjunction of $L_{ind}$. Definite determiners like *my*, *your*, etc., and the definite quantifier *each*, require an analysis from a complex structure in addition to lexical subjunction of $L_{ind}$.

(17)

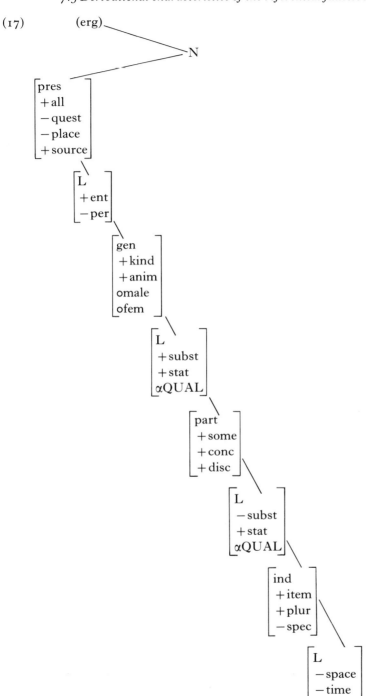

(18)

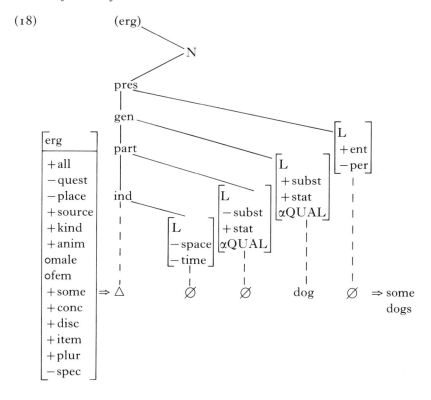

### 7.5.2 Delimitative serializations: quantifiers and E-classifiers.

Quantifier phrases deriving from complex structures include

(19)  (a)  some of the men

     (b)  one of the men.

In such phrases, *of* is considered the reflex of an underlying adnominal case, either absolutive, locative or ablative. Whether ergative can be adnominal or not is not an issue; since it accounts for transitivity we naturally assume that it cannot (cf. Anderson 1973: 57ff; 1974: 1).

A highly simplified representation of the structure underlying (19) is given in (20).

Apart from the overall principle – that delimitative serializations derive from complex structures – (19)(b) provides some further independent support that two Ns are involved in the derivation. If the phrase occurs as the subject NP of a present tense verb, that verb must be specified as singular. (19)(b) is, in short, a singular NP. Yet it contains a noun which is marked plural. Since the ascription of number

(20)                                         (erg)

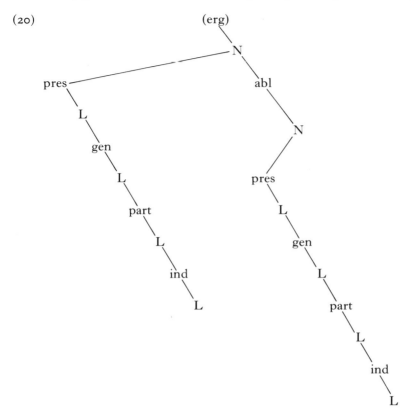

morphemes is guided by the feature on ind, it follows that (19)(b) must derive from a structure containing two occurrences of ind, or from a structure containing one occurrence of ind which then is equipped to carry two number specifications. Neither possibility is allowed for in a simple structure as here conceived, so (19) (b) must derive from a complex structure.

    Complex structures of the general form (20) give rise to a theoretical question of some interest. If the superficial appearance of the preposition marks the boundary between the lexical material deriving from the two Ns involved in deep structure, as seems a reasonable supposition, then how do we decide which N is eventually realized as which 'half' of the surface string?

    The assumption behind this formulation of the problem is, of course, that (19)(b) can be regarded as deriving from a structure which, if no 'reductions' occurred, would appear superficially as *one man of the men*, which, again, seems a reasonable supposition.

Relative to the example at hand, the decision might seem not too difficult: *the men* indicates the 'background group' from which a selection is made. Hence *the men* must be governed by abl and therefore be the realization of the lower N in (20). Conversely, *one*, as the part of the phrase which decides concord with the verb, could by virtue of this fact be regarded as deriving from the upper N, which is thereby given some kind of 'primary' status. Finally, this solution would accord well with natural serialization.

Consider now, however, (21) which contain *kind* and which are held to derive from a structure similar to (20):

(21)  (a)  that kind of car (is expensive)

      (b)  a car of that kind (is expensive).

I consider (21)(a) and (b) to be referentially identical, i.e. to have the same referential potential.

In these examples, *of* hardly realizes ablative, but rather absolutive (the appositive relation, cf. Anderson, 1974: 1), so it is not clear that we can speak of a 'background group' against which selection is made. It is also clear that the criterion of natural serialization cannot be made much use of. The only criterion of those used above to decide the question then seems to be the question of concord, or the ascription of number morphemes. In relation to phrases involving *kind*, this question is difficult, mainly because *kind of* (etc.) can have a function as 'downtoners' (Quirk *et al.* 1972: 452ff), in addition to their more 'full' function.

Each of (21) contains four number-sensitive elements, namely, *that*, *kind*, *car*, and *be*. Absolute lack of concord would therefore yield sixteen possible strings of each general structure. Of this theoretical total of thirty-two only the following seven are allowed, some of which are further regarded as 'colloquial' or even substandard:

(22)(a)  (i)    that kind of car is expensive

        (ii)   those kind of cars are expensive

        (iii)  those kinds of car are expensive

        (iv)   those kinds of cars are expensive

   (b)  (v)    a car of that kind is expensive

        (vi)   cars of that kind are expensive

        (vii)  cars of those kinds are expensive.

Substituting *make* for *kind* we find that (ii) and (iii) contain 'downtoner' *kind*, since these two disallow such substitution. I take these two to have low stress on *kind*. I also take (iii) to be of dubious non-deviancy.

The only generalization concerning concord which covers every instance of (22) is that the *first* and the *fourth* number-sensitive element agree in number. This means, in (a), that the determiner alone decides concord with the verb, whereas, in (b) verbal concord is decided by the number specification on the head noun (see below). If we maintain the assumption mentioned above, that the upper N is decisive for verbal concord, this generalization implies that whichever N we take to be subordinate in (20), it may be 'raised' to superordinate status by transformation, and further that number assignment to verbs is a later process than this transformational shift. But these considerations do not help us to decide *which* N should be above the other.

It seems, then, that different criteria must be searched for. Consider once more (19) and (22). They differ with respect to the number of 'nouns' (in traditional terms) that they contain: each of (19) contains just one (*men*), whereas (22) contain two (*kind* and *car*). I shall now say that *men* in each of (19) is the head noun (HN), in comparison with which *car* becomes head noun in each of (22). From a communicative point of view the head noun is the most important noun occurring in a NP since it denotes the kind of thing being mentioned. From a derivational point of view, the head noun originates under $L_{gen}$ in the superordinate N of a complex structure.

The immediate effect of this decision to have HN originate in the superordinate is a revocation of the apparently easy and straightforward account of the origin of each of the parts of (19)(a) and (b): it must now be the superordinate N that generates *the men* and the subordinate N governed by abl that generates *some/one*. The intuition which this new decision is in accord with is no longer that of natural serialization in relation to background groups, but rather with the organization of the referential structure itself. The progressive specialization, explained in relation to Jespersen's ladder above (p. 93), embodies the same principle of background groups, from which selection may be made, being denoted by categories 'higher' in the referential structure than those that denote the selections themselves.

We can now sketch the further derivational history of (19)(a) *some of the men* from the underlying structure (20). Note first of all that *some*, in this context, would be described in traditional terms as a pronoun.

Anticipating the discussion of the next section I shall regard this 'pronominal' status of *some* as a consequence of lexical subjunction of $L_{gen}$ to gen. $L_{gen}$ being specified generally as ([+subst] & [+stat]) and, in this case specifically by the set of features lexicalizable as *man*, is thus conflated with the functional categories under RP-subjunction, thus characterizing the lexical reflex of the complex node as a 'noun' with the recoverable denotative meaning *man*. The pertinent, if incomplete, representation of these steps is shown in (23).

(23)

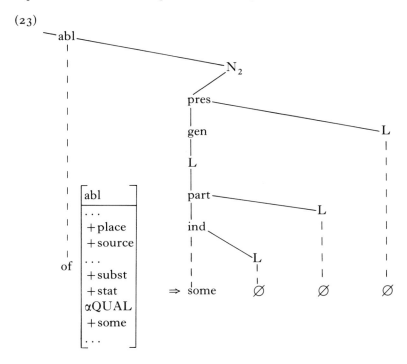

There are various ways in which we might describe a procedure by which a subordinate N is promoted to primary status, but suppose that we initially made allowance for the general processes of subjunction and adjunction to apply also to entire structures. In this way N is now subjoined to abl under observance of the MI-convention, the result being an explicitation. The next step would then be the adjunction of abl to a particular category in the superordinate N. Let us assume that this adjunction is decided on semantic grounds, such that a given case is adjoined to the category with which it shares some cognitive content. In the case of ablative, this category is part(itive): abl and part are, respectively, the syntactico-semantic and the referential–semantic categories which express *separation from*. In the same way, locative shares with $L_{ind}$ the cognitive content of location. The semantically neutral case absolute has no cognitive content to share, but I shall on occasion exploit the possibility of adjoining it to gen. The representation that these considerations give rise to is given in (24).

(24)

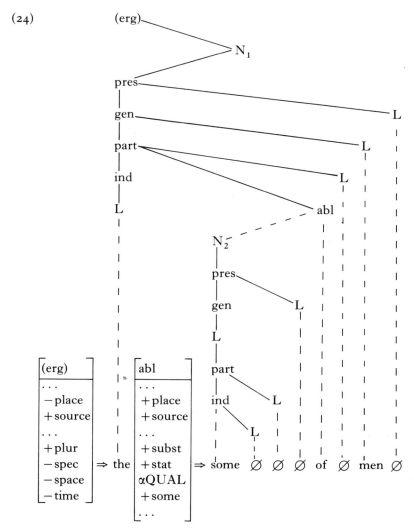

Example (24) also displays L-subjunction of the superordinate $L_{ind}$, and the full cycle of RP-subjunctions. The broken dependency lines connecting abl and $N_2$ symbolize the effect of the MI-convention.

Finally, the subordinate ablative structure is subjoined to part, again under observance of the MI-convention, the result being an explicitation (25). The effect of the MI-convention is again symbolized by broken dependency lines.

(25)

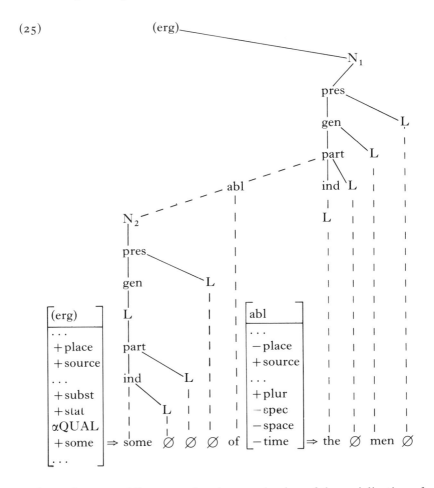

Apart from providing a precise characterization of the serialization of *some of the men*, (25) embodies a principle of some importance. Notice that the complex symbols of features in the morphophonemic compartments have changed places, except at one point: the case-specifications above the horizontal lines have remained in their original positions. Yet the case-specifications below the horizontal lines have changed. The

(26) (a)

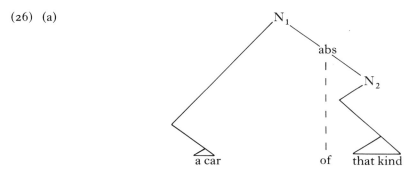

(b)

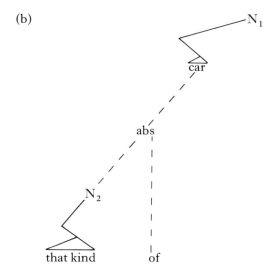

result of these processes is the creation of 'complex' case-specifications on nouns, a result which is explicitly allowed for by Anderson (1977). Yet Anderson fails to give very precise arguments for the ways in which such complex cases arise and also for what combinations may (not) occur. I do not wish to pursue these matters here, but I want to suggest that the superficial occurrence of a case-form may embody an underlying complex case-function, the complexity of which arises from mergings of case-features relevant to both the syntactico-semantic and to the referential–semantic functions performed by NPs. By way of empirical evidence for the proposed bi-partition of the morpho-phonemic compartment, consider the well-known fact that in some languages the 'possessor' is marked locative, while in others it is the 'possessed' which is so marked in possessive constructions. Assuming that possessive constructions originate in complex structures similar (except for details) to (20), these facts may be explained with reference to the subjunctional shift of the subcomponents of the morphophonemic compartments.

Let us now return to (21). Adherence to the principles just discussed implies that the two schematic representations (26)(a) and (b) are the final derived strings of (21)(b) and (a), respectively; where in (b), abs is adjoined and subjoined to gen in $N_1$ under the MI-convention, and where in (a), $N_2$ is neither adjoined nor subjoined to anything within $N_1$. In other words, the adjunction, and subsequent subjunction, of a subordinate N to a given category in the superordinate is optional. Consider now such phrases as:

(27)  (a)(i) a cluster of trees $\begin{cases} \neq \text{(ii)} & \text{a tree of that cluster} \\ \neq \text{(iii)} ^{if} & \text{a tree-cluster} \end{cases}$

    (b)(i) a cup of coffee $\begin{cases} \neq \text{(ii)} & \text{coffee of/from that cup} \\ \neq \text{(iii)} & \text{a coffee cup} \end{cases}$

    (c)(i) a nest of birds $\begin{cases} \neq \text{(ii)} & \text{a bird of/from that nest} \\ \neq \text{(iii)} & \text{a birds' nest} \end{cases}$

    (d)(i) a shoal of herring $\begin{cases} \neq \text{(ii)} & \text{a herring of/from that shoal} \\ \neq \text{(iii)} ^{if} & \text{a herring-shoal.} \end{cases}$

None of the (ii)–(iii) phrases, where well-formed, are referentially identical with their respective (i) 'counterparts'. The phrases in (27) are thus different from those in (21) with *kind*.

The head nouns in (27)(i) and (ii) are *tree, coffee, bird*, and *herring*, whereas, in (iii) it is *cluster, cup, nest*, and *shoal*. Let us now impose the requirement on E-classified phrases that number-oppositions with respect to the head noun are neutralized in them, that is, for a NP to be an E-classified phrase there can be no *semantic oppositions* of number in the head noun. Cf. then:

(28)  (a)(i) *a cluster of tree    $\neq$ (ii) two trees of that cluster

    (c)(i) *a nest of bird    $\neq$ (ii) two birds of/from that nest

    (d)(i) a shoal of herrings $\neq$ (ii) two herrings from that shoal.

(b) is excluded for reasons of countability. On the criterion of paradigmatic opposition between the members of grammatical categories, only (ii) display the presence of number on the head noun. In (i) no opposition can be found, either because the singular form cannot be used at all ((a) and (c)), or because no semantic opposition arises through the substitution of the plural form by the singular form. Thus the phrases in (27)(i) are all E-classified phrases on the criterion just established, those in (ii) (and (iii)) are not.

Generalizing on the various findings from the discussion of the derivation of (19) and (21), we say that complex structures which yield delimitative serializations generate either E-classified or quantified NPs. We now have to look into the difference between these two.

In contrast to the pronominal status of the quantifier in a delimitative serialization, the status of what I have called E-classifiers is traditionally that of a noun. The pronominal status of the quantifier was attributed to L-subjunction of $L_{gen}$ to gen in the subordinate N. It is in fact the same L-subjunction that accounts for the noun-like status of E-classifiers, but whereas the L-subjoined gen-L is conflated with the other functional categories during RP-subjunction in the derivation of quantifiers, it enters the MI-convention with them during RP-subjunction in the derivation of E-classifiers. Cf. (23) with (29) which is the non-final derived structure underlying *that kind of (car)*; where the broken dependency lines as usual symbolize the effect of the MI-convention.

(29)

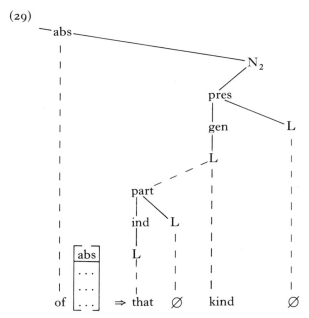

In the present instance, $L_{gen}$ is not independently subcategorized by lexical features, so *kind* simply reflects the 'lexical' content of gen.

However, since $L_{gen}$ is inherently specified as ([+subst] & [+stat]), *kind* comes out as a noun.

The derivational principle behind the existence of the fairly large number of E-classifiers commented upon above (§7.3.3) is the supposition that $L_{gen}$ *may* be independently subcategorized by lexical features in structures similar to (29).

Although in this way we explain why E-classifiers are syntactically nouns, we do not explain why a large number of recognized nouns should be E-classifiers (i.e. *functional* items), except in the definitional sense that they are dominated (after L-subjunction) by a FC and this would hardly count as a valid explanation alone.

There is, however, distributional evidence which may be brought to bear on the question. Consider first:

(30)  (a)  an embroidered bag vs. *an embroidered bag of pheasant

       (b)  a broken glass vs. *a broken glass of milk

       (c)  a green bucket vs. *a green bucket of water.

Depending on whether such nouns as *bag*, *glass*, and *bucket* function as 'full' nouns or as E-classifiers, different selectional rules apply to them.

(31)(a)  (i)  a number of {men, theories, police, . . .}

            (ii)  *a number of {water, knowledge, audience, . . .}

     (b)  (i)  a bevy of {birds, larks, girls}

            (ii)  *a bevy of {fish, herrings, boys, . . .}.

Here, too, there are co-occurrence restrictions, this time between the two nouns involved. It seems reasonable to say that an E-classifier is sensitive to what *kind* of thing is being denoted by the head noun, either in such general terms as countability, or in such more specific terms as 'natural class'. But this means that the subordinate structure must contain a replica of (a subset of) the features on $L_{gen}$ and part in the superordinate N. And since these features indicate *kind*, contingent kind in the case of part, essential kind in the case of $L_{gen}$, I take these features to be copied into *gen* in the lower structure. By lexical subjunction of the lower gen-L, this subset of kind-indicating features will then be 'inherent' to the E-classifier.

Finally, if (a) a wall of stone is a stone wall, why is (b) a wall of hostility not a hostility wall? I would suggest, firstly, that the case-relation involved in (a) is absolutive, whereas, in (b), it is ablative; secondly, that *wall* in (a) is the head noun, originating in the superordinate, whereas, in (b), it is an E-classifier, originating in the subordinate; and thirdly, that the reason why *a wall of stone* is not an E-classified NP is that no L-subjunctions of gen-L are involved in its derivation.

None of these distributional facts necessarily show that some nouns are E-classifiers (functional items). On the other hand, they are not incompatible with such a suggestion either. We conclude, therefore, that the postulation of a functional status as E-classifiers for a subset of nouns *may* be an explanation of certain distributional facts surrounding these nouns.

**7.5.3 Derivational characteristics of pronouns.** Let me quote a passage from Hjelmslev (1937: 196) by way of introduction to the present topic:

Leur base [des pronoms] doit donc être constituées, non par des morphèmes convertis, mais par un syncrétisme de tous les plérèmes nominaux de la langue. C'est ainsi qu'il faut expliquer leur rôle de nomina uicaria, c'est-à-dire le fait qu'ils renferment toutes les significations nominales possibles, prêtes à surgir alternativement a titre de variantes sémantiques selon les exigences du contexte.

The *plérèmes nominaux* are the minimal, non-autonomous, meaning-carrying elements which are involved in the constitution of nouns, or, simply, the semantic components that enter into a specification of all the lexical nouns in a language.

What Hjelmslev says here is in effect what I would express by saying that the referential phrase gen-L is lexically subjoined, and that the result of this subjunction is a conflation.

Pronouns may be either definite (the personal pronouns, for example), or indefinite (*something*, etc.). In derivational terms this distinction reflects a difference with respect to the occurrence, or non-occurrence, of L-subjunction of $L_{ind}$.

Apart from being characterized by these two instances of L-subjunction, pronouns are generally characterized also by L-subjunction of both $L_{part}$ and $L_{pres}$. In phrases like *lucky you, poor me*, etc., where the attributive adjectives are considered to originate under $L_{part}$, natural serialization might suggest that we do have L-subjunction of $L_{part}$, but that the MI-convention has applied.

By far the most interesting aspect of the derivation of pronouns, however, is the question of which referential phrases should be included in their underlying structure. I have already suggested several times that some pronouns derive from structures which do *not* contain the referential phrase gen-L. This suggestion might appear to be in conflict with the derivational characteristic just introduced (L-subjunction of $L_{gen}$). This conflict cannot be solved on derivational considerations, which are, in effect, quite mechanical. On the contrary it can only be solved on the basis of considerations of referential functions. I therefore postpone detailed discussion of it to chapter 10.

### 7.5.4 Juxtapositive serializations from complex structures.
Complex structures like that in (21) do not always yield delimitative serializations. Consider the following:

(32)(a) (i)   *each boy* was searched

(ii)  *each of the boys* was searched

(iii) *the boys* were *each* given a thorough search

(b) (i)   *neither boy* has the correct answer

(ii)  *neither of the boys* has the correct answer

(c) (i)   *my knife* is blunt

(ii)  *my knives* are blunt

(iii) *their knife* is blunt

(iv)  *their knives* are blunt.

The italicized phrases are all considered to be describable within the present framework, even (a)(iii), although further investigation will have to be carried out into the general problem of discontinuous constituents than I shall attempt to do.

If this is so, it seems that we can make the following generalization about concord: in a juxtapositive serialization, the number on the verb is decided by the number of the head noun, whereas, in delimitative serializations, the number on the verb is decided by the number of the referential functive.

The interesting point is then that we sometimes find differently serialized pairs of phrases (as in (a) and (b)) the members of which are referentially identical. Since two number specifications are clearly required in (a)(ii) and (b)(ii), and since these are referentially identical with their respective counterparts in (i) and (iii), it seems reasonable to suppose that also in these latter cases two number-specifications are called for. And these we can only get in complex structures.

The derivation of (32)(a)(ii) is quite similar to that outlined in (26)(b), with a final derived string like (33).

That is, $N_2$ is fully subjoined lexically, is then subjoined to abl under observance of the MI-convention, and finally abl is adjoined and subjoined to part in $N_1$, again under observance of the MI-convention.

(33)

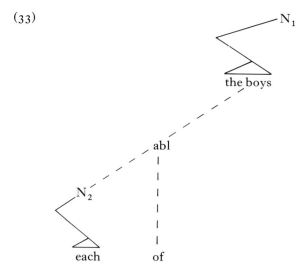

$N_1$ is specified as ($[+\text{plur}]$ & $[-\text{spec}]$) on ind, to which $L_{ind}$ is L-subjoined. $N_2$ is specified as ($[-\text{plur}]$ & $[+\text{spec}]$).

I suggest two derivational alternatives to (33), one which accounts for *each boy*, and one which accounts for *the boys each*. Suppose the derivation outlined for (33) were to stop at the step where $N_2$ is subjoined to abl, and that the 'instruction' for the break was that $N_2$ absorbed abl, rather than enter the MI-convention with it. We could represent this situation in a schematic structure like:

(34)

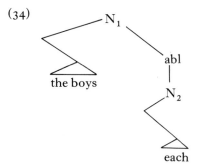

The other alternative exploits the possibility of L-subjoining the whole of $N_1$ rather than $N_2$. Also it differs from (33) in that the whole $N_1$ is absorbed by $N_2$. The final derived string of *each boy* is given in (35).

(35)

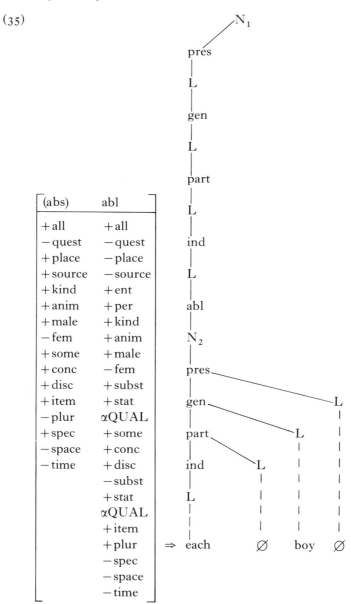

Before we leave the general area of the derivational characteristics of the referential functives, much more about which can be said, and much more about which *is* said in Thrane (1976: Part III), I should like briefly to discuss two points, one concerning the proper statement of meaning of the referential functives, and one more specifically concerning the special derivation of (34), which may have some general implications.

It is clear from (35) that a great deal of redundancy is included in the complex symbol which is held to contain a feature-specification of the meaning of *each*. However, if we went through a number of different phrases containing *each* in combination with various head nouns along the lines suggested above, we would find that the following is a statement of the meaning of *each* in the form of a list of the sufficient and necessary features that appear in any complex symbol of these analyses:

(36) 
$$
\begin{bmatrix}
\text{(case)} \\[4pt]
+\text{all} \\
-\text{quest} \\
+\text{place} \\
+\text{source} \\
+\text{ent} \\
\text{oper} \\
+\text{subst} \\
+\text{stat} \\
\text{oQUAL} \\
+\text{some} \\
+\text{conc} \\
+\text{disc} \\
+\text{item} \\
-\text{plur} \\
+\text{spec} \\
\text{ospace} \\
\text{otime}
\end{bmatrix}
$$

This symbol states that *each* is a positive ([+all]), countable ([+conc] & [+disc]), definite ([ospace] & [otime]) referential functive which carries the inherent meaning of partition ([+place] & [+source]), which may on occasion function as a pronoun ([+subst]), and which imposes a condition of specified singularity on the entities it is used to mention ([+ent], [oper], [+item], [−plur], [+spec]). It does *not* state that *each* combines individuality with universality. The ability of *each* to exhaust a definite background group I take, on balance, to be a necessary *presupposition* on its inherent meaning, explicable on the (derivational) fact that it always derives from $N_2$.

The structure (34) displays a situation where a subordinate N is not adjoined and subjoined to any category in the superordinate. It underlies the phrase *the boys each*. Now it seems to be a general characteristic of *each*, *all*, and *both*, which are all quantifiers on the present analysis, that they may follow their head nouns in juxtapositive serializations. This sets them off from all other quantifiers in (6). Carden (1973: 92 fn 2) even suggests that there are dialects of (American) English which permit only *the guests all*, not *all the guests*. They have another thing in common. They are all universal quantifiers, in the sense that they exhaust the sets they are used of. In contrast, all the other quantifiers are partitive. Reconsider in this light the discussion surrounding (21) and (27)–(28) above. All the phrases in (27)(a) may reasonably be called partitive, and I argued that they were E-classified phrases in virtue of adjunction and subjunction of $N_2$ to a category in $N_1$. The derivational principle I am arguing for here can now be stated concisely: any $N_2$ which generates a referential functive with partitive meaning must be adjoined and subjoined to part in $N_1$. Any $N_2$ which generates a referential functive which is universal, either inherently or by presupposition, may or may not undergo a similar process.

## 7.6  The notional content of the referential functives

In his paper 'Towards a "notional" theory of the "parts of speech"' (1966), Lyons seeks to bridge the gap between traditional ('notional') and more modern ('distributional') criteria for the establishment of word-classes. He does so by distinguishing two separate procedures which, he claims, are often confused: (a) the procedure of *establishing* classes of words; and (b) the procedure of *naming* these classes. Of these (a) is a purely distributional procedure, whereas (b) may be based on 'notional' characteristics. The general business of establishing word-classes should be conducted along the lines of the following schema:

(37)  It is a fact that all the words in English which ... fall into the same distributional class; taking those members of this distributional class which do ... as the nuclear members, we may call the entire class the class of __.

In this schema, ' ...' stands for a given 'notional' characteristic, '__' for a particular name which 'sums up' this characteristic.

I have argued for the existence of an overall class of referential functives the members of which are all distributionally defined with respect to a particular descriptive strategy (ultimate dominance by FC). More particularly, I have argued for the existence of four subclasses of referential functives, distributionally defined by the diagnostic frames in (3), and I have anticipated the present discussion in that I have already named these classes. The aim of the present section is to justify those names.

The overall class of referential functives has two pervasive notional characteristics: *enumeration* and *identification*. Cutting across these two characteristics is a third, namely, whether or not enumeration or identification is achieved through considerations of what *kind* of thing is being spoken of. Inserting these characteristics for the dots in (37) we get:

(38)  (a) It is a fact that all the referential functives in English which enumerate things or indicate amount of substance irrespectively of what kind of thing or substance is being spoken about fall in the same distributional class. Taking those that do this as the nuclear members of the class, we may call the entire class the class of *quantifiers*.

(b) It is a fact that all the referential functives in English which enumerate things or amounts of substance with regard to what kind of thing or substance is being talked about in terms of such characteristics as countability, weighability, measurability and the like, fall in the same distributional class. Taking those that do this as the nuclear members we may call the entire class the class of *E-classifiers*.

(c) It is a fact that all the referential functives in English which identify things or amounts of substance in terms of what kind of thing or substance is being spoken about, fall in the same distributional class. Taking those members which do this as the nuclear members, we may call the entire class the class of *determiners*.

(d) It is a fact that all the referential functives in English which identify things or amounts of substance irrespectively of what kind of thing or substance is being spoken about, fall in the same distributional class. Taking those members which do this as the nuclear members, we may call the entire class the class of *pronouns*.

The names chosen for these classes are quite common in discussions of (English) grammar, except for the term 'E-classifier', which is coined on the term 'numeral classifier' employed in the description of a large number of (non-Indo-European) languages. But it should be emphasized that, in this book, a quantifier is any referential functive that may be inserted in both diagnostic frames in (3). In addition it *may* have the notional content of (38)(a), namely, when it is one of the nuclear quantifiers.

# 8 *Indefinite expressions*

## 8.1 Indefiniteness: sortal and selective expressions

In chapter 4 we established a distinction between three referential functions, sortal, selective, and identitive, and in chapter 7 we found that four classes of referential functives can be identified on distributional grounds. In this and the following two chapters I shall attempt to synchronize the notions of referential function and referential functive. This endeavour, which might be described as an attempt to synchronize functional and formal phenomena, constitutes the synthesis of the present work.

Let me begin by reminding the reader of my use of the term 'referential expression' (§4.1). A referential expression is a NP considered as a distributionally defined syntagm, the meaning of which equips it as a potential linguistic correlate of non-linguistic entities. According to which kind of referential function a given NP is held to perform, we may speak of sortal, selective, or identitive expressions, and according to which type of referential functive forms (part of) a given NP, we may likewise speak of quantified, E-classified, determiner, or pronominal expressions. Instead of the latter designation we shall usually speak simply of pronouns, however.

It is clear already, for numerical reasons, that there is no one-to-one correlation between, on the one hand, sortal, selective, and identitive expressions, on the other quantified, E-classified, determiner and pronominal expressions. It is therefore not the case that, e.g. a determiner expression always performs one and only one type of referential function. It is not even always true that a NP containing a particular referential functive always performs one and the same referential function, though in many cases it is.

The ensuing discussion could be organized in several ways, but no matter which way we chose, a certain amount of overlapping and cross-reference between sections would be in evidence. To avoid this as far as possible I shall, for reasons of exposition only, avail myself of what is often taken to be the basic distinction in discussions of referentiality, the distinction between definiteness and indefiniteness.[1]

As already stated several times, indefiniteness and definiteness are regarded as two transformationally related notions, the distinction between them being brought out in configurational terms by means of non-application vs. application of L-subjunction of $L_{ind}$. It is in this light that the above suggestion should be seen that the distinction is not a basic one. I am not suggesting that, for a given NP, it is the case that it cannot be classified (in configurational terms) as either definite or indefinite. What I *am* suggesting is, firstly, that neither definiteness nor indefiniteness is a semantically primitive notion, as some would have it (see, e.g. Krámsky (1972); Perlmutter (1969); Postal (1966); Sørensen (1959a, 1963: 97)), and secondly, that the distinction on its own is too broad for it to serve as a tool by which to account exhaustively for the referential functions of NPs. For although it is the case, as we shall see, that indefiniteness is a necessary ingredient in selective expressions, and definiteness in identitive expressions, sortal expressions may be either. So the notions of definiteness and indefiniteness are only partly isomorphic with what I consider the basic referential distinctions, the notions of partitiveness, of categorial distinctions, and of spatio-temporal location.

In the present chapter I shall be concerned mainly with indefinite expressions (selective and sortal), but some points concerning definiteness will also be touched upon since they are presupposed by much which follows. Then, in chapter 9, I shall discuss definite expressions (sortal and identitive) excluding pronouns. These will be the subject matter of chapter 10.

## 8.2 The classes of sortal and selective expressions

The various types of expression – some of which are to be discussed in this chapter – may be tabulated as in (1). Here '$N_s$' stands for 'noun in singular form', '$N_p$' for 'noun in plural form'.

There are, of course, also 'indefinite' E-classified expressions, but since the E-classifiers are non-autonomous referential functives – in virtue of their 'noun-like' status – and require the presence of another

---

[1]  This distinction is (implicitly) basic to such previous important works as Christophersen (1939); Hawkins (1978); Krámsky (1972); and Robbins (1968).

referential functive with which to enter a juxtapositive serialization, they can be excluded from the discussion in this and the following chapters. E-classified expressions perform complex functions: either sortal (*kind*, etc.) or selective (*bag*, etc.), plus the function performed by the extra referential functive.

There are, however, no sortal pronouns. The reason for this will become clear in chapter 10, to which I also defer the discussion of the three selective ones quoted in (1).

| (1) | | selective | sortal |
|---|---|---|---|
| | quantified | $some + N_{s/p}$ <br> $many + N_p$ <br> $much + N_s$ <br> $one + N_s$ <br> $two + N_p$ <br> ... | $all + N_p$ <br> $any + N_{s/p}$ |
| | determiner | $a + N_s$ <br> $what + N_{s/p}$ | $a + N_s$ <br> $what + N_{s/p}$ <br> $no + N_{s/p}$ <br> $every + N_s$ |
| | pronouns | -thing <br> -body <br> -one | |

The lay-out of the present chapter is as follows: in §8.3 I shall present some points of derivational contrast in relation to expressions introduced by *some* and *all* which are presupposed by the discussion in subsequent sections; in §8.4 phrases introduced by *any* will be analyzed in relation to other (quantified and determiner) expressions; finally, in §8.5 the problems of 'specificness' will be discussed in relation to some of the traditional problems of 'genericness'. Many problems worthy of attention are left out. Some of them are discussed at various points in Thrane (1976), others I plan to treat in detail elsewhere.

## 8.3 *All* **and** *some*

I have already stated the appropriate derivation of expressions like *some dogs* (§7.5.1; (7:17) and (7:18)). In contrast with that I regard (2) as the final derived structure of *all dogs*.

(2)

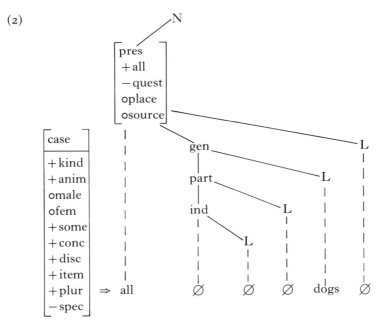

The most obvious aspect of (2) is that I have slackened the general requirement expressed in §6.2.3, that RP-subjunction is obligatory in English; more precisely, (2) implies that only the first, adjoining, step in the two-step process of RP-subjunction has applied to adjoin gen ( + its dependents) to pres, whereas the last, subjoining, step has not. There are, however, good distributional reasons for making the last, subjoining, step in the last application of RP-subjunction optional in English; cf.:

(3)    (a)  all the dogs
       (b) *if* some the dogs.

The derivation of (3)(a) follows the pattern of (2), except that $L_{ind}$ is L-subjoined, so we get (4) (omitting unnecessary details).

Notice now that, with L-subjunction of $L_{ind}$ in (7: 18), we would get (5) (again omitting irrelevant details).

The structure (5) would preclude *some the dogs* (and, indeed, *all the dogs*), as would also (4). I shall now begin to discuss some further issues around structures like (4) and (5), a discussion which will be concluded in §9.3.1.

(4)

(5)

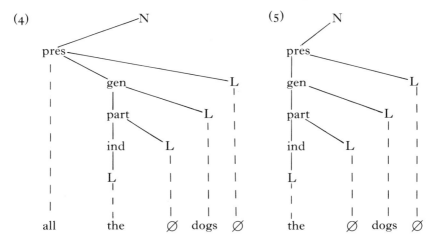

Consider first:

(6)(a) (i)   all the boys (brought sleeping-bags)
     (ii)  the boys all      –
     (iii) the boys      –
  (b) (i)   *if* some the boys      –
     (ii)  *if* the boys some      –
     (iii)  the boys      –
  (c) (i)   all boys (are noisy)
     (ii)  *if* boys all      –
     (iii)  boys      –

In §7.5.4 a derivation was suggested for expressions containing a universal quantifier in post-noun position, according to which such expressions derive from complex structures. While such a derivation is necessary for *each*, an alternative (additional) derivation might be suggested for expressions containing *all* (and *both*, which we disregard here), like (6)(a)(ii). It seems, from a comparison of (6)(a) and (c), that *all* can only occur in post-noun position when the head noun is definite. The main question we shall be concerned with is whether all the definite expressions in (6) derive from structures like (4) or (5), or whether both are necessary.

Initially, this latter possibility seems most promising. The well-formed (a)(i) example derives from (4), whereas the two definite (iii) examples derive from (5). But what about the well-formed (ii) example? Suppose we decide to derive not only (a)(i), but also (a)–(b)(iii) from a structure like (4), relating this decision to the status as a salient category attributed to pres in §4.4.2. As a salient category, pres may be lexicalized, but if it is, no referential opposition (or 'marking') accompanies the resultant string as against a string in which it is not lexicalized. This is precisely the case here: all of the three expressions under discussion have the same referential potential – provided we regard *all* and *both* as complementary variants, dependent on the number-specification on ind.[2] What we then need to account for the acceptable (a)(ii) example is the MI-convention, connected with the *optionality* of the last, subjoining, step of RP-subjunction commented upon above. When this step does apply, the MI-convention comes into force:

(7)

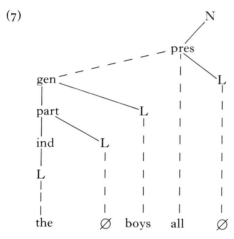

Carden's (1973: 92) footnote already referred to (p. 154), according to which certain American dialects allow only *the guests all arrived at eight*, is easily explained in this light. These dialects would here be described as having obligatory application also of the last, subjoining, step of RP-subjunction. Yet there are problems with this analysis. First

---

[2]   This may not be accepted. Whereas *all* is indefinite, *both* is definite; cf.

    (a) all the men ≠ all men

    (b) both the men = both men.

This inherent definiteness of *both* is due to a diachronic development, Old English *bā þā* > *both*, where *bā* is equal to *both* minus definiteness, and *þā* is the (plural) weak demonstrative article. It is this difference in definiteness which is behind the distributional non-parallelism noted by Carden (1973: 94)

    (c) *all Tom, Dick and Harry left

    (d) both Tom and Dick left.

Note also *all ten men* vs. *both two men*. It would be Old English *bā* and Modern English *all* that could be described as complementary. Cf. also Modern German *beiden*.

of all, $L_{pres}$ is required to appear to the right of *all*. Since it is usually empty it is difficult to give non-arbitrary solutions to this potential problem. And that it is a potential problem is evident from a comparison of (8)(a) and (b):

(8)    (a)  those three flying saucer things all appeared at dawn

(b) *if* those three flying saucer all things appeared at dawn.

The serialization involved in (b) is clearly ill-formed, as opposed to that in (a). Yet (b) is to be expected from the analysis just given.

Secondly, certain verbs may appear between head noun and *all*, as in *the boys were all extremely quiet*. This might suggest that *all* is far more loosely connected with the (rest of the) referential structure than has been assumed throughout.

To sum up, it seems that we can derive all the definite NPs in (6) from just the one structure (4), given the validity of a number of assumptions. Of these, the involvement of the MI-convention in the derivation of the (b) example requires the greatest suspension of disbelief. Yet to suggest that (5) would be an appropriate structure for such examples, without the participation of the MI-convention, would be unrealistic. I shall let the matter rest here for a while; but in §9.3.1 I shall take up some further points relevant to the issue.

## 8.4  *Any*

Expressions introduced by *any* are often said to be in complementary distribution with expressions introduced by *some*. Two distinct types of context may serve as criterial:

(9)(a) (i) *I have any apples
  { ≠ (ii)  I have some apples
  { ≠ (iii) I have sm apples

(b) (i) I don't have any apples
  { ≠ (ii)  I don't have some apples
  { ≐ (iii) I don't have sm apples

(c) (i) Do you have any apples?
  { ≠ (ii)  Do you have some apples?
  { ≐ (iii) Do you have sm apples?

(d) (i) If I had any apples I'd give you one
  { ≠ (ii)  If I had some apples I'd give you one
  { ≐ (iii) If I had sm apples I'd give you one.

This type of context may be called non-modal, as opposed to the modal type exemplified by:

(10)(a)  (i)   any horse can jump that fence
                 (cf. *any horse jumped that fence)
           (ii)  *any horses can jump that fence
                 (cf. *any horses jumped that fence)
      (b)  (i)   *some horse can jump that fence
                 (cf. some horse jumped that fence)
           (ii)  some horses can jump that fence
                 (cf. some horses jumped that fence)
      (c)  (i)   all horses can jump that fence
                 (cf. all *the* horses jumped that fence).

On a pragmatic ('ability') reading of the modal the distribution of deviancy is as stated; (b)(i) is likely to be non-deviant on an epistemic reading of *can*, but then (a)(i) would be deviant.

As suggested by the display in (9), the distribution of *some* and *any* in non-modal contexts is overlapping rather than complementary. This has been pointed out by others, e.g. R. Lakoff (1969). Furthermore, as also indicated by (9), discrimination is called for between an unstressed ('indefinite determiner') use of *some* (spelled *sm*), and a stressed ('quantifier') use, in terms of which (a)(ii) might be continued ' . . . but not enough to go round', whereas an appropriate continuation of (a)(iii) would be ' . . . in case I get hungry'. Also embodied in (9) is an indication that I take the (i)- and (ii)-examples in (b)–(d) to be non-deviant and well-formed, but referentially non-identical; and the (iii)-examples in these cases as non-deviant and well-formed, and perhaps referentially identical with their (i)-counterparts. That is, the implication of each of (b)–(d)(ii) is that the speaker (in (c) the hearer) has precisely one apple, whereas the implication of (b)–(d)(i) and (iii) is that the speaker (in (c) the hearer) has no apples. The question to be resolved now, given the validity of these implicational relationships, is whether (i) and (iii) *are* in free variation. R. Lakoff (1969) says they are not, and she relates the postulated difference between them to a conventional notion of speaker's presupposition, in conjunction with a rather ill-defined and vague new concept of synonymy. The argument that I shall develop is based on the distinction drawn in §4.2.2 between conditional and non-conditional referential functions, first applied to (10).

A conditional referential function is performed by a sign, S, if S *invites* the hearer to accept the categorial location established by S; a non-conditional referential function is performed by S if S *presupposes* such acceptance.

To say that (10)(a)(i) is a conditional expression is to say the following about the meaning of *any horse*: if you, the hearer, accept the categorial location C(HORSE), then, for whichever entity you might care to locate in it, wherever it is, it is the case that it can jump that fence.

In contrast, both *some* and *all* are non-conditional. To say this is to say the following: I, the speaker, assume that you, the hearer, accept C(HORSE); then, for some/all things you locate in it, wherever they are, it is the case that they can jump that fence. In derivational terms the differences are indicated as in (11); where [αconditional] is introduced as a feature on ind.[3]

If we now compare (10)(a)(i) to the (well-formed) (i) examples in (9), and particularly (d)(i), we find that, if we in these latter instances can speak about 'conditional' at all, it must be a different kind of condition

(11) (a)

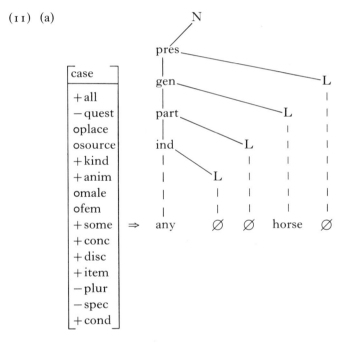

---

[3] Perhaps [αconditional] should be introduced as a factor which controlled the choice of [±plur]. The reason would be this: Provided [+cond] poses a condition on the categorial locations established by (the lexemes inserted under) $L_{gen}$ and $L_{part}$, the question of number becomes irrelevant. C-locations are either accepted or not, they are not accepted in numbers. This would explain the difficulties that native speakers of English have had of pointing to a clear notional difference between

    (a) any promise by our agents cannot bind the company
    (b) any promises by our agents cannot bind the company.

(b)

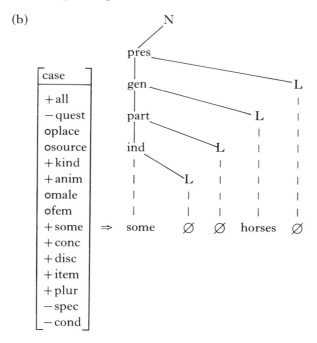

(c)

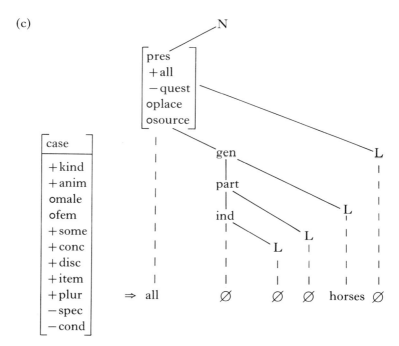

to that just discussed. It makes little sense to say of (9)(d)(i) that *any apples* imposes any condition on C(APPLE). The condition, in this case, is rather on the entity located in C(APPLE). This latter type of condition is, in Searle's terms, an illocutionary force on propositions, the illocutionary force indicator being *if . . . then* (Searle 1969: 30).

We can distinguish a conditional 'operator' which has propositions as its scope, and one that has arguments as its scope. In linguistic terms we might say that the feature [αconditional] characterizes both V – the verb being the sentence-constituting unit – and N, and we might generalize this notion of intra- vs. extra-nominal features to cover also [αall] and [αquest], thereby treating negation and interrogation both as illocutionary forces on propositions and as inherent features on nominals. It seems to me that this distinction, with respect to [αall], is necessary to account for the different implicational properties of:

(12)  (a)  there weren't any girls ⊃ there were no girls

      (b)  some girls weren't there ⊃ there were some girls there

where (a) is supposedly marked [−all] on pres in the structure generating *any/no girls*, and where (b) is marked [−all] – or perhaps rather [+neg] on V, but as [+all] on pres in the nominal structure. With respect to [αquest] the distinction is held to be associated with the distinction between *wh*-questions (intra-nominal) and *yes/no*-questions (extra-nominal).

Consider (12) once more. Whereas the two sentences in (a) have the same referential potential, this is not the case with (b). In (b) the implicate establishes a subclass of girls of which it is true to say of each member that she was there; the implicans, on the other hand, establishes a subclass of girls of which it is true to say of each member that she was not there. These two classes of girls are complementary. In other words, *some* imposes a division on a given *kind* of thing. It performs a selective function. In contrast, *any*, as well as *no*, imposes a distinction between a given kind of things and everything not considered to belong to that kind. They perform sortal functions.

The referential identity of the two NPs in (12)(a) can be accounted for in derivational terms in (13), which exploits the distinction between structures like (4) and (5) discussed above. I return in due course to the question whether one, both, or neither of these structures should be marked by the conditional feature.

We should now expect interrogative expressions to conform to the same two-fold derivation. In order to demonstrate that this is indeed the

(13)  (a)

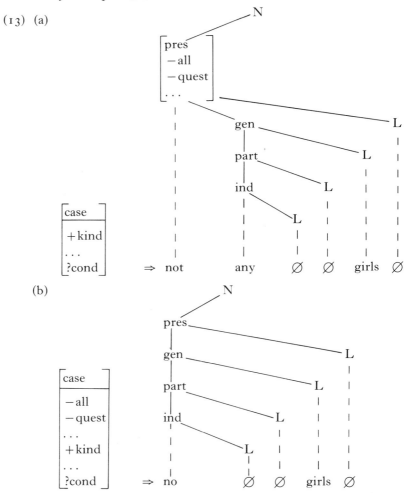

case, I shall present some data from Danish which, in contrast to English, has a question morpheme, *mon*:

(14)(a) (i) (α) hvilke piger (mon) (der)   kommer?
                  what   girls   (?)     (there) come?
              (β) hvilke piger kommer (der) (mon)?
                  Both = 'I wonder what girls are coming?'
        (ii)(α) *if* mon hvilke piger kommer?
              (β) *if* mon der kommer hvilke piger?
     (b) (i) (α) *if* nogen piger mon (der)   kommer?
                  any   girls  ?    (there) come?
              (β) *if* nogen piger kommer (der) mon?

(ii)(α) kommer der (mon) nogen piger?

(β) mon der kommer nogen piger?

Both = 'I wonder if there'll be any girls coming?'

As appears from (14), the placement of *mon* is to some extent free. Moreover, it is optional in all *wh*-questions – i.e. (a) – but obligatory in some *yes/no*-questions, namely those, like (b)(ii)(β), which would simply be statements were it not for the presence of *mon*. But despite this apparent freedom of placement, the serializations (a)(ii) and (b)(i) are clearly ill-formed in any dialect of Danish with which I am familiar. And it is precisely these two impossibilities which are interesting from a derivational point of view.

I take it that (14)(a) are derived from a structure with full application of RP-subjunction, including subjunction of gen to pres, i.e. a structure similar to (13)(b), except that it is [+quest]. The impossibility of (14)(a)(ii) is then a function of the MI-convention: if *mon* must be expressed it must be moved to the end of the string. In contrast, (14)(b) derive from structures similar to (13)(a). Hence *mon* – which is the realization of pres in the nominal underlying the subject NP when the verb is marked [+quest] and which must be expressed when this marking has not resulted in inversion – cannot appear after the quantifier *nogen*.

Let us now return to the conditional distinction. Consider the following:

(15)  (a)  Do you have any quasps?

(b)  I don't have any quasps

(c)  If I had any quasps I'd give you one.

If (a) is uttered by a customer in a general store the shop assistant will be hard put to it. He cannot say 'yes' without qualification, for that would commit him to producing something which he would be prepared to locate in C(QUASP). Nor could he say 'no' without further qualification, for that would prevent him from finding out what the customer actually wants. The question presents a catch not dissimilar to that presented by leading questions like 'When did you stop beating your wife?' And here, too, the reason for the quandary has something to do with presupposition. By the occurrence of *any*, the hearer knows that the *speaker* does not necessarily commit himself to acceptance of C(QUASP), he leaves it up to the hearer. What *any* does is to call for one-sided acceptance, and the hearer feels uncomfortable because he knows that the speaker may blame him afterwards for accepting C(QUASP), no matter which answer he gives. In contrast, the same question, with *some* instead of *any*, also commits the speaker to acceptance of C(QUASP). An unqualified 'no' will therefore not place the hearer in a situation where he can be blamed (by the speaker) for accepting C(QUASP).

The difference between (9)(iii)(a) *Do you have any apples?*, and (c) *Do you have sm apples?*, can now be brought out in terms of different communicative effects by an unqualified 'yes' in the two instances:

> An unqualified 'yes' in reply to (9)(c)(i) informs the (original) speaker that the (original) hearer not only accepts sole responsibility for regarding the phonetic sequence /æpl/ as the bearer of the meaning which establishes C(APPLE), but that he also has some things he would be prepared to locate in it.

> An unqualified 'yes' to (9)(c)(iii) informs the (original) speaker that the (original) hearer has some things that he would be prepared to locate in C(APPLE), and that he agrees with the speaker that /æpl/ is the phonetic sequence the meaning of which establishes that C-location.

The difficulties over sentences like (9)(b)–(d) are then that negative, interrogative, and (propositionally) conditional contexts are compatible not only with conditional but also with non-conditional signs.

In the light of these considerations we may give the following specification of the meaning of *any*, contrasted with the specifications for *all* and *some*:

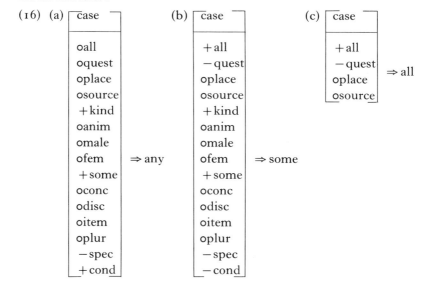

(16)  (a) [ case
          oall
          oquest
          oplace
          osource
          +kind
          oanim
          omale
          ofem        ⇒ any
          +some
          oconc
          odisc
          oitem
          oplur
          −spec
          +cond ]

      (b) [ case
          +all
          −quest
          oplace
          osource
          +kind
          oanim
          omale
          ofem        ⇒ some
          +some
          oconc
          odisc
          oitem
          oplur
          −spec
          −cond ]

      (c) [ case
          +all
          −quest
          oplace
          osource ]    ⇒ all

We note first, in relation to these specifications, that the initial statement concerning the lexical reflexes of the functional categories – as presented in §5.1.5 – was imprecise. I had not yet introduced the notions of subjunction and adjunction, which are prerequisites of lexical insertion. The 'semantic primitives' embodied in these categories are not the English *words* 'all', 'some', 'kind', and 'one', but rather those components of their meaning which might be isolated as 'universality', 'division', 'genus', and 'itemization'.

We note next, in relation to the specification attributed to *any*, that it is characterized by a high degree of unspecified features, which makes it compatible with all the contexts of *some*, provided that these contexts permit both conditional and non-conditional signs. But this high degree of unspecified features is due to the fairly great derivational differences between *any* in modal and non-modal contexts. If we take the modal contexts as those which bring out the 'true' nature of *any*, a specification of its meaning would have to include [+conc], [+disc], and [+item] whereas the features on pres would be irrelevant.

With respect to the specification attributed to *all* we note, not very surprisingly, that it is a referential functive that expresses universality, pure and simple. Yet to say this is also to say that *all*, in itself, performs neither sortal nor selective functions. It does so only in combination with lexical nouns. Since *all* may nevertheless occur alone, as in *there he stood, gumboots and all*, it might be suggested that there are, in fact, more referential functions than the three recognized here.

## 8.5 Specificness and 'genericness'

We are sometimes told that a NP introduced by the indefinite article can have either specific or non-specific reference:

(17)  I want to catch a fish.

The two different readings of *a fish* are brought out by Baker (1973) by means of the following paraphrases:

(18)  (a)  There is a fish that I want to catch (specific)
      (b)  I want there to be a fish such that I catch it (non-specific).

Another type of criterion suggested (Lyons 1977: 187ff) for the identification of the two functions relies on the form of an associated anaphoric pronoun (ex. from Lyons 1977: 188):

(19)  Every evening at six o'clock a heron flies over the chalet. *It* nests in the grounds of the chateau.

The occurrence of *it* may be taken as supporting a specific interpretation of *a heron*, according to Lyons. This criterion is only half. We cannot take an occurrence of anaphoric *one* as supporting a non-specific interpretation of the antecedent NP, for in that case *the fish* would be (indefinite?) non-specific in:

(20)  I caught the fish. My wife caught one, too.

A different criterion is based on considerations of scope under negation:

(21)  John didn't buy a car

is said to be capable of either of the following paraphrases:

(22)  (a)  There is a car that John did not buy (specific)
      (b)  There isn't a car such that John bought it (non-specific).

Common to analyses such as these is the fact that they do not explain why NPs introduced by the indefinite article should be both specific and non-specific; they assume the validity of the distinction and go on to present certain (logico-)semantic consequences of it. Moreover, by focusing on NPs introduced by the indefinite article, such analyses invite the view that only such NPs are ambiguous in this way.

I shall take the view that the distinction between specific and non-specific $a(n)$ is just one manifestation of a pervasive phenomenon which characterizes most types of referential expressions. An informal statement of this pervasive phenomenon would be that there is a systematic vacillation in the emphasis placed on C-locations and ST-locations by speakers as well as by hearers in their production (reception) of referential expressions.

I shall also attempt to give reasons why NPs introduced by the indefinite article (and other expressions) may receive either a specific or a non-specific, or even a 'generic' interpretation. For these purposes I take my starting-point in the following – supposedly non-controversial – observations, concentrating, for the moment, on expressions introduced by the indefinite article.

I take it that no one can know the precise meaning of *a* in:

(23)  a child.

I also take it that everyone would know the meaning of *a* in (24) if they were uttered on particular occasions:

(24)  (a)  a child is missing
      (b)  she wants a child
      (c)  a child is a blessing.

In current terminology, (a) would often be specific, (b) often non-specific, and (c) often 'generic'. If this is so, context would seem to be decisive for a given interpretation. And this means that $a + N_s$ must have a referential potential that allows a certain context-dependent fluctuation.

What each of (24) 'does' in the terminology developed here must be either one or the other of the following:

(25)  (a) The sign *a child* establishes C(CHILD) and ST(x); it presupposes the hearer's acceptance of C(CHILD), inviting him to assign some things to it; and it further invites him to assign *all the things* assigned to C(CHILD) to ST(x) at TU;

(b) = (a), except that *all the things* is substituted by *some of the things*.

If the pertinent formulation is (25)(a) then *a child* is a non-conditional sortal expression whereas, if it is (b), it is a non-conditional selective expression. Making allowance also for a conditional function, there would be four possible formulations.

The first noteworthy thing about (25) is that the distinction between *all the things* in (a) and *some of the things* in (b) – on which depends the distinction between sortal and selective function – is neutralized in practice. The instruction to assign *some things* to C(x) by signs like *a child* is, in practice, an instruction to assign just *one* thing to C(x) – and subsequent assignment of *all* or *some* of the things assigned to C(x) is therefore pragmatically the same. This is not to say that no communicative difference can be found from one occurrence of $a + N_s$ to another with respect to the sortal/selective distinction. It is rather to say that the context decides whether emphasis should be placed on *all* or on *some*. In contexts like '__ is a blessing' (i.e. (24)(c)), the emphasis would typically be placed on *all*, yielding a 'generic' interpretation of *a child*. In contexts like '__ is missing' or 'she wants __', on the other hand, the emphasis is on *some*, yielding selective interpretations of *a child*. This change of emphasis has some interesting implicational consequences:

(26)  (a) a child is missing ⊃ some children are not missing

(b) a horse is an animal ⊅ some horses are not animals.

One more comment is needed concerning 'generic' *a(n)*. Contexts defining the indefinite article as 'generic' are typically of the structure $a + N_s$ *is* Predicate, as in:

(27)  (a) a child is innocent

(b) a lion is dangerous

(c) a horse is an animal.

It was with respect to such sentences that the conditional distinction was first introduced and explained (§4.2.2 (4: 7)(b)). The conditional nature of such 'generic' expressions is emphasized by their referential identity with expressions introduced by *any*:

(28)  (a)  any child is innocent

(b)  any lion is dangerous

(c)  any horse is an animal.

However, as also mentioned in §4.2.2, not all occurrences of $a(n)$ are conditional. When they are not they are 'non-generic'. In terms of referential potential this means that $a(n)$ is in itself neutral with respect to the conditional distinction. Still exploiting the notational suggestion of p. 67 above I incorporate the value [ocond] in a specification of the meaning of $a(n)$:

(29)

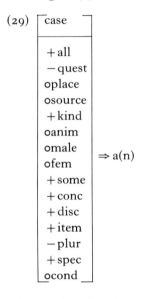

$$\Rightarrow a(n)$$

The specification for *one* would be the same, except that it would be [−cond].

What this complex symbol of features states is this:

(30)  *A(n)* is an indefinite referential functive (determiner) which indicates a specified number (one), and which is neutral with respect to the conditional distinction. It signals discreteness and concentration (i.e. countability), and it posits a division within a given kind, K, in the sense that it establishes a one-member class, k, of K. If communicative emphasis (for contextual reasons) is on

[+all], k becomes the representative of K, and $a(n)$ performs a sortal function. If communicative emphasis (for contextual reasons) is placed on [+some], the implication is that $a(n)$ establishes not only k, but also its complement class, k', and $a(n)$ performs a selective function.

The referential potential of a sign like *a child* might then be characterized as follows:

(31) The sign *a child* either invites H to accept, or presupposes H's acceptance of, C(CHILD); it invites H to assign one entity (person) to C(CHILD); it invites H to accept that entity either as the representative of *all* entities locatable in C(CHILD), or as being a one-member selection from C(CHILD); it finally invites H to assign that entity to ST(x) at TU.

In this way I have sought to establish a distinction between traditionally 'generic' ( =sortal) and 'non-generic' ( =selective) functions of the indefinite article. And this distinction will be seen, on reflection, to be one manifestation of the vacillation between C-locations and ST-locations – or between *kinds* and *individuals*, in less doctrinaire terms. Yet it was with respect to the specificness distinction that I mentioned this vacillation above. It seems, therefore, that I associate non-specificness with 'genericness', opposing both of these to specificness in terms of the distinction between C-locations and ST-locations. Let us go more explicitly into the matter.

I have not, up to now, provided the means by which the specific and the non-specific functions of the indefinite article can be distinguished, for the simple reason that no such distinction *can* be established inside the complex symbol of features recognized as the specification of the meaning of $a(n)$. It must, consequently, be looked for elsewhere.

Consider initially once more the traditional statements on specificness, in particular the one that reserves the distinction for indefinite descriptions (or perhaps expressions). Although the distinction between specific and non-specific reference can be subsumed under the general distinction between communicative emphasis on ST-locations and C-locations, and thus is comparable to certain differences within the referential potential of definite expressions, the systematic fluctuation of scope assignment (exemplified in (18) and (22) above) is peculiar to indefinites.

There is, in the present account, just one thing that distinguishes a definite from an indefinite expression, application vs. non-application of

L-subjunction of $L_{ind}$. Since the features in terms of which $L_{ind}$ is subcategorized, [αspace] and [αtime], might be held to play a significant role in the derivation of existential sentences like those in (18) when they are directly lexicalized (cf. below, §9.1.2), and since they are 'inside' the nominal structure, although 'outside' the complex of features realized by $a(n)$, such paraphrases are quite natural. Yet what is important to the specificness distinction is the values of these features on particular occasions. I take (32) as a general representation of the final derived structure of *a child* (unnecessary details omitted).

(32)

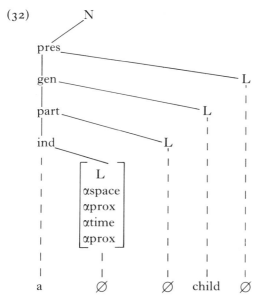

The distinction between specific and non-specific reference of indefinite descriptions can now be characterized in terms of different values of [αspace], [αtime], and [αprox] on particular occasions. More generally, the difference between specific and non-specific reference is a function of the difference between assigning things of C(x) to a *particular* ST-location, or to *no* particular ST-location. If $L_{ind}$ on a given occasion is subcategorized as ([−space] & [−time]), assignment of things is to no particular ST-location. This is the basis of non-specific reference. When $L_{ind}$ is subcategorized by at least one positively marked feature, assignment of things is to a particular ST-location. This is the basis of specific reference.

The sense in which the specificness distinction reflects the general vacillation between emphasis on C-locations and ST-locations can now be made clear. If a speaker in uttering *a child* mentions an individual whose actual location in space and time is irrelevant to the utterance situation (cf. §§9.2.2–3 for a precise characterization of these points), it is clear, by implication, that what matters to him is that the entity he mentions should be a *child*. The communicative emphasis is on the locatability of the entity mentioned in C(CHILD). It is likewise clear how non-specific and 'generic' indefinite descriptions overlap. Whereas a 'generic' occurrence of $a(n)$ invites the hearer to accept one entity as the representative of *all* the entities potentially locatable in a given category, no such representative function is imputed to the thing mentioned by means of a non-specific indefinite description. But apart from this, both types of function emphasize the C-location involved.

It is clear, since there is no overt morphological distinction between specific and non-specific indefinite descriptions, that ambiguities and misunderstandings arise. It can be exasperating for a speaker, who intends a given indefinite description as non-specific, to have it challenged by the question 'What X ?', which frequently happens when the hearer is a child. But the reason for these misunderstandings is now clear: it stems from the fact that the semantic features which control specificness, though 'present' and retrievable, are no integral part of either $a(n)$ or the lexical noun involved. Cf. §9.2.3 for a pertinent comment on *this*.

# 9 Definite expressions

## 9.1 The influence of $L_{ind}$

A NP containing one of the following referential functives is definite in the sense of deriving from a N in which $L_{ind}$ is L-subjoined (1).

| (1) | | Identitive | Sortal |
|---|---|---|---|
| | Quantifiers | both<br>each<br>(n)either<br>which? | both<br>each<br>(n)either<br>which? |
| | Determiners | the<br>that<br>this<br>those<br>these<br>my<br>your<br>her<br>. . .<br>(the) same | the<br>that<br>this<br>those<br>these<br>my<br>your<br>her<br>. . .<br>(the) same<br>such |

The pronouns (personal, reflexive, possessive, and relative) are also definite in this sense, as are proper names. These are all identitive expressions. They will be discussed in chapter 10. E-classified phrases may also be definite, of course, as for example *that kind of car*.

This chapter will be concerned with determiners, and it is quite obvious from (1) that they are considered capable of performing two referential functions, identitive and sortal. All except *such*, that is.

The centre of interest in the account of the referential potential of the definite determiners is $L_{ind}$, or, more precisely, the indicating features on $L_{ind}$. These features, to recapitulate briefly, are the following (cf. (5:28)(C)(2)(d)):

(2)    $L_{ind}$ ([αspace] & [αprox] & [αtime] & [αprox])

where [αprox] is introduced only by a positive value of [αspace] and [αtime].

The position to be taken on these matters here owes much to Lyons (1973), but nevertheless some departures from the exposition there will be in evidence. Let us therefore begin by justifying these departures and additions.

**9.1.1 The justification of [αspace] and [αtime].** First of all, Lyons operates with a feature [αentity]. So do I. But whereas Lyons has it as one of the features eventually realized by a demonstrative determiner, I have it as the basic denotative feature on $L_{pres}$. Lyons' approach leads naturally to the appositive analysis he proposes for such phrases as *that dog*, which can be underlyingly represented by an appositive structure like *that entity − that dog* (or a number of other possibilities due to varying applications of appositivalization and adjectivalization which need not concern us).

However, instead of placing too much reliance on the traditional concept of apposition − which I have elsewhere shown to be lacking in clarity (Thrane 1976: §§1.22; 4.431−2) − I have introduced the notion of juxtapositive serialization. The consequence of this change which interests us here is that there is then no longer any need to incorporate [αentity] in the demonstratives. We can see it, rather, as the feature which indicates what sort of thing (entity or place) is being introduced into the universe of discourse (cf. (5:23)).

Secondly, Lyons does not operate with a feature [αspace]. In fact, his feature [αentity] in a sense covers not only my feature [αentity] but also my feature [αspace]. That this is so will be clear from a closer look at Lyons' need for introducing a feature [αdistal] *in addition to* [αproximate]. Lyons relates this need to the Boolean conditions on binarism. I think the need arises from something else.

The feature [αdistal] is introduced by [−proximate] (Lyons 1973: 76).[1] Its introduction is designed to account for the distinction between

---

[1] Unless otherwise stated, all page references in the present section are to the edition of Lyons' paper printed in Keenan (1975) 61–83. An earlier version appeared (1973) in *LAUT*.

the strong and the weak non-proximate deictics, of which the weak adverb (*there*$_1$) is later (p. 80) associated with existence. Next Lyons states, 'Just as the meaning of the weak demonstrative pronoun *that*$_1$ is derived by abstraction from the gesture of pointing, so the weak demonstrative *there*$_1$ is derived by abstraction from the notion of location in the deictic context' (1973:80).

The phrase 'the deictic context', it seems, must mean 'the physical, spatio(-temporal) context'; cf. p. 79: 'We begin by introducing the notion of deictic existence: location in a physical space, whose co-ordinates are established by the utterance of sentences of a given language-system.'

The feature-specification lexicalized as *there*$_1$ is

$$(3) \quad \begin{bmatrix} +D \\ -\text{entity} \\ -\text{proximate} \\ -\text{distal} \end{bmatrix} \Rightarrow there_1$$

where [+D] is the deixis-indicator (p. 76).

Now, if we re-interpret Lyons' appeal to 'the deictic context' in terms of the feature [$\alpha$space], and incorporate this in Lyons' original specification for *there*$_1$ in (3) we get

$$(4) \quad \begin{bmatrix} +D \\ +\text{space} \\ -\text{entity} \\ -\text{proximate} \\ -\text{distal} \end{bmatrix} \Rightarrow there_1$$

at least if I have interpreted correctly the phrase '*by abstraction from* the notion of location in the deictic context' from the passage quoted above (my emphasis). To abstract from something is to imply that it is there.

This feature-specification – i.e. (4) – commits its proponents to a view according to which existence is dependent upon location, or 'abstracted from' it; cf. p. 25 above.

This conflict, it will have appeared, stems from Lyons' use of [−entity] to specify the deictic adverbs. Put in different terms, Lyons' feature-specification, it seems to me, cannot account for the fact that entities may be seen as places and vice versa (cf. §5.3.2, in particular (5:25) and discussion).

These considerations constitute the justification for introducing the feature [αspace]. It enables us to give a specification of the 'existential' deictic adverb which is unmarked for physical, spatial location, namely, [−space], which may be part of a nominal subcategorization which involves, in addition, either [+entity] or [−entity]. In this way we maintain the fundamental equivalence between existence and location, or C-locations and ST-locations.

The third and last point I shall comment on relative to Lyons' paper concerns my introduction of [αtime] as a parallel to [αspace]. Lyons does not discuss the temporal deictics, but it is natural to try to accommodate them in the same way as the spatial deictics, especially in view of the fact that the feature [αproximate] is equally relevant to both. However, by introducing such a feature I commit myself to demonstrating the validity of a set of temporal deictic adverbs corresponding to the spatial adverbs; in particular, I commit myself to demonstrating the presence of a weak and a strong non-proximate temporal adverb, *then$_1$* and *then$_2$*. The justification of [αtime], therefore, will take the form of justifying the presence of these two adverbs. The temporal feature is usually unexpressed, though it need not be. Cf.:

(5)   (a)  the Prime Minister
      (b)  the present Prime Minister.

The referential potential of (b) is included in that of (a), which is tantamount to saying that whatever accounts for the superficial appearance of *present* may be left unexpressed, yet is retrievable.

The feature that quite naturally could be regarded as the central feature of *present* is [+time]. Furthermore, it expresses proximity in the temporal sense. Thus an appropriate, if possibly incomplete, feature-specification of *present* would be

$$(6) \quad \begin{bmatrix} +\text{time} \\ +\text{proximate} \end{bmatrix}$$

Let us now see whether any candidates offer themselves as possible lexicalizations of ([+time] & [−proximate]). In fact, several do:

(7)   (a)  the former Prime Minister
      (b)  the then Prime Minister
      (c)  the late Prime Minister.

The salient points for this discussion in respect of these three – and there are others, e.g. *previous, recent, past*, etc. – can be expressed by means of a time-line. Let PM stand for the predicate *be Prime Minister*, E for the physical existence of the person who is the carrier of PM, and

TU for time of utterance:

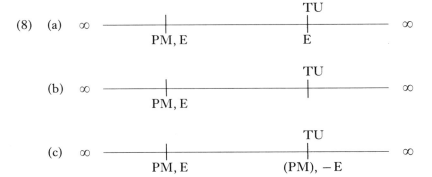

Rough paraphrases of (7) corresponding to these time-lines would be
(9)    (a)  the x who has been Prime Minister

(b)  the x who was Prime Minister at time t (where t is prior to TU)

(c)  the x, who was Prime Minister at (or before) the time of his death.

Whereas (a) and (b) carry only positive existential presuppositions or implications, (c) carries both a positive and a negative one: (c) implies (or presupposes) that someone who was (recently) alive *and* a Prime Minister, is now dead. But this, in fact, is the overriding implication. The reference to time is only concomitant with that. In contrast, (a) and (b) are primarily time-indicators. I suggest that both *former* and *then* realize the temporal deictic features ([+time] & [−proximate]) – i.e. *then₂* – whereas *late* realizes the temporal deictic feature [−time] – i.e. *then₁*. *Then₁* is a temporal existential.

In addition to [−time], *late* embodies a number of other denotative features at least one of which is negative in some sense. As for the possibility of expressing the temporal existential in its naked – or at least in a positive – form, cf. §9.1.2 below.

The distinction between *former* and *then* correlates with the distinction in the aspect-system of English between imperfective and perfective.

I shall not go into a more detailed discussion of these phenomena here. Suffice it to say that the distinction between three orders of entities is relevant to an assessment of the semantic properties of these and other lexemes that embody [αtime], probably supplemented by considerations of the distinction between essential and contingent qualities.

Notice finally that by associating the adjectives *former, then, late*, etc.

with $L_{ind}$ – rather than with $L_{part}$ – through [αtime], a derivational criterion is provided which may account for the (well-known) fact that these adjectives in attributive position cannot be derived from a predication by relative clause reduction and adjective movement, and which correlates with their intuitive relationship with adverbs (cf. e.g. Bach 1968: 101ff).

**9.1.2 Positive expression of [αtime].** I have hitherto assumed that the indefinite article is derived from structures without lexical subjunction of $L_{ind}$. I shall now present an alternative that recognizes lexical subjunction of $L_{ind}$ to ind, plus application of the MI-convention. The derived structures which arise from this alternative look like (10).

(10)

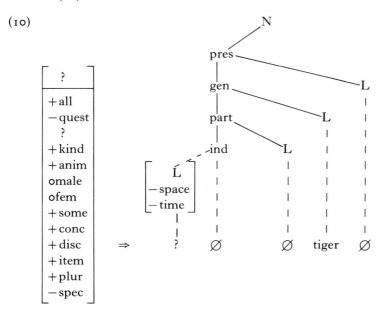

The superficial expression of (10), I suggest, is *there are tigers*, i.e. an 'absolute' existential sentence. *Be* as an existential verb is arguably non-tensed, neutral, as it were, to the question of temporal proximity; it realizes the temporal existential in its naked form. This derivation goes some way towards showing, on linguistic grounds, that existence is not a property: *there are tigers* is derived from a non-predicational structure. Moreover, it accounts naturally for the special properties of number-concord displayed by such sentences.

However, we are left, as indicated, with the question of deciding whether or not a case-specification is relevant, and if so, which. This question is no more difficult to decide – in principle – than the comparable question within a predicational derivation of existential sentences. As long as pres is the case-preserving node within the referential structure we can say that, unless N is governed by a case, the potential of pres to carry a case is actualized by the most neutral case-category, i.e. abs.

From the basic configuration (10) we can derive other 'absolute' existential sentences like *tigers exist* by appeal to a subordinate locative branch which generates *in existence*. By subjunction to $L_{ind}$ and normalization of the surface order of the ensuing string on the pattern of the serialization of English predicational structures we eventually get *tigers exist*. (For a different – predicational – derivation of such existential sentences which also invokes the concept of (lexical) subjunction, see Anderson 1974; cf. also Allan 1971.)

As pointed out by Lyons (1968: §8.4.3; 1973: 80) sentences introduced by *there is* more often than not involve an explicit locative phrase as well, in contrast to what I called 'absolute' existential sentences above. Exploiting the timeless derivation and its possible extension by a subordinate locative branch, we might suggest a parallel derivation for nominals marked [ −plur] and [ +time]. Thus, *there is a fly in the soup* will derive from a complex structure in which the superordinate generates *there is a fly* along the lines of (10), and where the subordinate locative branch generates (*in*) *the soup*. The tense of *be* in such sentences will then reflect the feature [αproximate]. Whatever else this proposal might do it would certainly explain why there are no existential sentences of the form *there are the . . .*, or *there is the . . .* (although there are 'functional' sentences of this form, cf. Atkinson & Griffiths 1973: 51ff).

## 9.2 Identitive *the*, *this*, and *that*

After this, largely justificatory, introduction we shall now look at the identitive function of the definite determiners *the*, *that*, and *this*. I assume that *these* and *those* differ from *this* and *that* only with respect to the number-specification on ind, and that some special determination rule prevents *this* and *that* from occurring as pronouns with human referents.

The initial presentation will take the form of a critical discussion of the most recent work on definiteness, Hawkins (1978), chapter 3 of which specifies a number of uses of the definite article, develops what is referred to as the 'locational' theory of the definite article, isolates a predicate in terms of which the function of the definite article should be defined, and establishes a set of appropriateness conditions on the use of the definite article, all of them questions of high relevance to the present study.

After discussing a number of uses of *the*, Hawkins finally settles for the following eight as essential (the examples, and the numbers in square brackets, are from Hawkins (1978: ch. 3), as are, indeed, all quotations in the present section):

(11)(a)  The Anaphoric Use

[3.01] Fred was discussing *an interesting book* in his class
[3.02] I went to discuss *the book* with him afterwards

(b)  The Immediate Situation Use

[3.39] Pass me *the bucket*, please

(c)  The Larger Situation Use

[n.n.] *the Prime Minister* has just resigned

(d)  The Associative Anaphoric Use

[3.61] The man drove past our house in *a car*. *The exhaust fumes* were terrible

(e)  – with Referent-Establishing Relative Clauses

[3.16] What's wrong with Bill? Oh, *the woman he went out with last night* was nasty to him

(f)  – with Associative Clauses

[3.83] I remember *the beginning of the war* very well . . .

(g)  – with NP-Complements

[3.87] Bill is amazed by *the fact that there is so much life on earth*

(h)  – with Nominal Modifiers

[3.115] I don't like *the colour red*

Of these, (a)–(d) are subsumed under the label 'familiarity uses', whereas (e)–(g) are called the 'unfamiliar uses', these two labels being taken in the sense of Christophersen (1939). We shall be mainly concerned with the familiar uses. The NPs in all of (e)–(g) derive from complex structures of various sorts, some of which we return to.

It is now Hawkins' aim to establish a set of conditions on the appropriate use of the definite article such that each of these 'traditional' uses will be explained by it.

To achieve this end he establishes his 'locational' theory of the definite article, the foundation of which is the following statement: 'the hearer is being instructed to "locate" the referent [of a definite NP] in the immediate situation of utterance' (Hawkins 1978: 114).

The agent of this act of instruction is, apparently, either the definite article itself or the speaker. Cf.: 'Thus, in addition to these uses of *the* acting as an instruction to the hearer to locate the referent in the relevant situation . . .' (Hawkins 1978: 128), and 'Thus, when the speaker uses . . . *the* . . . in these cases he is instructing the hearer to locate the referent in that situation of utterance . . .' (Hawkins 1978: 128).

I think, as I tried to make clear in chapter 4, that it is only indirectly that the speaker can be said to be the agent in this instruction. The direct agent is the sign itself. Although this may appear to be a slight point it is not, since it is the basis of setting down appropriateness conditions on *speakers*. To say that a speaker instructs a hearer to locate the referent in the relevant situation by his use of *the*, is to give the speaker the entire blame on the occasions where such instructions misfire. It goes wrong because the *speaker* has not observed all the relevant rules. If only in the name of fairness I think we should operate with a system whereby the blame can be evenly divided between speaker and hearer. We do that by appointing the sign as the agent of the act of instruction.

In order to examine the 'location' theory in more detail we must now look at the speech acts performed by a speaker when he uses a definite description and the specification of the conditions that must be fulfilled for those acts to be appropriate and successful:

According to my location theory the speaker performs the following acts when using a definite article. He (a) introduces a referent (or referents) to the hearer; and (b) instructs the hearer to locate the referent in some shared set of objects (as we have defined them in the course of this chapter) [for a discussion of Hawkins' definition of these notions, see below]; and he (c) refers to the totality of the objects or mass within this set which satisfy the referring expression. These acts will only be successful if the following appropriateness conditions are fulfilled:

(1) *Set existence condition*: the speaker and hearer must indeed share the set of objects that the definite referent is to be located in.

(2) *Set identifiability condition*: the hearer must be able to infer either from previous discourse or from the situation of utterance which shared set is actually intended by the speaker.

(3) *Set membership condition*: the referent must in fact exist in the shared set which has been inferred.

(4) *Set composition conditions*: (i) there must not be any other objects in the

shared set satisfying the descriptive predicate in addition to those referred to by the definite description, i.e. there must not be fewer linguistic referents referred to by the definite description than there are objects in the shared set; and (ii) the number of linguistic referents referred to by the definite description must not exceed the number of objects of the appropriate kind in the shared set; and (iii) the hearer must either know or be able to infer that the intended object has the property that is used to refer to it in the descriptive predicate. (Hawkins 1978: 167–8)

Of these conditions, (1) is said to be a prerequisite for the fulfilment of the others, so naturally the immediate interest centres around (1). Is it clear, relevant, and informative?

Its clarity depends on a precise characterization of the notion 'shared set of objects'. What does it mean for a speaker and a hearer to share the same set of objects? Hawkins (1978: 129) suggests that there are in fact two slightly different, but comparable situations to be taken into account, each one associated with a 'basic' use of the definite article, what we might call the 'situational' use (subsuming (11)(b) and (c)) and the 'anaphoric' use (subsuming (11)(a) and (d)). In connection with the 'situational' use, the set of objects to be shared by speaker and hearer is now either the objects actually there, in the vicinity of the interlocutors, or the objects common to speaker and hearer in virtue of their (cultural, national, regional, and/or local) background. In connection with the 'anaphoric' use, the set of objects to be shared is 'there' only in the derivative sense of having been previously mentioned. It is peculiar to the Associative Anaphoric Use (11)(d) that it involves both 'anaphoric' and 'situational' features: it depends on previous mention, combined with associative links which may be culturally (nationally, etc.) defined. Although Hawkins does not do so himself, this peculiarity might be taken as a piece of positive evidence in favour of 'situational' and 'anaphoric' objects being subsumed under the same treatment.

However, this notion of 'shared sets of objects' rests on an important assumption, which he himself states, but which I see no reason to accept: 'the objects available to speaker and hearer to which linguistic expressions with the definite article can refer, are arranged in these discrete mental or physical sets defined by shared knowledge and the shared situation of utterance' (Hawkins 1978: 130).

This assumption places far too much reliance on a mental patterning of objects for my liking. Reference is *not* to things directly, but only 'indirectly', via reference to some sort of 'mental' replica of the referent which is part of a 'mentally' located set of objects. On the one hand, such a view completely disregards the facts of lying. On the other, it simply represents yet another version of the existential presupposition on definites: any definite NP must have a referent which exists, at least in some mental set of 'objects'; cf. also Hawkins' condition (3), the Set Membership condition.

This whole existential question leaves the notion of a shared set of objects. unclear, in general. Consider now a more specific instance of, say, an English-speaking foreigner who, on his first visit to England, turns on his car radio on arrival at Dover to hear the following:

(12) Westbound motorists are advised to leave *the motorway* at Hungerford because of a serious accident.

He has never spoken to the announcer (we assume), he does not know where (or what) Hungerford is. Does this use of the definite article count as an instance of appropriate usage? And is it successful? That would seem to depend on whether our tourist and the announcer can be said to share the same set of objects, this set being presumably of the larger situation variety. I find it difficult to attribute any sense to the notion of 'sharing objects' in such a case as this – except in just one respect: the announcer and the tourist, we may assume, both know what *a* motorway is. But this cannot be a properly shared object for, whereas the announcer is probably aware which British motorway he is mentioning, this is not the case for the tourist. What they have in common is not some *object* which they share knowledge of, it is simply knowledge of the meaning of the English sign 'motorway'. There is therefore no reasonable sense, it seems to me, in which we can say that the tourist and the announcer share a set of objects, and consequently this occurrence of the definite article is inappropriate or at least unsuccessful as a reference marker. Nevertheless I find it highly probable that the tourist, driving west along the M4 later in the day, would react to the sign of the Hungerford exit by wondering whether the road had been cleared. And if he did not, it is more likely to be that he forgot what had been said on the radio than that the act of reference had been unsuccessful.

Is it the case that only definite articles require the presence of some 'shared set of objects'? I think not. I would ask for *two cakes* in a baker's shop, *some herrings* at a fishmonger's, *six pounds of potatoes* at a greengrocer's. I would do this because I 'share a set of objects' with the respective shopkeepers.

Is condition (1) informative? No, it is not. It is vacuously true that we all 'share sets of objects' with each other, and it is vacuously true that we sometimes wish to say something about some of the objects in our 'sets'. My wife and I 'share' a vast set of objects, but we do happen sometimes to use an indefinite article, even when mentioning objects which we know to be in each other's 'sets'.

Because the Set Existence condition is neither clear, exclusively relevant, nor informative in relation to definite descriptions, and because he himself regards it as a precondition on the other conditions, Hawkins' version of the location theory of definiteness fails. Yet it should be clear from chapter 4 – the terminology of which was developed long before Hawkins' book appeared – that I am highly sympathetic to what might probably be called an even stronger version of the locational theory of reference than Hawkins brings forth. I have already mentioned one point of disagreement between Hawkins' version and that presented here. I shall now explain how, in my view, a locational theory should account for expressions introduced by the definite article.

**9.2.1 Identitive *the*.** To say that a referential expression introduced by *the* performs an identitive function is to say the following (cf. (4:16)(c)):

(13) The sign *the* N invites the hearer to assign some thing(s) (substance), located at ST(n) at TU, to C(N).

Here C(N) is the categorial location established by N in *the* N, and ST(n) is an abbreviation of 'no particular spatio-temporal location'.

The derivational reality covered by (13) is that *the* is the lexical reflex of a complex category which contains $L_{ind}$ by lexical subjunction, and where $L_{ind}$ is subcategorized by the weak deictic features [−space] and [−time]. What interests us here, however, is the communicative reality covered by it.

Consider once more (12). The reason why *the motorway* does not necessarily lead to a communicative breakdown is that our tourist understands it. And what is involved in this act of understanding is, at least, the following:

(14)(a) From the welter of all things that surround you, consider one that you would be prepared to call a motorway;

(b) accept that, although one such is situated at a particular point in space and time, the actual location of it is irrelevant to the present utterance situation.[2]

---

[2]  A precise characterization of the notion 'irrelevance to the present utterance situation' will be given in §9.2.3 below.

But there is more to it than this. It might be said, for example, that the actual location of the motorway in question is highly relevant to the motorists for the benefit of whom (12) was uttered in the first place. How can I seriously claim, then, that it is irrelevant? Because I distinguish between the utterance situation and what we might call loosely, in this connection, the 'situation of transport' of the motorists. If our tourist were an extremely careful and cautious motorist he might call the BBC and ask for further information as to *which* motorway had been mentioned by the announcer, and the announcer (or his representative) would be committed to supply the information desired. This information, needless to say, would ultimately be reducible to a precise space and time specification, say *the motorway which connects London and Bristol*. But this commitment on the announcer is built into his use of *the*. In other words, we may supplement (14) with the following:

(14)(c) If the actual space/time location of the motorway is of relevance to you (in your 'situation of transport') then the use of *the* commits the speaker to retrieve it and supply it on demand.

But even this supplement does not exhaust the proper use of *the*, mainly because, so far, it is implied that everything mentioned by a definite description *does* occupy a particular point in space/time: we come up against the existential problem once again. What is needed to counter it is a reformulation of (14)(b):

(14)(b') Accept that, *even if* one such is situated at a particular point in space and time, the actual location of it, should it have one, is irrelevant to the present utterance situation.

If (14)(a), (b') and (c) are explicit characterizations of what is involved in the understanding of (12), we now have to show how these characterizations can be generalized to cover other uses of *the* than that exemplified by *the motorway*. I shall do this with reference to the examples quoted from Hawkins in (11). Common to them all, *qua* identitive expressions, is their signalling of non-relevance to the utterance situation of the actual space/time location of the referent. Where they differ is with respect to the way in which the speaker provides information as to the actual ST-location of the referent, should he be requested to do so. In other words, we are interested in finding how the speaker of each of (11) will cope with the question 'what (which) N?'

(15) [3.02] I went to discuss the book with him afterwards.

The immediate reaction by the speaker to the question 'what book?' is likely to be, 'I just told you. The book that Fred was discussing in his class'; but this, in Strawson's (1959: 18) terms, would count only as an instance of 'story-relative' identification, and although in many cases such identification is sufficient, the hearer is *still* entitled to ask, 'yes, but which one was that?'. Ultimate identification would involve a reply like 'the book written by X in 1978, called . . .'. But the point is that the speaker, having provided this information, is within his right to continue, ' . . . but that is totally irrelevant to what I want to tell you'.

[3.39] Pass me the bucket, please.

Here the speaker's reaction would be totally different to that just considered, more likely something like 'that one, are you blind!', accompanied by a pointing gesture. Although we have not yet said anything about *this* and *that* we may anticipate matters by saying that what the speaker does here is to convert irrelevance into relevance to the utterance situation of the actual ST-location of the referent. If [3.39] on occasion may lead to the correct handing over of the bucket, it is because the hearer draws a number of justifiable inferences concerning the speaker's intentions. The occasional success of [3.39] does not stem from *the* indicating the actual ST-location of the bucket.

[n.n.] The Prime Minister has just resigned.

In this case the desired information cannot be given by means of *this* or *that Prime Minister*, but must be given by means of expressions like *our PM*, *the PM of Great Britain*. Again, [n.n.] may successfully tell someone that the British PM has resigned, but this, too, is due to inferences drawn by him, not to the communicative content of *the*. An Englishman could not reasonably be blamed for telling lies if he used [n.n.] to inform another Englishman that the Canadian PM had just resigned.

[3.61] The exhaust fumes were terrible.

Further specification of the actual ST-location of these exhaust fumes would be likely to be related to the actual ST-location of the car which emitted them. This is the basis for the associative link involved.

All the examples of 'unfamiliar uses' of the definite article (11)(e)–(h) have one feature in common which sets them off against the 'familiar' instances dealt with so far: they do not allow reformulation as *which*-questions unless the modifying element is excluded; cf.

(16)(a) (i)   *which woman he went out with last night
        (ii)  which woman

        (iii) the one he went out with last night

(b) (i)   \*which beginning of the war

    (ii)  which beginning

    (iii) of the war

(c) (i)   \*which fact that there is so much life on earth

    (ii)  which fact

    (iii) that there is so much life on earth

(d) (i)   \*which colour red

    (ii)  which colour

    (iii) red.

The deviancy of each of the (i)-examples is of a semantic nature: *which*-questions are requests for information which will enable the (original) hearer to identify the thing mentioned. But in each of the above cases, the modifying element contains just this information, as suggested by the (iii)-examples. The questions in (i) are vacuous. With a term adapted from Hawkins (1978) we might call these modifying elements 'ST-location establishing' elements. I take such elements to derive from a subordinate N adjoined in various ways to (various categories in the) superordinate. Although a great many details are unclear I shall return to one or two pertinent points during the discussion of relative pronouns.

**9.2.2 The utterance situation.** In the course of the preceding chapters I have used the term 'utterance situation', undefined and without further clarification. This notion becomes important for the discussion of the demonstrative determiners and pronouns. I shall therefore make this brief digression to explain what I mean by it.

A situation, in the relevant sense, is a delimited, static organization of concrete phenomena which stand in specific relationships to each other. An *utterance* situation is a situation in which these relationships are concerned with communication.

An utterance situation is brought about by the occurrence of an utterance, and an utterance must have an origin. I shall call the point in actual space occupied by this origin the *deictic centre*. An utterance is said to be *orientated* towards a receiver, the point in actual space occupied by which I shall call the *point of orientation*. These, the utterance, the deictic centre (plus occupant) and the point of orientation (plus occupant), are the necessary and sufficient concrete phenomena in an utterance situation.

A situation, I said, is static. What I mean by this is that the progress of time is arrested within a situation. Everything in a situation is temporally co-occurrent with everything else in it. Given the features in terms of which $L_{ind}$ is subcategorized, i.e. [$\alpha$space], [$\alpha$time] and [$\alpha$prox], we now define the deictic centre as ([+space] & [+prox] & [+time] & [+prox]). The static nature of situations then guarantees that every NP used to mention a thing in an utterance situation derives from a N in which $L_{ind}$ is marked ([+time] & [+prox]).

A situation, I also said, is delimited. But what sets the bounds for an utterance situation? To answer this question we must return to a reconsideration of the necessary and sufficient ingredients in an utterance situation. Imagine a situation where a man in a shower wants his wife to bring him a bar of soap. If he says, 'Please bring me a bar of soap, Emily' in his normal, everyday voice at a volume he would use if they were chatting over the dinner table, the desired result would hardly follow (if the water was running, the door shut, etc.). His voice would not carry to the point of orientation. Although in one sense there would be a point of orientation, in another, important one, there would not. I would like to impose the requirement on the occurrence of an utterance situation that the utterance in fact *reaches* the point of orientation. Otherwise, as an utterance situation, it would be null and void. The extent of an utterance situation can now be precisely characterized as the (three-dimensional) space within which the speaker believes his utterance will carry. It is this three-dimensional space, with its content of deictic centre, utterance and point of orientation, which *is* the utterance situation. And it is the speaker who *decides* the actual size of a given utterance situation by adjusting his volume of speech to a level where he seriously believes that the utterance will reach the point of orientation.

**9.2.3 Identitive *this* and *that*.** Apart from the things occupying the deictic centre and the point of orientation in an utterance situation there may be something else, namely, something which is mentioned in the utterance. Let us call such potential ingredients *objects of discourse*. However, due to the design feature of 'displacement of referent', an object of discourse *need* not be present in the utterance situation: we may mention things which are not 'there'. (17) is an attempt to give a graphic representation of an utterance situation.

The main point I wish (17) to capture is that the point in actual space occupied by an object of discourse may be either *inside* or *outside* the three dimensional space of the utterance situation as this is delimited by the volume of the utterance.

(17)

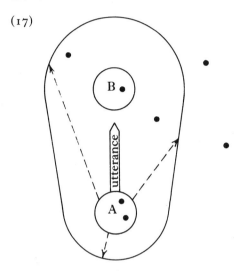

A = deictic centre
B = point of orientation
● = object of discourse
– – – ►= lines defining the volume of speech

One of the uses Hawkins discusses (1978: 110ff) – and later conflates with the Immediate Situation Use – is what he calls the 'visible situation use'. This is one of the few uses where *the* is in competition with the demonstrative determiners *this* and *that*, according to Hawkins. It is concerned with such situations where the referent is (must be) visible to the *hearer*, and Hawkins concludes:

> The demonstrative instructs him [the hearer] to identify the object itself, and thus it actually has a visibility requirement built into it as part of its meaning. But whether visibility is simultaneously required by the definite article depends on factors which are extraneous to the meaning of *the* itself. This important point has not been appreciated in the literature. (Hawkins 1978: 115)

I think it is wrong to speak about a visibility *requirement* in either case. Visibility is a factor contingent upon the facts of the utterance situation. Consider once more (14)(b'). In the light of (17) I shall now characterize the notion 'irrelevance to the present utterance situation' attributed to *the* as a communicative effect whereby the point in actual space and time occupied by the referent, should it occupy one, is unspecified with respect to the distinction between being *inside* and *outside* of the utterance situation. By the employment of a demonstrative determiner, on the other hand, the speaker wishes to inform the hearer that the point in actual space and time occupied by the referent is *either* inside *or* outside of the utterance situation. If it is inside it will, in the normal case, be visible. But it is quite possible, I think, for me to say 'Give me that candle' to someone I am with in a pitch dark room, provided that I know that the other one knows that there is a candle close at hand although neither of us can actually see it.

I shall now discuss what I take to be the normal uses of the demonstrative determiners and then return to some rather less normal ones which might appear to run counter to the norm.

If the referent is considered by the speaker to be inside the utterance situation, he may refer to it by means of either *this* or *that*. If he uses *this* it is because he considers it to be located at the deictic centre. The deictic centre, therefore, is not a mathematical point but a point in actual space where things may be located. The same holds for the point of orientation. If he considers it not to be located at the deictic centre he must use *that*. This is a characterization slightly different from the traditional one, according to which *this* may be used to refer to that of two (or more) things of the same kind which is nearest to the speaker. But how 'near' must a thing be to be referred to by *this*? I do not know. Although nearness is a matter of measurement, I do not think that any precise measures can be given by which *this* and *that* can be kept apart. They are kept apart by subjective judgement on the part of the speaker. And the basis of this judgement is only contingently a matter of measurement. The actual basis for it is whether or not the speaker is prepared to consider a thing located at the deictic centre – where he himself is – or not. The extent of the deictic centre is not absolute. The feature [αprox] should be reinterpreted in this light.

Anything inside the utterance situation but considered to be outside the deictic centre must be referred to by means of *that* (if demonstrative reference is required). If there are two (or more) objects of discourse of the same kind inside the utterance situation, reference to one of them by means of *that* must be disambiguated by ostension, or by an explicit ST-location establishing description, as in *that chair in the corner*. This necessity makes it clear that, wherever the referent is in the utterance situation (except inside the deictic centre), *that* must be a lexicalization of the same feature specification. We can now give the deictic feature specifications for *this* and *that* when they are used to refer to things inside the utterance situation:

(18)(a) $\begin{bmatrix} +\text{space} \\ +\text{prox} \\ +\text{time} \\ +\text{prox} \end{bmatrix} \Rightarrow$ *this*    (b) $\begin{bmatrix} +\text{space} \\ -\text{prox} \\ +\text{time} \\ +\text{prox} \end{bmatrix} \Rightarrow$ *that*

But this is only the lower part of the complex symbols of features which are realized by *this* and *that*. A full specification would include, in particular, the features in terms of which gen is subcategorized. The implications of this statement will become clear during the discussion of *I*, *you*, and the proper names in the next chapter.

If an object of discourse is located at a point in actual space which the speaker considers to be *outside* the utterance situation, it should in the nature of things only be possible to refer to it by means of *that*: if it is not even inside the utterance situation it cannot be inside the deictic centre. And this, indeed, is the normal state of affairs. I can point upwards and say 'that plane is a Boeing 747'. This instance of *that* would be specified as (18)(b). However, it is only by accident that the occurrence of the plane at that particular point in space is co-temporaneous with the utterance situation. I could, even when the plane had long gone, say 'that plane was a Boeing 747' and I could emphasize my words by pointing upwards (at the exhaust trails, say). What I would be doing in such a situation seems to be this: I indicate a particular point in actual space, and I say, with respect to this point, that the thing that was located at it at some time prior to the time of utterance, was a plane of a certain type. But the plane referred to would itself be at a different point in space at the time of utterance. This use of *that* would have the following specification:

(18)(c) $\begin{bmatrix} +\text{space} \\ -\text{prox} \\ +\text{time} \\ -\text{prox} \end{bmatrix} \Rightarrow$ *that*

It might be objected that this specification simply reflects (or is?) the tense specification on the verb. While I concede this I still want to maintain that there may be a 'tense-specification' on the NP which is different from the tense of the verb. It is perfectly possible to say 'that plane was in the Battle of Britain' while pointing at a Spitfire (in a museum, for example). So there is no reason to suppose that there may not be a 'tense-specification' on a NP which is identical to that on the verb.

The three specifications in (18) are behind what I have taken to be the normal uses of *this* and *that*. But they can be used in other ways as well. Consider:

(19)  that dog of yours has been chasing my sheep again.

An utterance of (19) would be appropriate no matter whether the dog in question was inside or outside the utterance situation, provided the hearer owns just one dog. The point in space occupied by the dog up to and including the time of utterance is totally irrelevant to the utterance situation. What matters is that, at the time of utterance, one dog owned by the hearer can be located in time. If the hearer can truthfully reply that he knows, that he is sorry, and that he had the dog shot only yesterday because of it, the complaint embedded in (19) loses its force. Since the point in actual space occupied by the dog at the time of utterance is irrelevant, the question of temporal proximity likewise becomes superfluous. I therefore suggest the following specification:

$$(20) \quad \begin{bmatrix} -\text{space} \\ +\text{time} \\ \text{oprox} \end{bmatrix} \Rightarrow that$$

where [oprox] signals unspecified significance.

It is now interesting that none of the native speakers of English I have consulted on the matter were able to state a tangible difference between (19) and (21):

(21)  this dog of yours has been chasing my sheep again.

Various suggestions of a stylistic nature were made, the most persistent of which was that (19) showed a higher degree of outrage than (21). Be that as it may, it seems to be the case that the usually clear difference between *this* and *that* is suspended in cases such as these. Why? If (20) is accepted as a feasible specification of (19), I suggest that the reason is that (22) is a sufficiently precise specification of (21):

$$(22) \quad \begin{bmatrix} -\text{space} \\ +\text{time} \\ +\text{prox} \end{bmatrix} \Rightarrow this$$

where the spatial occurrence, wherever that is, of the dog referred to is made explicitly, rather than implicitly, co-temporaneous with the utterance situation.

I think, also, that (22) is behind the use of *this* in cases like

(23)(a) I sat very quiet like, and then *this bloke* comes up . . .

(b) Now there was *this girl*, see, . . .

Especially (b) is suggestive. As Hawkins. (1978: 150f) notes, *this* in examples similar to (23)(a) is a competitor of the *in*definite article, rather than of *the*. We can supplement Hawkins' argument with the observation that *this* can occur in existential sentences like (b), a possibility not normally open to definite determiners. In the light of the discussion of §8.5 above we might even suggest that *this*, in this usage, is a competitor of *a(n)* with *specific* reference, in fact that it is becoming a form of *in*definite specific article. Its occurrence in existential sentences can then be explained derivationally with reference to the proposals of §9.1.2: *there was this N* derives from a structure in which $L_{ind}$ is L-subjoined under observance of the MI-convention. But this process must be described in two steps, where the 'specificness' features (*in casu* the positive element of [+time] and [+prox]) are left behind on the complex symbol of categories when next the MI-convention moves only the 'definitemarkers' [−space] and [−time]. Such a proposal would presumably be in accord with the 'trace' theory being developed by Chomsky (1976).

I have now argued that six of the possible nine combinations of the space, time, and proximate features are lexicalized in modern English (counting ([−space] & [−time]) as well as ([−space] & [+time] & [−prox]), which latter is implicit to (20)). Of the remaining three, two are impossible on the present assumptions:

(24(a)
$\begin{bmatrix} +\text{space} \\ +\text{prox} \\ +\text{time} \\ -\text{prox} \end{bmatrix}$
  (b)
$\begin{bmatrix} +\text{space} \\ +\text{prox} \\ -\text{time} \end{bmatrix}$

Spatial proximity − i.e. occupation of the deictic centre − is incompatible with both temporal distance and non-temporality.

The third one, ([+space] & [−prox] & [−time]), I suggest, is excluded on logical (commonsense) grounds: nothing can be located physically in space without being located in time.

If it is true that no demonstrative realizes these three feature specifications, we can generalize our findings as follows:

The feature which sets off the demonstrative determiners from the definite article is [+time]. The feature that sets off *this* from *that* is [+prox], introduced by [+time]. *This* signals necessary *temporal*, rather than spatial, co-occurrence of the referent with the time of utterance.

## 9.3 Sortal *the*, *this*, **and** *that*

To say that a NP of the form *the N* is a sortal expression is to say the following (cf. (4: 16)(a)):

(25)  *The N* invites the hearer to assign some thing(s) (substance) to categorial location C(N), and to assign *all* things of C(N) to ST(y) at the time of utterance.

In most discussions of English grammar, much attention is devoted to so-called generic reference of expressions introduced by *the*, *a*, or *zero*. No attempt is made to investigate whether also other determiners may be involved in expressions with generic reference, with the possible exception of *all* (which is not a determiner), probably because no very clear guidelines have been found by which to describe the semantics of genericness.

I have already stated several times that there is a systematic vacillation in the emphasis placed on categorial and spatio-temporal location. The present account of 'genericness' will be based on the assumption that, whenever communicative emphasis is placed on the C-location involved, then we have an expression with 'generic' (or sortal) reference. Before we go on to discuss such expressions in detail, we need to examine (25) more closely.

I have tried to show that the defining characteristic of an *identitive* expression in communicative terms was that the hearer is required to *accept* that the referent is located in space and time at the time of the utterance act. Essentially the same kind of acceptance is implicit to (25). Although (25) states that it is the hearer who assigns things to categorial locations, it is the case, since things do not change their categorial locations in the same way as they may change their spatio-temporal locations – though cf. p. 50 above – that we may in fact interpret it as an invitation to the hearer to *accept* that some things *are* located at a given C-location at the time of utterance, and further that he is invited to assign *all* the things located in it to ST(y).

**9.3.1 Sortal** *the.* The most typical traditional examples of generic *the* involve a lexical noun (in the singular) which denotes a natural species:

(26)  (a)  the tiger is a dangerous animal

(b)  the rose is the queen among flowers.

The further away we get from such natural species, the more careful we must be in choosing a predicate which will make a generic interpretation of the subject NP likely:

(27)  (a)  the castle is a prominent feature of Welsh scenery

(b)  the home is the Englishman's castle

(c)  the garden is the symbol of order

(d)  the young couple in denims is the badge of the sixties.

Each of these, I hold, may be used on occasion in a generic sense. As it stands, (27)(a) will probably always be given a generic interpretation, but if *Welsh* is substituted by *Edinburgh's*, it could only be non-generic. Is *the home* in (b) generic? I suppose so, since we would hardly use (27)(b) to refer to a specific home, and since we seem to refer to the home of *the Englishman*, which is a generic NP. But then it could be said that it is the *specific* home that each Englishman has, and would it not then be non-generic? As it stands (c) can be used either generically or specifically, depending on the general context of utterance. A lecturer on seventeenth-century English literature might use it, for example, as a general statement about symbolic usage during that period, but the same lecturer might use it in connection with a lecture just on Marvel's poem *The Garden*. The immediate reaction to (d), I think, is that this cannot be a generic subject NP, but I am sure it could be so used. Yet a specific reading would be much more likely of this phrase out of context.

The obvious conclusion I want to draw is that a NP introduced by *the* is not 'in itself' either specific or generic. It has a referential potential that allows the hearer to interpret it in either way. The hearer must decide whether he wants to place the emphasis on the C-location or the ST-location involved.

What are the criteria by which a given NP is classified as either generic or specific? There seems to be just one grammatical criterion, namely, that it must co-occur with a verb in a non-perfect tense (i.e. if the NP in question is subject, then it can only be generic if the verb is either simple past, present, or future). The following subject NPs are not generic on this criterion:

(28)  (a)  the tiger has always been a dangerous animal

(b) the rose has been considered the queen among flowers for centuries

(c) the castle has been a prominent feature of Welsh scenery since the twelfth century.

Another criterion is of the 'question-and-answer' type. If we can meaningfully ask 'what (which) N?', then the article in the original NP is non-generic, otherwise it is generic. On this criterion the following NPs are generic:

(29)  (a)  *a girl* stopped me to ask me where Liberty's is

   (c)  *the man who killed Smith* must be insane.

Both of these criteria presuppose the assumption that there are two articles *the* in English, one inherently generic, and one inherently non-generic, an assumption which I do not share. I shall therefore seek to establish a different criterion, which specifies – on derivational grounds – when *the* is *used* in a generic sense and in a non-generic sense.

A common remark about genericness is connected with countability: a NP introduced by *the*, and containing a countable noun, can only be generic if the noun is singular. If the noun is uncountable, genericness is expressed by the zero determiner. The same holds for countable nouns in the plural. An exception from this general principle is said to be when the lexical noun denotes nationalities. Employing the terminology adopted here, we can set up the following paradigm:

(30)(a) (i)   the tiger          indentitive or sortal
      (ii)  the Finn          identitive or sortal
   (b) (i)   the tigers        identitive
      (ii)  the Finns         identitive or sortal
   (c) (i)   tigers                          sortal
      (ii)  Finns                           sortal
   (d) (i)   the water         identitive
      (ii)  water                           sortal
   (e) (i)   some tiger(s)  selective
      (ii)  some Finn(s)   selective
      (iii) some water    selective

We can now continue the discussion of the derivational characteristics of such NPs begun in §8.3. Theoretically, four different final derived structures are pertinent to the description of all the NPs in (30), namely, two with lexical subjunction of $L_{ind}$ and two without, and, cutting across these, two with adjunction vs. two with subjunction of gen to pres. The four relevant structures, filled in with lexical material in accordance with the discussion in chapter 8, are given in a simplified form in (31).

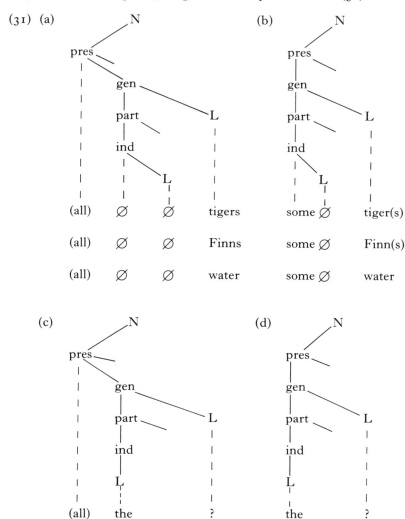

A comparison between (30) and (31) now shows that (31)(a) is the final derived structure of indefinite, countable plural or uncountable NPs. Let us call it *the purely sortal* derivation. And that (31)(b) is the final derived string of indefinite, countable singular and plural as well as uncountable NPs. Let us call it *the purely selective* derivation. We are then left with the two definite structures (c) and (d) and in particular, as indicated by the question marks, with the problem of determining which type of noun (countable/uncountable; singular/plural) should be inserted in them.

Consider first countable plural and uncountable definite NPs like *the water*, *the tigers*, and *the Finns*. There is no occurrence of these, I claim, which is incapable of expansion by *all*. The question mark in (31)(c) should therefore be substituted by either *water*, *tigers*, or *Finns*. It would then seem to be just a matter of substituting the question mark in (31)(d) by a countable, singular noun, say *tiger* or *Finn*. But it is not as simple as that. Cf.:

(32)  (a) all the car was smashed to bits

(b) all the house is in an uproar

(c) all the book is filled with beautiful drawings

(d) all the pig is eaten

where a definite *singular* NP is expanded by *all*.

It is now interesting that none of the NPs in (32) can reasonably be given a traditional generic interpretation. It must be a specific car which is smashed, a specific house in uproar, a specific book filled with drawings and a specific pig that is eaten.

Compare (32) with:

(33)  (a) all the car was an important advance in transport

(b) all the house is the centre of non-nomadic civilization

(c) all the book is mightier than the sword

(d) all the pig is the foundation of Denmark's economy.

All of these are odd and, in the light of (31), I suggest that they are in fact ill-formed, rather than merely deviant. However, each of (33) – without *all* – is likely to be given a generic interpretation.

The conclusion to be drawn from this is now clear. The question mark in (31)(c) is to be substituted by either an uncountable noun, a countable plural noun, or a countable singular noun, whereas that in (31)(d) can only be substituted by a countable singular noun. NPs deriving from (31)(d) are the traditional singular, definite, generic expressions.

But what are those deriving from (31)(c)? If it were the case that only those NPs in (30) which are marked *identitive* derived from it, we could, in analogy with the names given to (31)(a) and (b), call it *the purely identitive* derivation. But *the Finns* derives from it, and that is said to have either an identitive or a sortal function. What is the reason for attributing sortal (generic) meaning to *the Finns*, in contrast to *the tigers*? There seems to be just one. Cf.:

(34) (a) the Finns are great athletes
　　 (b) the tigers are dangerous animals.

In my terminology, (b) presupposes a spatio-temporally delimited set of animals, some of which are tigers. These latter are said to be dangerous, in contrast to the other animals in the set. In contrast, and still in my terminology, (a) presupposes the occurrence of a natural class of things, all of which, wherever they are, are great athletes. Insofar as these formulations sum up the recognized difference between (34)(a) and (b), I think it is a spurious difference. First of all, nationality is not a question of 'natural class', it is an accidental property based entirely on spatio-temporal considerations: being a Finn is simply a matter of having been born at a particular place at a particular time (or having lived there for a certain amount of time). Secondly, there is nothing to prevent us from giving a valid paraphrase of (34)(a) along the lines of that given for (b) above: (a) presupposes a spatio-temporally delimited set of people, some of which are Finns. These latter, in contrast to the other people(s) in the set, are said to be great athletes. *The Finns* is (*pace* Quirk *et al.* 1972) a purely identitive expression, like *the tigers*. Only the spatio-temporal limits are wider.

Three points remain relative to (31). I am aware, of course, that the identification of *the* as sortal or identitive on a given occasion is not a mechanical matter of trying to insert *all* before it: if it works, *the* is identitive, if it does not it is sortal. What I am arguing is that, whereas in *some* cases *all* may be successfully inserted before an occurrence of (identitive) *the*, this insertion is *in principle* impossible in any imaginable connection with sortal *the*.

This leads on to the second point. Lawler (1973) tries to analyze generic *the* in terms of an underlying universal quantifier, and it is clear why, from (31)(d): pres, the 'universally' marked category, is included in the complex category realized by it. However, so are both the linguistic parallels of the existential quantifier, part and ind. And so is gen. If we should give an explicit formulation of the communicative function of sortal (generic) *the* which not only takes these points into consideration but also the various findings of the preceding sections, it would be something like this:

(35) Accept that *some* things are located at C(x) at TU. Consider *one* of these, located at no particular ST at TU, the representative of *all* the things in C(x).

Finally, it might be objected that (31)(d) – which is held to generate *sortal* expressions, has nothing in common with the purely sortal derivation (31)(a), whereas it has significant features in common with both the purely identitive derivation (31)(c), and the purely selective one (31)(b). We might, indeed, call (31)(d) the *identitive-selective* derivation. The reply to this objection has two parts. First, it is to be expected that *the car* (sortal) differs derivationally from *(all) cars* (sortal), partly because of internal structure, partly because of difference in syntactic potential. Cf. e.g. *\*cars were an important advance in transport* with (33)(a). Secondly, the emphasis on *kind*, common to all sortal expressions, is a consequence of the representative function of the thing mentioned: it is only in virtue of belonging to a given kind that a thing may represent all the things in that kind.

Let me finally, and without discussion, suggest that those definite, singular descriptions to which Donnellan (1966) assigns an attributive function, also derive from structures like (31)(d) but, in contrast to the 'truly generic' expressions, that they are conditional.

**9.3.2 Sortal *this* and *that*.** Consider first expressions like:
(36) (a) you can get *this camera* much cheaper in Japan
(b) they are building *that house* in France, too
(c) he has *her eyes* (cf. *\*he got a fly in her eye).

I shall not say anything about the sortal function of the possessive determiners except point to the (macabre) ambiguity of (36)(c). In the (non-macabre) sense, *her* must be a sortal determiner.

In cases like (a) and (b) it is true that demonstrative reference is made to particular things along the lines of §9.2.3. Yet the context makes it clear that it is in fact the categorial membership of the things in question which is of prime importance. It seems therefore not out of the question to allow for both (31)(c) and (d) as the source of demonstrative expressions, especially since (36)(a) and (b) seem to me to be equally impossible with the NPs expanded by *all*. I therefore venture to conclude that the systematic vacillation between C-location and ST-location attributed to definite descriptions is a pervasive phenomenon which covers *all* (derivationally) definite expressions. For reasons of space I shall not here discuss the remaining definite determiners. A detailed account of the derivational properties of all of them can be found in Thrane (1976: 343–77). It should be emphasized, though, that although the general approach is the same, the exposition there differs from the present one in several respects.

# 10 *The pronouns*

## 10.0 Introductory

In §7.3.4 (7:13) the pronouns were displayed in a tabulation which was based on two criteria: the number of referential phrases in the referential structure that generates them, and the minimal structure (simple or complex) required for their derivation. With respect to these criteria I shall in the present chapter speak about three subtypes of pronouns: simple categorial, simple non-categorial, and complex pronouns. A simple categorial pronoun is a pronoun deriving from a simple structure in which gen-L is present, a simple non-categorial pronoun is one deriving from a simple structure in which gen-L is absent, and a complex pronoun is a (categorial or non-categorial) pronoun deriving from (the lower branch in) a complex structure. In addition, simple non-categorial pronouns may be either definite or indefinite. In contrast, simple categorial and complex pronouns are always definite.

## 10.1 Categorial vs. non-categorial: evidence for the distinction

Consider the following statement from Hjelmslev (1937: 198): '*ego* et *tū* ne sont que deux formes paradigmatiques d'un même pronom'. If we accept this statement we reduce what is at first sight a three-fold distinction between first (I), second (II), and third (III) person to a two-fold distinction between I + II as against III.

There are two good reasons to accept Hjelmslev's statement. In the (Indo-European) languages with gender distinctions – either in the system of personal pronouns or in the nominal system in general – I and II are characterized by being insensitive to gender. If we assume, as I do, that it is basically the same gender system that characterizes nouns and (personal) pronouns in languages which have the distinction in both classes, so that there is no special pronominal gender system,[1] the conclusion to be drawn is, in my terms, that I and II derive from referential structures which do not contain the referential phrase gen-L, the phrase responsible for gender distinctions.

Secondly, the necessary and sufficient number of things in an utterance situation (as this was defined in §9.2.2) is two, one located at the deictic centre, and one located at the point of orientation. In addition there may be other things in the utterance situation, both at the two criterial points and outside them, but they are considered to be there only by accident.

## 10.2 Simple non-categorial signs in English

Although the present chapter is primarily concerned with pronouns, the title of this section implies that there are other signs besides pronouns in English which are simple and non-categorial. These are proper names. Among the pronouns the following are definite, simple, and non-categorial: *I* and *me*; in addition I shall look at *we*, *us*, and *you*, which are classed as determiners on distributional criteria. In particular, we shall look at why these have a determiner function. The following are indefinite, simple, and non-categorial: *-thing*, *-body*, and *-one*.

### 10.2.1 Definite simple non-categorial signs: *I* and *me*. The non-categorial status of simple definite signs is closely related to the question of necessary presence in the utterance situation of the things to which they are used to refer. As this necessity may be viewed as a denotative condition on things, we may try to formulate it by means of a semantic feature. Suppose we just introduce the feature [$\alpha$nec(essary presence)], and let its insertion in the referential structure depend on the absence of gen-L. Since the necessary presence is defined relative to the utterance situation, we regard the feature [$\alpha$nec] as being introduced on $L_{ind}$, the category subcategorized by the features defining the utterance situation. Two more preliminary comments should be made relative to non-categorial signs. Since gen-L is not involved in their derivation they cannot perform sortal functions. I shall therefore assume that the full cycle of RP-subjunctions apply, including the last step to pres, without

---

[1] This, of course, is a position that implies that the gender-system which characterizes Modern English personal pronouns is a remnant of the gender-system which in Old English characterized nominal structures in general.

this implying a sortal interpretation (cf. §9.3.1); all definite non-categorial signs perform only identitive functions. And, since $L_{gen}$ is absent, $L_{pres}$ is subcategorized as ([ +subst] & [ +stat]). Cf. §5.3.2.

With these preliminaries over I can now state what I take to be the final derived string underlying *I* (and *me*) (1).

(1)

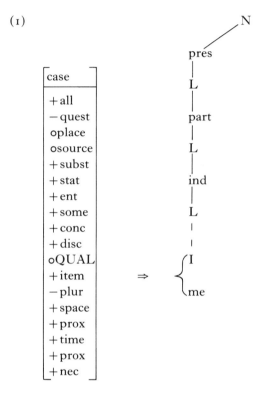

Some comments relative to (1) – and especially to the complex symbol of features – are in order, but perhaps these could better be made with respect to the referential function of which the complex symbol purports to be the abbreviation:

(2)   The sign *I* invites the hearer to accept one entity, which may be either an object[2] or an 'itemized' mass, as the entity necessarily located at the deictic centre, or simply to identify it as the sender of the utterance in which *I* occurs.

---

[2]   I shall use the term 'object' in this chapter and in formulae like (2) as an abbreviation of the term 'spatio-temporally discrete object of discourse', thereby subsuming both things and people.

The sign *I* does not invite the hearer to locate (or accept the location of) anything in a categorial location. In other words, *I* does not in any way indicate what *kind* of thing it is which is necessarily located at the deictic centre. Of course we generally assume that only humans can speak. But this is purely an accidental fact relative to the meaning of *I*. In fairy-tales all sorts of things may speak, animals, trees, the water, a cloud, and the pronoun which it is relevant for them to use to refer to themselves *qua* senders of the utterance would be *I*. Hence the irrelevance of the feature [αperson] – symbolized by absence of it from (1) – usually introduced by [+entity]. There are, however, some contingent properties that the sender must be understood to possess: it must be 'concrete' in the sense of being concentrated and discrete. If water can speak in a fairy-tale, it must be a specific *body* of water, and, from a Biblical sphere, it is not just wilderness that cries, it is 'the voice of one crying in the wilderness'. Whether it is unconditionally true that the sender must be understood to be just *one* entity is a question I return to in connection with the discussion of *we*. Notice finally that $L_{part}$ is lexically subjoined; and further that it may or may not be lexically specified, indicated by [oQUAL]. I take it always to be L-subjoined, but expressions like *poor me, lucky you*, etc., indicate that it undergoes the MI-convention when it is not lexically empty.

**10.2.2** *We, us,* **and** *you.* The reason for considering these traditional pronouns determiners is the occurrence of expressions like *you fool, we men, us guys*, which play a significant role in Postal's (1966) 'pronoun-as-article' theory. Such phrases receive a perfectly natural interpretation in the present framework. Let us assume, initially, that *we, you,* and *us* are, in fact, primarily pronouns (of the same kind as *I*). On this assumption, the minimal referential structure that would generate them would be (1), and different feature specifications would account for the differences in form. In particular, *you* would derive from a structure which was specified as ([+space] & [−prox] & [+time] & [+prox]). To say that (1) is the *minimal* structure capable of generating *we*, etc., is not to say that it is the *only* structure that could do so. I am suggesting, in fact, that these forms may also derive from a structure which contains gen-L; but, since the structure *without* gen-L in itself generates the pronominal forms, it is not L-subjoined. We get (3). I return (§10.3) to the reason for this peculiarity.

(3)

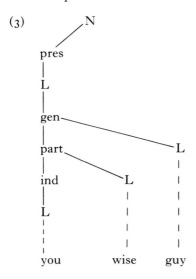

Accepting the primary status of *we*, *you*, and *us* as pronouns on these premises, we now have to specify their referential function:

(4)    The sign *you* (sg.) invites the hearer to accept one entity, which may be either an object or an 'itemized' mass, as the entity necessarily located at the point of orientation, or simply identify it as the entity which the sender considers to occupy the point of orientation.

Again, it is no necessity that the entity occupying the point of orientation should be a person. I can say *you* to my cat, my plants, to a recalcitrant screw, or whatever. Of course I do not expect a screw in any way to 'react' to my addressing it by *you*, but this point does not affect the fact that the sign issues just that invitation to it. One important feature is embodied in (4), namely, that it is the speaker who decides – by his choice of point of orientation – what thing should be considered the 'receiver'. This is the fact behind the occasionally effective rhetorical trick of *addressing* a message at something (or somebody) within earshot of the person(s) for whom the content of the message is in fact *intended*. But this does not make this (these) person(s) 'receivers' in the sense that they are considered to occupy the point of orientation, except in one case. If the speaker deliberately 'enlarges' the utterance situation by speaking more loudly than the location of the 'overt' receiver requires in order to 'include' in the utterance situation the person(s) for whom the message is in fact intended, then I suppose we could speak of an 'oblique' point of orientation, in addition to the 'overt' one.

This leads to a reconsideration of two points concerning the term 'the hearer' in formulae like (2) and (4), for obviously someone may hear an utterance which is not addressed to them. However, it follows from the formulation of (4) that such 'eavesdroppers', in virtue of being *hearers*, may in fact also successfully identify the referent of *you* as an object different from themselves, considered by the speaker to occupy the point of orientation. The second point concerns the necessary presence imputed to the *object* occupying the point of orientation. In fact a speaker may 'address a point in blank space', or 'speak to the wall', but I think that in such cases we typically *convert* the 'locations' addressed in this way to 'entities' occupying 'themselves', as, indeed, the expressions just quoted indicate.

Natural language, needless to say, has means of sorting out the organization of the utterance situation. *Are you talking to me?* may be just a question, but it is a question whose primary function is to have the structure of the utterance situation sorted out. *Pardon?* invites the sender of a preceding utterance to adjust (enlarge) the utterance situation. Incidentally, I do not think that this function is covered by any of the six functions recognized by Jakobson (1960); cf. (*Introduction*: 1).

*We* and *you* (pl.) are not, as often observed, simply the plurals of *I* and *you* (sg.) in the same sense as that in which *boys* is the plural of *boy*. Distinctions are usually drawn between *inclusive we/you* and *exclusive we/you*, depending on which (grammatical) persons can be identified in their reference. Since the situations are not entirely symmetric with *we* and *you*, I should prefer the following schema:

(5)  (a) all-inclusive *we*:  $+$ I $+$ II $+$ III
     (b) inclusive *we*:    $+$ I $+$ II $-$ III
     (c) exclusive *we*:    $+$ I $-$ II $+$ III
     (d) inclusive *you*:   $-$ I $+$ II $+$ III
     (e) exclusive *you*:   $-$ I $+$ II $-$ III

It may be, but I am not sure, that an 'all-inclusive' *you* can be identified in the use of *you* which is translatable by German *man*, Danish *man*. Since nothing of what I have to say on these matters hinges on the presence or absence of an 'all-inclusive' *you*, I prefer to disregard it.

Since the grammatical category of person may be defined on the basis of the organization of the utterance situation (see below), I should want to regard the two attributes (*all-*)*inclusive* and *exclusive* as being also

definable from the same source. This is hardly unreasonable, considering the fact that for something to be included (excluded), it must be
included (excluded) *in* (*from*) something. The referential function of *we*
can then be characterized:

(6)    The sign *we* invites the hearer to accept one entity, which may be
       either an object or an 'itemized' mass, as the entity necessarily
       located at the deictic centre, and further to accept some entity(-ies)
       as the entity(-ies) which the sender considers to be located with it
       at the deictic centre;

whereas that of *you* (pl.) would be:

(7)    The sign *you* (pl.) invites the hearer to accept one entity, which
       may be either an object or an 'itemized' mass, as the entity
       necessarily located at the point of orientation, and further to accept
       some entity(-ies) as the entity(-ies) which the sender considers to
       be located with it at the point of orientation.

These formulations create some immediate problems which we must
try to solve. Firstly, and most obviously, (6) locates not only the speaker
but also the receiver at the deictic centre if *we* is (all-)inclusive.
Although such a suggestion might appear self-defeating it is not, due to
the subjective extent of the deictic centre (and the point of orientation,
as well as of the utterance situation itself). It is the speaker's prerogative
to decide the extent of all three locations. And he may well decide to let
the deictic centre extend so far as also to include the point of orientation.

Secondly, and in a sense the reverse problem of that just discussed,
both (6) and (7) suggest that things and/or people not physically in the
utterance situation are in fact 'located' at the deictic centre/the point of
orientation. Again, the speaker's prerogative should be emphasized, in
connection with the suggestion much discussed above that the *actual*
point in space/time occupied by an object of discourse at the time of
utterance may be irrelevant to the utterance situation. If I phone a
married friend and say 'Can you come over for bridge tonight?', *he* must
know that his wife is considered by *me* to be located with him at the
point of orientation, although in actual fact she may be away at work at
the time of utterance. If he did not understand this, and said yes, he
would turn up alone, and we would have some misunderstandings to
sort out. And these, of course, do occur, precisely in such situations.

Thirdly, and perhaps most importantly, since it may jeopardize the
supposition that first and second person pronouns are non-categorial,
(6) and (7) do not preclude the situation that I may refer to myself and

my typewriter by means of *we* in an utterance of *we have had a hard time of it lately*. That is, can things of different *kinds* be subsumed under the reference of *we* (and *you*)? If they cannot, these pronouns would seem after all to be sensitive to gender, and that therefore gen-L should be included in the structure that generates them. But it seems to me entirely possible that I *can* refer to myself and my typewriter in the way described, provided it is clear – by gesture, position, or whatever – that I consider my typewriter to be located with me at the deictic centre at the time of utterance. If this is indeed true, then this point, rather than being detrimental to our hypothesis concerning gen-L, supports it.

If the objections to (6) and (7) have been adequately stated (and met), we can now, on the basis of them, define the members of the grammatical category of person:

(8)(a) A first person sign is a sign the meaning of which includes the denotative condition that at least one of the things to which it is used to refer on a given occasion *must* be located at the deictic centre;

   (b) a second person sign is a sign the meaning of which includes the denotative condition that at least one of the things to which it is used to refer on a given occasion *must* be located at the point of orientation;

   (c) a third person sign is a sign the meaning of which includes the denotative condition that the thing(s) to which it is used to refer on a given occasion *may* be located at either the deictic centre or at the point of orientation, but need not.

Let me finally try to forestall the objection that the meaning of *I*, *we*, and *you* cannot be defined (away), and that they are therefore semantic primitives, as represented by Sørensen (1963: 95ff). The reason why these signs cannot be defined away is that they are the only first and second person signs (in English), and that for that reason they cannot be semantically identical with any other sign by which we might try to define them. We cannot, for example, define away the meaning of *I* by means of the sign *the person who is speaking now*, according to Sørensen, for the following reason: 'Either B [i.e. the hearer] will take "the person who is speaking now" literally – that is, he will take it to be intended to denote a person C [i.e. a person distinct from both speaker and hearer] – or he will consider it the result of an attempt to be funny. He will not accept it as a genuine equivalent of "I"' (Sørensen 1963: 96).

I shall refrain from going into an argument on this issue and instead simply quote an example of what Sørensen apparently thinks is a sign which 'defines away' another sign. Thus, in Sørensen (1958: 36) the sign '(his) uncle' is held to be 'defined away' by the following: 'the male person who has, or who is married to the female person who has (or to one of the female persons who have), the same first-degree male ancestor and the same first-degree female ancestor as the first-degree male ancestor or the first-degree female ancestor he has has'. I leave it up to the reader to decide whether he, as hearer, would be inclined to think that the person who uttered this paraphrase was trying to be funny, or whether he would be prepared to accept it as 'a genuine equivalent' of '(his) uncle'.

**10.2.3 Proper names.** Proper names are third person signs, which means that whatever they are used to refer to on a given occasion may or may not be located at the deictic centre, the point of orientation, or in the utterance situation outside these two points. This, I think, is a fairly non-controversial characterization. Proper names are non-categorial signs, which means that they do not in any way indicate what *kind* of thing they are being used to refer to on a given occasion. This is not a non-controversial statement. Yet it is true.

The main division within the recognized class of proper names is between personal and geographical (place) names. Yet there is no non-contextual way in which the hearer may learn whether I visited a friend or a town if I say *I visited Sydney on my way home*.

The second division is between names 'for boys' and names 'for girls' (with such names as /lezli/ and /dʒəu/ doing service in both categories). It is, of course, purely by convention that some names are considered boys' (girls') names. And if a girl, for example, is generally known under what is conventionally exclusively a boys' name (for whatever reason), then this fact does not imply a concordial link with *he*: *John says she is ill* is ambiguous to the hearer who knows that this instance of *John* is used, in the face of convention, to refer to a girl.

Everything can be given a name; ships, planes, and cars often are. A large Scandinavian furniture store has given conventionally girls' names to their various models of sofas, tables, and whatever, and the same holds for a large Danish supermarket chain. A customer in each of these stores who bought 'Marie', for example, would come away with, respectively, a bed and a packet of sausages.

Proper names are sometimes said to be uniquely referring. This view is dismissed by Linsky:

But surely when I say 'Tommy Jones is not the king of England' I am not claiming that exactly one person of any circle is named 'Tommy Jones'. What is indeed necessary, if I am to make a definite assertion, is not that one person only be named 'Tommy Jones'; but that I be referring to just one person, however many others there may be with the same name as his. *It is a mistake to think that the 'referring expression' itself can secure and guarantee this uniqueness. This is obvious in the case of proper names, for here we cannot appeal to meaning. 'Tommy Jones' does not have a meaning,* and many people share it. Proper names are usually (rather) common names. (1967: 118; my italics)

I find this dismissal quite convincing; but then Linsky continues:

One can ask, 'To what city does the phrase "The City of the Angels" refer?' The answer is 'Los Angeles'. *Such expressions are on their way to becoming names,* e.g. 'The Beast of Belsen'. They are what a thing or person is called often and repeatedly, and that is why one can ask to what they refer. (1967: 120f; my italics)

There is a strange inconsistency between these two passages, hinging on the word 'name'. On the one hand we are told that there is no one-to-one correspondence between a name and whatever bears that name. On the other hand, *because* it is 'on its way to becoming' a name, there is apparently a one-to-one correspondence between 'The City of the Angels' and Los Angeles. To put it as directly and as paradoxically as possible: Although 'Tommy Jones' *is* a name, we cannot sensibly ask 'To whom does "Tommy Jones" refer?'; but *because* 'The City of the Angels' is *almost*(?) a name, we can sensibly ask 'To what city does "The City of the Angels" refer?' This paradox is in need of clarification, but Linsky provides none.

The paradox stems from the widespread – but wrong – assumption expressed in the first quotation, that proper names do not have 'a meaning'. If they did not have a meaning they would not be signs. No, what proper names lack is indication of – or the ability to establish – a categorial location, and that is not the same as not having a meaning. In contrast, signs like *The City of the Angels* contain indications of categorial locations (CITY and ANGEL), so such expressions are not proper names, despite the fact that they have 'grown capital letters', in Strawson's memorable phrase.

The structure generating a proper name is (1), but the associated complex symbol of features is rather different:

(9)    case

$\begin{array}{l} +\text{all} \\ -\text{quest} \\ \text{oplace} \\ \text{osource} \\ +\text{subst} \\ +\text{stat} \\ \text{oent} \\ +\text{some} \\ \text{oconc} \\ \text{odisc} \\ \text{oitem} \\ \text{oplur} \\ \text{ospec} \\ \text{ospace} \\ +\text{time} \\ \text{oprox} \\ -\text{nec} \end{array}$

What this complex symbol states is this:

(10)   A proper name invites the hearer to accept the (spatio-)temporal
       location of some entity(-ies) or place(s) which are not necessarily
       present in the utterance situation.

A proper name is the linguistic sign which imposes the *least* specified
denotative conditions on whatever it is used to refer to. Nevertheless,
the invariable specification by [+time] of a proper name has some
interesting consequences which we return to during the discussion of
the third person personal pronouns (§ 10.3.3).

**10.2.4 Indefinite simple non-categorial pronouns.** The large group
of pronouns formed from these suffixes constitute the pronominal
suppletives of quantifiers and – in the case of *no-* – determiners and E-
classifiers. They derive from a string similar to(1), except that $L_{ind}$ is not
Lsubjoined. The most interesting thing about them, however, is the
question of what feature-specifications the suffixes are lexicalizations of. In
general, I think they provide moderate support for $L_{pres}$, the category
of those we work with whose existence I suppose is the most in doubt.

Apart from the features [ +subst] and [ +stat], which guarantee the 'noun-like' status of these pronouns, $L_{pres}$ carries the specification ([αent] & [αper]). These are quite sufficient to separate the meaning of *something* on the one hand, *someone* and *somebody* on the other. If we then also consider the 'proadverbs' like *somewhere*, the following picture emerges:

(11)  (a)  -thing  ([ +ent] & [ −per])
      (b)  -body   ([ +ent] & [ +per])
      (c)  -one    ([ +ent] & [ +per])
      (d)  -where ([ −ent])

The temporal adverbs (*sometimes*) cannot, however, be derived in the same way, which may be considered a weakness.

The two forms (11)(b) and (c) must be kept apart by reference to some other feature, provided that a (referential–)semantic opposition is involved. The distinction between them is described by Schibsbye (1961: §9.2.3) as a tendency to employ *-one* when reference is made to a person considered to be a member of a delimited group, whereas *-body* is used when no such implicit delimitation is present. We might relate this description to the suggestion that *-one*, in addition to the features in (11)(c), requires a positive specification of the feature [αspec] on ind, which has so far been considered the origin of *one* and *a*, whereas *-body* is [ −spec]. In this way *-one* is regarded as the manifestation of the progressive delimitation said to be embodied in the referential hierarchy. No such implication pertains to *-body* since it is the realization of a positive specification of only the 'highest' features.

By way of example of the referential function performed by these pronouns I quote what I take to be the pertinent one for *something*:

(12)  *Something* invites the hearer to locate an entity, which may be either a thing or an 'itemized' substance – i.e. mass or abstract – at no particular ST-location at TU.

## 10.3 The simple categorial pronouns: *he, him, she, it, they*

These pronouns differ distributionally from *you, we,* and *us* − but not from *I, me* − in that they are incapable of a determiner function: *$^{if}$he boy*, *$^{if}$him stallion*, etc. Although in this respect *I* and *he* have the same distributional properties, they have them for different reasons. Whereas *I* invariably derives from a structure from which gen-L is excluded, *he* derives from a structure in which gen-L is invariably included but L-subjoined. I shall argue below that $L_{gen}$ in structures generating categorial pronouns is also empty, in the sense that it is not subcategorized by any of the features subsumed under the variable term [αQUAL]. But why should *I* and *you* differ in this distributional respect, especially as they are considered to be two paradigmatic variants of the same 'abstract' pronoun? The reason is this: although *you* (sg.) enables the hearer to identify uniquely an entity as the entity occupying the point of orientation (that is, in space/time terms), the speaker may nevertheless wish to make it understood what categorial location he considers that entity to be in at the time of utterance. It is therefore the case that only categorial locations in which entities may be temporarily located can occur in such cases; cf. *ⁱᶠyou fisherman, ⁱᶠyou baker*. The expression *you woman* cannot be used to refer to a woman, only to a man who is behaving temporarily in ways considered to be 'unmanly'. From a semantical point of view, such expressions have the same status as non-restrictive, descriptive relative clauses (which is not to say that they derive from such). In the plural the situation is slightly different, because there such expressions may serve to make explicit what entities the speaker considers to occupy the point of orientation or the deictic centre. Although a similar wish might be entertained by the speaker with respect to himself, fulfilment of it for some reason leads to slightly different constructions, like *I missed it, clown as I am*. In Danish, however, expressions like *jeg klovn tabte den* ('I clown dropped it') are perfectly normal. With the categorial pronouns, however, gen-L plays an entirely different role, as we shall see.

All categorial pronouns are definite; and they do not, *qua* categorial signs, involve the feature [αnec]. With the exception of *he*, they are always identitive expressions. In gnomic contexts, *he* may perform a sortal function, but I do not consider this very productive; cf. *he who stands and runs away lives to fight another day*. But it would seem, from the occurrence of such expressions, that both the purely identitive and the identitive-selective derivations (9: 31)(c) and (d) may be pertinent to the derivation of categorial pronouns.

**10.3.1** *He, him, she*. Keeping in mind the various points made in the last section we can now give the final derived structure for *he/him* (13). The specification for *she* is exactly the same, except that [+male] is [−male] and [−fem] is [+fem].

Again, a number of comments on the complex symbol are required. *He* may be used to refer to either humans or non-humans, animates or inanimates. Hence the specifications [oper] and [oanim]. $L_{part}$ may be specified or not by denotative features, but it is always L-subjoined. When it is positively specified, it undergoes the MI-convention: *poor him.* This categorical statement may need qualification, though, in the light of emphatic expressions like *him poor!,* i.e. *are you seriously suggesting that he should be poor?* I am not sure, however, that such expressions are amenable to the present kind of analysis. It is likewise a condition on the entity to which *he/him* is used to refer that it should be

(13)

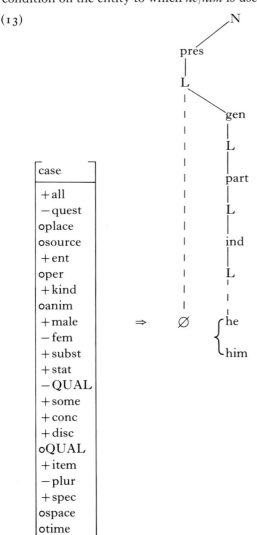

one specified object which is concentrated and discrete. By far the most interesting features in (13), however, are [−QUAL] and [ospace] and [otime]. I shall devote the next section to a discussion of the former, while the two latter will be discussed in §10.3.3.

**10.3.2 The anaphoric function: 'categorization'.** The present discussion will be built around just one very simple example:

(14)   the boy thought that he was ill.

On an analysis based on the notion of co-reference, (14) will be characterized as ambiguous: *he* may be understood to refer either to the same person as is referred to by means of *the boy*, or to a different (male) object. On an analysis based on the notion of substitution, the question of ambiguity is played down and the focus will be on the (intra-linguistic) relation holding between *the boy* and *he*. Despite this difference, these two types of analysis are essentially the same in one important respect: they both take *the boy* as the starting point for the analysis. In an explicit co-referential account, this fact is embodied in the metaphoric language in which the analysis is couched: if two NPs, $NP_1$ and $NP_2$, in the deep structure of a sentence are lexically identical and have the same referential index, then $NP_1$ must (may) *pronominalize* $NP_2$. In (14), *the boy* would be $NP_1$, so it is *the boy* which is the 'agent' of pronominalization. In a substitutional account, *he* is said to be the *substitute* for *the boy*, a metaphor which implies that *the boy* is the 'real' thing. Although details may differ in particular versions of these two types of analysis, they do not differ on this fundamental issue. Generally, I think it is true to say that, throughout the history of linguistics, the pronoun has played second fiddle to the NP to which it is said to bear an anaphoric relation. Needless to say, I also think that this is the main reason why the problems of pronominalization have appeared to be so great.

The implication of this criticism is that the *pronoun* should be given priority in the descriptional procedure. We do this by proposing the following initial formulation of the referential function of *he*:

(15)   *He* invites the hearer to locate one specified, concentrated and discrete entity, which may be either a thing or a person, located at ST(x) at TU, in one of the categorial locations which subsume male entities.

The point in this formulation which interests us here is the reality covered by the invitation 'to locate one . . . entity . . . in one of the categorial locations which subsume male entities'.

Once again Hjelmslev is pertinent. In the passage quoted at the beginning of §7.5.3 from Hjelmslev (1937: 196), the pronouns of a given language are regarded as a syncretism of all the lexical nouns in that language. The nature of this syncretism, in the terminology of (6: 13), is a conflation, since the morphological structure of a pronoun is distinct from that of all the lexical nouns that enter the syncretism. By analogy from this general characterization of the pronouns, German *er*, for example, must be a conflation of all German masculine lexical nouns. In English, which is not a gender language, the situation is different. It would make little sense to say that *he* is the conflation of all English masculine lexical nouns, for there *are* no masculine lexical nouns. What I shall say instead is this: *he* is the conflation of all the lexical nouns in English which the speaker is prepared to accept as denoting male entities. This, I believe, is the precise characterization of the English sexually based 'gender' system, at least when it is supplemented by a comparable characterization of *she* and a (negatively defined) characterization of *it*. Since there are many lexical nouns in English which may be considered to denote male entities, and since categorial locations are established by signs in virtue of their (denotative) meaning, it follows that we are justified in speaking about 'one of the categorial locations . . .'.

It is only to a certain extent true that it is solely the speaker's prerogative to decide what categorial locations may subsume male entities. Some sort of concordial (i.e. language-determined) tie holds between lexemes like MAN, BOY, HUSBAND, WIDOWER, etc. on the one hand, and *he* on the other. But already at the next step down the 'animateness hierarchy' speaker's choice is relevant. In speaking about bulls, stallions, rams, and other higher domestic animals he may choose between *he* and *it*. We should therefore modify the last part of (15) to ' . . . one of the categorial locations which subsume, or which are considered by the speaker at TU to subsume, male entities'.

Let us now reconsider the requirement of lexical identity sometimes imposed on pronominalization in the light of the present discussion. To say that *he* in (14) may refer to the same entity as *the boy* refers to is to say that *he*, in this case, invites the hearer to locate one entity in C(BOY). To say that *he* in (14) may also refer to an object distinct from the person referred to by *the boy* is to say that *he* invites the hearer to locate one entity in – what? Possibilities are infinite, out of context. And notice that, even in this case, C(BOY) is not excluded. It may just happen to be another boy. But is it really true, in a given context, that *he* is ambiguous in precisely so many ways as there are categorial locations considered by the speaker at the time of utterance to subsume male entities? No it is not. What possibilities there are, are restricted by the context of the utterance. And by the context of the utterance is here understood the situational, as well as the textual context. I therefore suggest the following reformulation of (15):

(16)   *He* invites the hearer to locate one specified, concentrated and discrete entity, which may be either a thing or a person, located at ST(x) at TU, in one of the categorial locations established in the context of the utterance in which *he* occurs, and which subsume, or are considered by the speaker at TU to subsume, male entities.

I have said, up to now, that it is *signs* that establish categorial locations, in virtue of their meaning. I want now to claim that also *things* establish categorial locations, but that they do so in virtue of our knowledge of which sign(s) they are denotata of.

The syntactic process of 'pronominalization' is now seen to be a referential process of 'categorization', i.e. of the hearer assigning things to C-locations. The real problem of pronominalization, in this light, is the problem of specifying what guidelines the hearer may have for deciding *which* of possibly several potential C-locations established in the context of utterance the entity referred to should be located in. I shall not even begin here to explore what possibilities there may be for specifying such guidelines.

I have reached what I consider my main objective, which was to show that there is no principled difference between the anaphoric and the referring functions of the personal pronouns. What difference there is between these two functions is a difference in the ways in which C locations are established: either by a sign in the textual context, or by a thing in the situational context within which the pronoun occurs. I conclude, therefore, that an anaphoric sign is a referring sign. Anaphora depends on reference.

**10.3.3 *He* vs. *John*.** Although *John* imposes no conditions of either animateness, humanness, or maleness on the thing to which it is used to refer on a given occasion, it is nevertheless the case that it is most often used – by convention – to refer to a single, male person. It is therefore often used as a competitor of *he*. Given a boy christened *John*, I shall now investigate whether *John* and *he* are in free variation as expressions by means of which reference to that boy may be achieved, and, if not, why not.

We note first that *John* cannot be used instead of *he* in (14) on the assumption that *the boy* and *he* refer to the same boy. In general, proper names cannot have an anaphoric function, and it is clear why not: as non-categorial signs they contain no information as to what set of categorial locations established in the context of utterance should be considered pertinent for the hearer's location of the referent. For the same reason *I* and *you*, *we* and *us* can have no anaphoric function. But even in the non-anaphoric function *John* and *he* are not in free variation as referring expressions. There is a politeness factor which separates them, and although such a notion may be considered more appropriate in stylistic rather than semantic enquiries, I shall nevertheless argue that it is centrally concerned with the deictic features on $L_{ind}$.

Compare the lower parts of the feature-specifications for *he* and *John*, repeated here for convenience as:

(17)       *he*                *John*

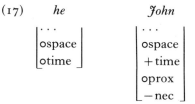

What these specifications state is that, whereas *he*, on particular occasions, may be specified by means of all the combinations possible between ([−space] & [−time]) and ([+space] & [+prox] & [+time] & [+prox]), *John* does not allow a specification which contains [−time]. I suggested above that the only instances of NPs being *necessarily* specified as [+time] are those in which they are used to refer to an object of discourse inside the utterance situation. They are then also [+prox].

Consider in this light the piece of polite linguistic behaviour inculcated in us at a very early age, according to which we are not allowed to say *he* or *she* about persons who are 'present'. We *may* use expressions like *the gentleman* or *the lady*, which at least locate them in acceptable categorial locations, but preferably we should use a *name*. But where is the boundary between *he* and *John* in this connection? I suggest that it is isomorphic with the utterance situation, as that was defined in §9.2.2: we should not say *he* about a person when he is within earshot.

These observations perhaps relate most clearly to the inter-personal (Halliday) or social (Lyons) functions of language. By using a proper name we emphasize the necessary temporal co-occurrence of the referent with the utterance situation, we 'include' the referent. By using a personal pronoun we fail to stress this necessary inclusion and hence, by implication, we 'exclude' the referent from the intimacy of the utterance situation. But this aspect of the social function of language is ultimately based on the referential properties of language.

**10.3.4** *It,* **they,** and *them.* At least four different grammatical functions of *it* may be distinguished, of which three seem to be related:
(18)(a) Entity-referring: he kicked *it*
    (b) The Great 'It' of Nature: *It* is raining
    (c) Preliminary subject *it*:
        (i) Clefting: *It* was Jóhn who broke the window
        (ii) Extrapositional: *It* happened that John was late.
The three functions I take to be related are (b) and the two in (c). However, I am not convinced that all of these functions are in fact amenable to our kind of analysis. If they are, the two types in (c) must be analyzed within a framework which also allows for analysis of whole sentences. What I shall do here, then, is to discuss various aspects of (18)(a) and (b), give a feature-specification of *it* which would also make allowance for the referential content of *it* in (c), and finally suggest, in a tenative fashion, ways for an overall analysis of the sentences quoted as examples under (c)(i) and (ii).

*It*, in its entity-referring function, is similar to *he* and *she* in deriving from a structure like (13). It is negatively specified for maleness and femaleness, and it imposes no conditions of concentration and discreteness on its referent. It likewise imposes no conditions of itemization, and consequently no conditions of specified numbers of referents, unless, of course, on a given occasion it is specified as [ +item]. So far, then, the complex symbol for *it* would contain a very high degree of unspecified features.

This characterization assumes the validity of ([ +ent] & [ −per]). I want now to consider whether *it* must in fact always be [ +ent]. Consider the type of sentence which Strawson (1953/4: 38) labels 'feature-placing sentences'. Among the examples of such sentences given by Strawson we find not only *It is raining*, but also *There is gold here*. By way of general characterization of sentences such as these

Strawson says (1953/4: 39) '*Such sentences as these do not bring particulars into our discourse*' (Strawson's italics). I have already suggested that even 'concrete' existential sentences, like *There is gold here*, may not in fact be sentences at all – in the sense of deriving from an underlying predicational structure – but rather sentential realizations of underlying nominal structures; cf. §9.1.2. Suppose we regard all feature-placing sentences as sentential realizations of underlying nominals. We might do that on the assumption that such sentences all contain a 'feature', Strawson's term for what I would call a categorial location, which is located at a 'place'. A 'sentence' like *It is raining here/there* would then contain the following elements: [−ent], realized by *it*, *raining*, a transform of RAIN, which is dominated by $L_{gen}$, *is* a realization of the temporal features, and the deictic adverb a realization of the spatial features on $L_{ind}$. The implication of this proposal, of course, is that *it* is specified as [oent]. We can then quote the entire specification of *it* :

(19)

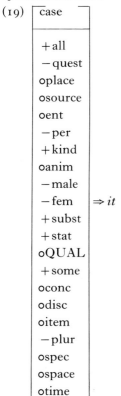

$$\begin{bmatrix} \text{case} \\[4pt] +\text{all} \\ -\text{quest} \\ \text{oplace} \\ \text{osource} \\ \text{oent} \\ -\text{per} \\ +\text{kind} \\ \text{oanim} \\ -\text{male} \\ -\text{fem} \\ +\text{subst} \\ +\text{stat} \\ \text{oQUAL} \\ +\text{some} \\ \text{oconc} \\ \text{odisc} \\ \text{oitem} \\ -\text{plur} \\ \text{ospec} \\ \text{ospace} \\ \text{otime} \end{bmatrix} \Rightarrow \textit{it}$$

Despite Rosenbaum (1967) and Huddleston (1976), the grammar of complementation is not very clear (to me), but I suppose that both of the two examples quoted under (c) in (18) would have to be analyzed in terms of complementation, at least if relativization is seen as a special type of complementation. Part of the argument in the analysis of them might then be that there are transformational relations between the following sentences:

(20)(a) (i)   It was Jóhn who broke the window
       (ii)  It was the window John broke
       (iii) It was Jóhn broke the window
       (iv)  Jóhn broke the window
    (b) (i)   It happened that John was late
       (ii)  John happened to be late.

Clefting would presumably be described as a topicalization transformation. What is of interest to me, however, is that (a)(i) and (iv) cannot be said to be synonymous. Nor can (b)(i) and (ii). The (i) examples might be described in terms of an extension of the notion of 'feature-placing sentence': (a)(i) stresses the existence of a 'place', or occasion, characterized by Jóhn breaking a window, and (b)(i) stresses the existence in the past of 'places', or occasion*s* which were characterized by John being late. No comparable stress can be found in (a)(iv), and (b)(ii) can only be used of a *single* occurrence of John's being late, unless a frequentative adverb is included. I take (21)(a) and (b) to be rough approximations to the (case-grammatical) deep structures of the (i)-examples.

The internal structure of $N_1$ is the same in both of these cases. It generates *it* (*was*) from $[-\text{ent}]$ (and the temporal features), plus a dependent clause-structure. In both cases one of the NPs in this lower clause structure (or *the* NP in the case of (b)), may be 'raised' into the superordinate $N_1$ (to give (20)(a)(ii) and (b)(ii)), or it may not (to give (20)(a)(iii) and (b)(i)). Our original example, (20)(a)(i) may be analyzed as involving 'raising' in combination with the 'trace' theory. But (20)(a)(iv) would be analyzed without the presence of $N_1$.

*They* presents no problems that cannot be satisfactorily dealt with by the apparatus as it has been developed so far. *Them*, on the other hand, presents one problem, in that it may, albeit in substandard and (perhaps) regional dialect, have determiner function: *them fellers*. This goes against the supposition that $L_{gen}$ is L-subjoined and (lexically) empty. I am not sure how much weight to give examples such as this. I

(21)  (a)

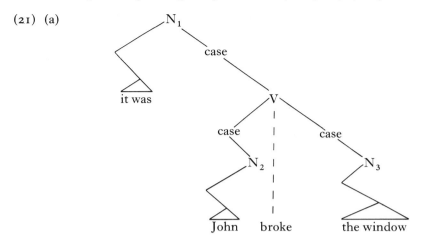

(b)

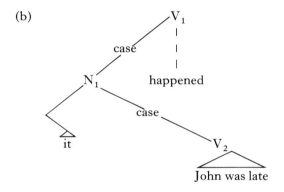

shall in the next section comment on a phenomenon which may be connected with it.

**10.3.5 The 'prop-word' *one*.** In some accounts of pronominalization, noun reduction to *one* plays a major role (e.g. Stockwell, Schachter & Partee 1973). In such accounts reliance is placed on the fact that at least two kinds of *one* may be kept apart on grammatical grounds: a numeral, and one which may appear in the plural. I, too, shall avail myself of this fact, but I shall, following Sommerstein (1972) rather than Postal (1966) and Stockwell, Schachter & Partee (1973), regard the pertinent process as *one*-insertion, rather than reduction.

NPs like *the green one* are easily analyzed within the present framework, provided we allow $L_{gen}$ to be lexically empty *without* being

L-subjoincd. In this way we also stress the intuitive affinity that there is between personal pronouns and constructions such as these. We also highlight another aspect of the present analysis, namely, the role of $L_{part}$. So far we have assumed that it is always L-subjoined in pronominal derivations, and that, if it is lexically specified, it undergoes the MI-convention to give phrases like *poor him*. I take (22) as the final derived structure of *the green one*.

(22)

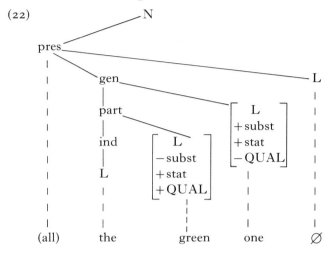

The complex symbol would be highly unspecified, but it would contain [+spec].

## 10.4 The complex pronouns

The pronouns which require a complex referential structure for their proper analysis are the possessive, the reflexive, and the relative pronouns. For reasons of space I shall not discuss these in any great detail. I shall restrict myself to giving fairly schematic representations of what I take to be their main derivational characteristics.

**10.4.1 The possessive pronouns.** The possessive pronouns (*mine, yours*, etc.) stand in a relation of complementary distribution to the class of possessive determiners (*my, your*, etc.). A description of the members of these two classes should provide an explanation of this fact. At the same time the description should provide an explanation of the relationship between possessive determiners and genitive expressions, and of the relationship of these latter with delimitative serializations involving *of*. Thus the following NPs are pertinent to the present discussion:

(23) (a) hers, mine
(b) her life, my life
(c) (for) the life of her, (for) the life of me
(d) the horse's mouth
(e) the mouth of the horse.

All of these derive from the same kind of complex structure. And whenever we have a derivation from a complex structure we are faced with the problem of identifying the head noun, i.e. the noun held to originate from $L_{gen}$ in the superordinate N (henceforth $N_1$). If we take (23)(c) as the basis for solving this problem, however, it is not so great, for in these cases there is only one noun, namely, *life*. By analogy, *mouth* is the head noun in (e); and if all of (23) derive from the same kind of structure, then *mouth* and *life* are also head nouns in (d) and (b). A schematic representation of the structure immediately underlying (23)(c) and (e) is given in (24).

(24)

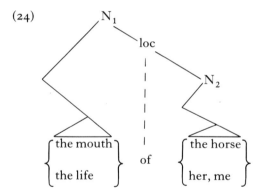

The difference between them is that, whereas $L_{gen}$ in $N_2$ is absent for *me*, and lexically unspecified and L-subjoined for *her*, it is lexically specified and not L-subjoined for *the horse*.

In §7.5.2 allowance was made for the possibility that a subordinate case-phrase (i.e. loc + $N_2$ in this case) may be adjoined and possibly subjoined to a given category in $N_1$ with which it shares some cognitive content. There are two categories in a nominal with which loc may be said to share some cognitive content, $L_{pres}$ and $L_{ind}$. Due to the very modest role played by $L_{pres}$ in general, I shall take the pertinent category to be $L_{ind}$. This is further supported by the fact that the head noun in a genitive construction like *the horse's mouth* is always definite. If a subordinate locative is adjoined and subjoined to $L_{ind}$ in $N_1$, this adjunction may be regarded as an instruction to L-subjoin $L_{ind}$. On the validity of these assumptions we then get (25); where, at the point of subjunction of $N_2$ to loc, the MI-convention has applied.

(25)

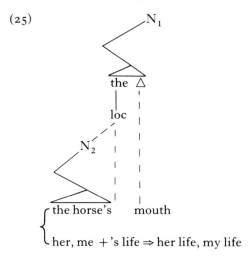

$\left\{\begin{array}{l} \text{the horse's} \quad\quad \text{mouth} \\ \text{her, me } +\text{'s life} \Rightarrow \text{her life, my life} \end{array}\right.$

In both (24) and (25), $L_{gen}$ in $N_1$ has been lexically specified and not L-subjoined. If we have a pronominal derivation of $N_1$, however, we would get (26) rather than (25).

(26)

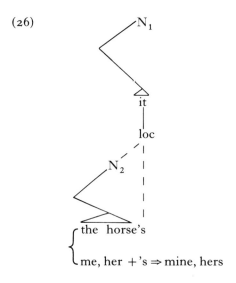

$\left\{\begin{array}{l} \text{the   horse's} \\ \text{me, her } +\text{'s} \Rightarrow \text{mine, hers} \end{array}\right.$

The possessive pronouns are thus seen to derive from a complex structure in which $L_{gen}$ (provided there is one) is lexically unspecified and L-subjoined in both $N_1$ and $N_2$. For the possessive determiners this holds only for $N_2$; and for genitive constructions it holds for neither $N_1$ nor $N_2$.

**10.4.2 The reflexive pronouns.** Although the reflexive pronouns (*myself, yourself*, etc.) function as NPs, the whole notion of reflexivity is so tightly linked with the syntax of the verb that no account of them can be satisfactory without due notice being given to various matters of clause-structure. More specifically, any account of the reflexive pronouns must provide the basis of a reasonable explanation of the following grammatical facts:

(27)(a) *-self* can never function as subject, only as (direct and indirect) object, complement to a preposition, and subject complement;

   (b) the *-self* forms *always* refer to an entity which is also referred to by some other expression in the same (simple) sentence. Hence they are often seen as clearly anaphoric;

   (c) the forms in *-self* with reflexive function are in complementary distribution with the forms in *-self* with emphatic function: *if the barber himsélf shaved himself*;

   (d) any NP introduced by the definite article can be associated with an emphatic *-self* form, no matter which grammatical function it performs:

     (i) the duchess hersélf wrote the letter to the count

     (ii) the duchess wrote the letter itsélf to the count

     (iii) the duchess wrote the letter to the count himsélf

     if not all at the same time;

   (e) no NP introduced by the indefinite article can be associated with an emphatic *-self* form, no matter which grammatical function it performs:

     (i) *a duchess hersélf wrote a letter to a count

     (ii) *a duchess wrote a letter itsélf to a count

     (iii) *a duchess wrote a letter to a count himsélf;

   (f) any subject NP introduced by the indefinite article can be associate with a reflexive *-self* form:

     (i) a duchess wrote a letter to herself;

   (g) when a reflexive *-self* form refers to the same entity as the subject NP, the latter must be ergative.

In addition, the analysis might be formulated in such a way as not to contravene three diachronic facts:

(28)(a) the fact that *same* – a loan from Old Norse in Middle English – came to supersede the vernacular *self* in a number of contexts (Mustanoja 1960: 176);

   (b) the fact that *self* alone had a reflexive function throughout Middle English, without *my-* etc. (Mustanoja 1960: 145);

   (c) the fact that the old Indo-European locative came to be expressed in Germanic by either the genitive or the dative case-form.

And finally, some importance might be attached to the fact that Danish (and German) – which have both retained the Germanic reflexive system of pronouns – distinguishes the emphatic from the purely reflexive function by morhological means. Cf.:

(29)(a) (i)  Jeg keder mig (reflexive function)
           I   bore  me 'I'm bored'
      (ii) Jeg keder mig selv (emphatic function)
           I   bore  me  self 'I (even) bore mysélf'
   (b) (i)  *if*Han er ikke sig (reflexive function)
           He  is not  –  ( = himself )
      (ii) Han er ikke sig selv (emphatic function)
           He  is not  –   self ( = himself )

I want now to consider what implications might be drawn from (27). To say, (c), that emphatic and reflexive *-self* are in complementary distribution is to suggest that they derive from the same underlying unit. To say, (d), that any NP introduced by the definite article may be associated with an emphatic *-self* form irrespectively of grammatical function is to suggest that the emphatic *-self* form in fact 'grows out of' the NP with which it is associated. Connected with this point, and further implied by (e) and (f), is the suggestion that a *-self* form is always (derivationally) definite. The reason why the examples in (e) are deviant is that there an indefinite and a definite form not only are used to refer to the same person or thing, but also perform the same grammatical function. In (f), on the other hand, an indefinite and a definite sign refer to the same entity, but they do not perform the same grammatical function. Given a model for syntactico-semantic analysis in which NPs are dependents on verbs (via a case-relation), all these points suggest the same conclusion: *-self* is a realization of a NP which is *not* directly dependent on the verb in the (semantic) deep structure, but is rather a dependent on some other NP which latter is directly dependent on the verb. A rough first approximation might be (30).

(30)

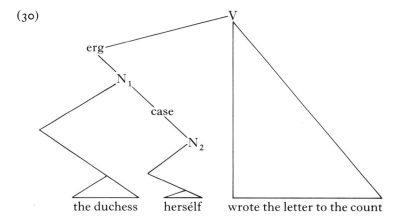

the duchess    hersélf    wrote the letter to the count

Consider now the verb *shave*. It is a transitive verb, requiring two arguments, one governed by erg, the other by abs. However, it is a semantically reflexive verb in the sense that, when it is associated with only one argument, the verb is interpreted as reflexive. I take the deep structure of both of (31) to be (32):

(31) (a) John shaved
     (b) John shaved himself.

(32)

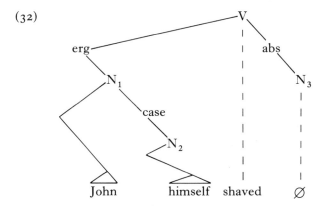

John    himself  shaved    ∅

There are two possible transformational developments of (32). Either $N_2$ is copied into the empty $N_3$ to yield (31)(b), or it is subjoined to $N_1$ and absorbed by it to yield (31)(a). Generally, a *-self* form in reflexive function derives from a subordinate N ($N_2$) which is promoted to superordinate ($N_1$) status. It is on this analysis easy to see why a reflexive pronoun must have a 'co-referent' NP within the same clause: it *derives* from that NP, and it is promoted to be directly governed by the verb which already governs the NP from which it derives.

During the preceding outline of what I take to be the main factors in the syntactic process of reflexivization, nothing has been said about the internal structure of $N_2$, the subordinate from which the reflexive pronoun is said to derive. It is on this question that the diachronic points raised above become pertinent. In view of these I suggest that $N_2$ is in fact itself a complex structure (33). Reflexivization is the linguistic

(33)

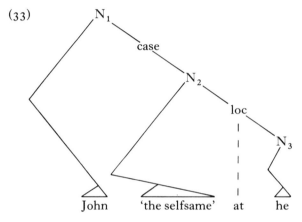

embodiment of the principle that everything is identical with itself. A given nominal structure, $N_1$, can be 'reduplicated', in principle *ad infinitum*, if it had any practical significance. What does have practical significance is the possibility of expressing the idea that an agent does something to himself. The English reflexive system avails itself of *two* such 'reduplications', represented in (33) by $N_2$ and $N_3$. Although productive in Old and Middle English – as it still is in Danish and German – the relationship between these two 'reduplications' has become fossilized in a subjunction whereby loc + $N_3$ is subjoined to $L_{ind}$ in $N_2$. The fluctuation in the modern reflexives between *my-* (genitive form) and *him-* (dative form) is due to the two-fold Germanic realization of the old locative. But these matters are primarily diachronic, as stated. What is of essence to a purely synchronic account of reflexivization are the configurations (30) and (32), plus the associated transformations which either promote the (diachronically complex) $N_2$ to primary status or subjoin it to $N_1$.

**10.4.3 The relative pronouns.** The structure (21)(a) displays a situation in which a verb is dependent on a nominal. It is this situation in general which is the derivational basis of (restrictive) relativization. Like reflexivization, relativization trades on the notion of structure identity, or 'reduplication'. One of the Ns dependent on the subordinate V must be identical to the N on which V depends, but since identity is a definite notion – cf. *the same* vs. **a same* – the 'reduplicated' structure must always be definite in the derivational sense, even if its 'source' is derivationally indefinite. The relevant deep structures of (34) are (35).

(34)  (a) the maid who kissed the butler (was fired)
      (b) the maid (whom) the butler kissed (was fired).

(35)  (a)

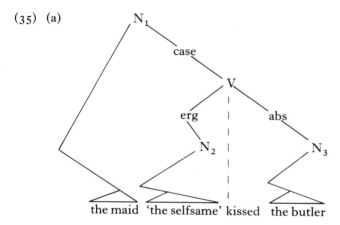

(b)

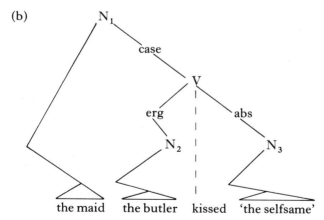

There are various ways in which further to develop these, but due to the need in (b) for some kind of 'fronting' of the structure underlying the relative I take it that some kind of movement transformation is always involved. Recall now that reflexivization involved a transformation which moved an originally subordinate N to superordinate status. As we shall see below, relativization and reflexivization have some important referential characteristics in common, a fact so far captured by the employment of 'reduplication' of structures. But the referential affinities might be brought out further by suggesting that essentially the same type of movement of structures is involved in both processes. I shall therefore suggest that relativization involves a movement transformation which degrades a deep structurally superordinate N to subordinate status. In (35) $N_2$ and $N_3$ are both superordinate relative to the V that governs them. But by the transformation just proposed, one of these will be adjoined to $N_1$, thereby in effect undergoing a degradation. The condition on this transformation is, of course, structure identity, so it is $N_2$ which is moved in (35)(a), whereas it is $N_3$ which is moved in (b). We may now relate the option of expressing the relative pronoun in (34)(b) to the nature of the case that governs $N_3$ in (35)(b), abs. As the semantically neutral case it may be adjoined and subjoined to $L_{gen}$ in $N_1$. If it is, the result will be *the maid the butler kissed*, in which *maid* has absorbed abs + $N_3$. If it is not, the result will be *the maid who(m) the butler kissed*. Ergative, as a non-referential case, cannot be adjoined or subjoined to any category in $N_1$. Hence we invariably get *the maid who kissed the butler* from (35)(a).

This rough outline of the process of relativization cannot account for non-restrictive (appositive, descriptive) relative clauses. These I take to be associated with co-ordination (rather than subordination), and although certain aspects of co-ordination invite a referential–semantic analysis, I shall not pursue this question here. I shall, however, mention one or two pertinent facts in the 'further prospects' section.

Let me finally sum up what I take to be the referential function of relative, as well as reflexive, pronouns:

(36)    A relative (reflexive) pronoun invites the hearer to accept an entity, which may be either a thing, a person, or an 'itemized' substance, as the same as an entity whose ST- (and C-) location is established by a sign in the textual context of the relative (reflexive) pronoun.

A description of relative and reflexive pronouns as primarily anaphoric is thus not amiss. They are signs the main function of which is to 'abbreviate' ST- (and C-) locations established in the context of utterance. But in contrast to the personal pronouns, this establishment of locations is based entirely on the linguistic context. Yet since the 'abbreviation' embodied in relative and reflexive pronouns is an abbreviation of the referential properties of other signs, we are justified, even in these cases, in maintaining the catch-phrase that anaphora depends on reference.

# Conclusion : summary and further prospects

My main concern in the present work has been to argue in favour of recognizing a distinction between two equipollent types of linguistic analysis. Of these, the syntactico-semantic analysis is well established and has been throughout the history of linguistics. In contrast, the referential–semantic analysis has received only sporadic and informal treatment, more often than not by philosophers rather than by linguists. Furthermore, when linguists have concerned themselves with the analysis of data that lend themselves to RS-analysis, they have more often than not conducted their enquiries within the framework which is designed to account for SS-phenomena. This has led to a certain amount of inconsistency within the SS-analysis while at the same time complicating the issues unnecessarily.

The area of English nominal composition which has provided data for an empirical assessment of the validity of the theoretical framework established in Part II has been restricted to the area in which the referential functives play a major part. This area is at the same time one of the areas least satisfactorily dealt with by current SS-practice.

Yet it is not only with respect to the referential functives that the referential–semantic theory may contribute with new insights into linguistic structure. Another general area where this type of analysis can reasonably be expected to yield felicitous results comprises many aspects of adjectival constructions. The serialization of attributive adjectives is clearly bound by a system of rules which the SS-analysis has no obvious way of accounting for. The referential theory offers the immediate possibility of subcategorizing the cover feature [$\alpha$QUAL] in various ways which, *a priori*, would seem to involve reference to such notions as permanent vs. transient properties.

Adjectival comparison and reinforcement by elements like *very* and *too* likewise fall within the province of referential analysis, where such matters might be related to a scalar feature [$\alpha$degree] on $L_{ind}$ in connection with a refinement of the notion of recursion.

The general area of nominal compounding is susceptible of analysis in RS-terms, and the relationships between apposition and (phrasal) co-ordination is likely to be captured by RS-analysis rather than by SS-analysis. Notice in this connection the relation of mutual exclusion that holds between the NP-constructions in

(a)  (i)  Harry planted his garden with roses and other flowers
     (ii) *Harry planted his garden with flowers and (other) roses
(b)  (i)  *Harry planted his garden with roses – flowers, actually
     (ii) Harry planted his garden with flowers – roses, actually.

Quite obviously the hyponymical relations between lexical nouns involved in compositions such as these impose restrictions on the serialization-order allowed in co-ordination (a) and apposition (b). Apposition implies restriction, co-ordination implies generalization. Compare this statement to the (obsolescent) use of relative *which* in determiner function: *Harry planted his garden with roses, which flowers his wife liked most*, vs. *\*Harry planted his garden with flowers, which roses his wife liked most*. These relative clauses are non-restrictive.

Finally, when sufficient insight into the referential structure of NPs has been reached and a serious attempt can be made to integrate the RS- and SS-analysis in greater detail than attempted here, I suspect that also certain aspects of VP-structure will prove susceptible of RS-analysis, in particular with respect to the functions performed by the verbal categories of tense, mood, and aspect.

Tentative considerations such as these invite us to broaden the scope of RS-analysis beyond the restricted area investigated in Part III. More important than this, they point towards sufficiently varied and interesting areas for further investigation into the referential structure of language.

# Bibliography

## A. Lexica

*NED*: *The Oxford New English Dictionary on Historical Principles*
Onions, *Etym.*: *The Oxford Dictionary of English Etymology* OUP, 1966
Webster's *Dictionary of Synonyms*. Springfield, Mass., 1951

## B. Bibliographical abbreviations

*AJ*: *Acta Jutlandica*
*AL(H)*: *Acta Linguistica (Hafniensia)*
*BGdSL*: *Beiträge zur Geschichte der deutschen Sprache und Literatur*
CUP: Cambridge University Press
*ES*: *English Studies*
*EWPL*: *Edinburgh Working Papers in Linguistics*
*FL*: *Foundations of Language*
*GL*: *General Linguistics*
*Idg J*: *Indogermanisches Jahrbuch*
*IULC*: *Indiana University Linguistics Club*
*JL*: *Journal of Linguistics*
*L&P*: *Linguistics and Philosophy*
*LA*: *Linguistic Analysis*
*LAUT*: *Linguistics Agency, University of Trier*
*LI*: *Linguistic Inquiry*
*Lg*: *Language*
*Lg M S*: *Language Monograph Series*
*OSCULD*: *Outfit for Scandinavian Underground Linguistics Dissemination, University of Gothenburg*
OUP: Oxford University Press
*Ph P*: *Philologica Pragensia*
*SL*: *Studia Linguistica*
*TCLC*: *Travaux du Cercle Linguistique de Copenhague*
*WW*: *Wirkendes Wort*

## C. References

Akmajian, Adrian & Lehrer, Adrienne (1976) 'NP-like quantifiers and the

240

problem of determining the head of an NP', *LA* 2.4, 395–413

Allan, Keith (1971) 'A note on the source of *there* in existential sentences', *FL* 7, 1–18

- (1977) 'Classifiers', *Lg* 53.2, 285–311

Anderson, John M. (1971a) *The grammar of case*. CUP

- (1971b) 'Dependency and grammatical functions', *FL* 7, 30–7
- (1971c) 'Outline of a proposal for the lexicalization of complex structures', *SL* 15.1, 1–8
- (1973) *An essay concerning aspect*. Mouton: The Hague
- (1974) 'Existential quantifiers', *AL(H)* 15, 1–27
- (1977) *On case grammar*. Croom & Helm: London

Anderson, Stephen (1976) 'On the notion of subject in ergative languages', in Li (1976), 1–23

Atkinson, Martin & Griffiths, Patrick (1973) 'Here's here's, there's, here and there', *EWPL* 3, 29–73

Austin, J. L. (1962) *How to do things with words*. OUP 1970

Bach, Emmon (1968) 'Nouns and noun phrases', in Bach & Harms (eds.) (1968) 91–122

- & Harms, Robert T. (eds.) (1968) *Universals in linguistic theory*. Holt, Rhinehart & Winston: New York

Baker, Carlos, L. (1973) 'Definiteness and indefiniteness in English', *IULC* June

Bar-Hillel, Yehoshua (1953) 'On recursive definitions in empirical sciences', in Bar-Hillel (1970) 302–7

- (1967a) 'Dictionaries and meaning rules', *FL* 3, 409–14
- (1967b) Review of *The structure of language*, *Lg* 43.2, 526–49
- (1969) 'Universal semantics and philosophy of language', in Bar-Hillel (1970) 181–201
- (1970) *Aspects of language*. Magnes Press/North-Holland: Jerusalem

Bauer, Laurie (1979) 'Some thoughts on dependency grammar', *Linguistics* 17 (1979) 301–15

- & Boagey, Winifred (1977) Review of *The grammar of case*, *L&P* 1 (1977) 119–52

Baumgärtner, Klaus (1970) 'Konstituenz und Dependenz', in Steger (ed.) (1970) 52–77

Bierwisch, Manfred (1967) 'Some semantic universals of German adjectives', *FL* 3, 1–36

- (1971) 'On classifying semantic features', in Steinberg & Jakobovits (eds.) (1971) 410–35
- & Heidolph, Karl (eds.) (1969) *Progress in linguistics*. Mouton: The Hague

Bloomfield, Leonard (1933) *Language*. Unwin: London 1967

Botha, Rudolph P. & Winckler, Walter K. (1973) *The justification of linguistic hypotheses: a study of nondemonstrative inference in transformational grammar*. Mouton: The Hague

Brinker, Klaus (1971) 'Aufgaben und Methoden der Textlinguistik', *WW* 21, 217–37

Bühler, Karl (1918) 'Kritische Musterung der neuern Theorien des Satzes', *Idg J* 6, 1–20

– (1934) *Sprachtheorie*. Gustav Fischer: Stuttgart 1965

Carden, Guy (1973) *English quantifiers: logical structure and linguistic variation*. Taishukan: Tokyo

Carnoy, A. J. (1927) 'Psychologie de l'article grec', in *Symbolae Grammaticae in honorem Ioannis Rozwadowski* I, Drukarnia Universytetu Jagielleńskiego: Krakow

Chafe, Wallace L. (1970) *Meaning and the structure of language*. University of Chicago Press

– (1976) 'Givenness, contrastiveness, definiteness, subjects, topics, and points of view', in Li (1976) 25–56

Chomsky, Noam (1964) *Current issues in linguistic theory*. Mouton: The Hague 1970

– (1965) *Aspects of the theory of syntax*. MIT: Cambr. Mass.

– (1970) 'Remarks on nominalization', in *Studies in semantics in generative grammar*. Mouton: The Hague 1972

– (1972) 'Conditions on transformations', *OSCULD*

– (1976) *Reflections on language*. Temple Smith: London

– & Halle, M. (1965) 'Some controversial questions in phonological theory', *JL* 1, 97–138

Christophersen, Paul (1939) *The articles*. OUP

Cole, P. & Morgan, J. (eds.) (1975) *Syntax & semantics 3: speech acts*. Academic Press: New York

– & Sadock, J. (eds.) (1977) *Syntax & semantics 8: grammatical relations*. Academic Press: New York

Collinson, W. E. (1937) *Indication: a study of demonstratives, articles, and other 'indicaters'*. Lg M S 17

Crymes, Ruth (1968) *Some systems of substitution correlations in modern American English*. Mouton: The Hague

Dahl, Östen (1971) 'Some inconclusive arguments for dependency structures', *Gothenburg Papers in Theoretical Linguistics* 2

Delisle, Gilles L. (1973) 'Discourse and backward pronominalization', *IULC*, October

Derwing, Bruce (1973) *Transformational grammar as a theory of language acquisition*. CUP

Donnellan, Keith (1966) 'Reference and definite descriptions', in Steinberg & Jakobovits (1971) 100–14

Emeneau, M. B. (1951) *Studies in Vietnamese (Annamese) grammar. University of California Publications in Linguistics* 8, University of California Press: Berkeley and Los Angeles

Fillmore, Charles J. (1968) 'The case for case', in Bach & Harms (1968) 1–88

– (1977) 'The case for case reopened', in Cole & Sadock (1977) 59–81

Frege, Gottlob (1891) 'Function and concept', in Geach & Black (1966) 21–41

– (1892a) 'On concept and object', in Geach & Black (1966) 42–55

– (1892b) 'On sense and reference', in Geach & Black (1966) 56–78

Friedrich, Paul (1970) 'Shape in grammar', *Lg* 46.2, 379–407

Frye, Northrop (1957) *Anatomy of criticism : four essays.* Atheneum: New York 1969

Gaifman, H. (1965) 'Dependency-systems and phrase-structure systems', *Information and Control* 8, 304–37

Geach, Peter & Black, Max (1966) *Translations from the philosophical writings of Gottlob Frege.* Blackwell: Oxford

Givón, Talmy (1972) 'Opacity and reference in language'. *IULC*, June

Goyvaerts, D. L. (1968) 'An introductory study on the ordering of a string of adjectives in present-day English', *Ph P* 11.1, 12–28

Greenberg, Joseph H. (1972) 'Numerical classifiers and substantival number problems in the genesis of a linguistic type', in *Preprints of the 11th International Congress of Linguistics, Bologna 1972*, 1–19

Grice, H. P. (1975) 'Logic and conversation', in Cole & Morgan (1975) 41–58

Haas, W. (1973) Review of Lyons *Introduction to theoretical linguistics*, *JL* 9, 71–113

Halliday, M. A. K. (1961) 'Categories of the theory of grammar', *Word* 17, 241–92

– (1970) 'Language structure and language function', in Lyons (1970) 140–65

Happ, Heinz (1976) *Grundfragen einer Dependenzgrammatik des Lateinischen.* Vandenhoeck & Ruprecht: Göttingen

Hartmann, Peter (1971) 'Texte als linguistisches Objekt', in Stempel (1971) 9–29

Harweg, Roland (1968) *Pronomina und Textkonstitution.* Wilhelm Fink: Munich

Havers, Wilhelm (1926) 'Zur Bedeutung des Plurals', in *Festschrift für Paul Kretschmer : Beiträge zur griechischen und lateinischen Sprachforschung*, Deutscher Verlag für Jugend und Volk: Vienna, 39–62

Hawkins, John A. (1978) *Definiteness and indefiniteness : a study in reference and grammaticality prediction.* Croom & Helm: London

Hays, D. (1964) 'Dependency theory: a formalism and some observations', *Lg* 40, 511–25

Helbig, Gerhard (ed.) (1971) *Beiträge zur Valenztheorie.* Mouton: Berlin

Heltveit, Trygve (1953) *Studies in English demonstrative pronouns : a contribution to the history of English morphology.* Universitetsforlaget: Oslo

Heringer, J. T. (1969) 'Indefinite noun phrases and referential opacity', in Robert I. Binnick, Alice Davison, Georgia M. Green & Jerry L. Morgan (eds.) *Papers from the 5th Regional Meeting, Chicago Linguistics Society*, 87–97

Hjelmslev, Louis (1928) *Principes de grammaire générale.* Det Kgl. Danske Videnskabernes Selskab, Hist.-Fil. Medd. xvi.1. Munksgaard: Copenhagen 1968

– (1935/7) 'La catégorie des cas', *AJ* 7 (1935) and 9 (1937)

– (1937) 'La nature du pronom', in Hjelmslev (1959) 192–98

– (1939) 'La notion de rection', *AL(H)* 1, 10–23

– (1941) 'De grammatiske kategorier', *Translatøren* 3.1, 8–16

– (1943) *Omkring sprogteoriens grundlæggelse.* Akademisk: Copenhagen 1966

– (1956) 'Om numerus og genus', in *Festskrift til Christen Møller.* Borgen: Copenhagen

– (1959) *Essais Linguistiques* I. *TCLC* 12, Nordisk Sprog- og Kulturforlag: Copenhagen 1970
– (1972) *Sprogsystem og sprogforandring*. *TCLC* 15, Nordisk Sprog- og Kulturforlag: Copenhagen
Hockett, Charles F. (1958) *A course in modern linguistics*. Macmillan: New York
Householder, F. W. (1973) 'On arguments from asterisks'. *FL* 10, 365–76
Huddleston, Rodney (1972) Review of Seuren *Operators and nucleus*, *GL* 12.2, 96–105
– (1976) *An introduction to English transformational syntax*. Longman: London
Ibrahim, Muhammad Hassan (1973) *Grammatical gender*. Mouton: The Hague
Ivić, M. (1970) 'On the part–whole relation and its linguistic consequences', in Jakobson, Roman & Kawamoto, S. (eds.) *Studies in general and oriental linguistics*, TEC Company: Tokyo
Jackendoff, Ray S. (1971) 'Modal structure in semantic representation', *LI* 2, 479–514
– (1972) *Semantic interpretation in generative grammar*. MIT: Cambr. Mass.
Jakobsen, 'A. Lykke (1977) 'An analysis of hypostasis forms'. Mimeo; Dept. of English, Univ. of Copenhagen. (To appear in *AL(H)*.)
Jakobson, Roman (1960) 'Closing statement: linguistics and poetics', in Sebeok, T. (ed.) *Style in language*. MIT: Cambr. Mass. 1960
Jespersen, Otto (1924) *Philosophy of grammar*. Allen & Unwin: London 1968
– (1949) *A modern English grammar* VII. Allen & Unwin: London/Copenhagen 1965
Karttunen, Lauri (1971) 'Definite descriptions with crossing coreference: a study of the Bach-Peters paradox', *FL* 7, 152–82
Katz, Jerrold J. (1972) *Semantic theory*. Harper & Row: New York
Keenan, Edward L. (ed.) (1975) *Formal semantics of natural language*. CUP
– (1976) 'Towards a universal definition of "Subject"', in Li (1976) 303–33
Kempson, Ruth (1974) *Presupposition and the delimitation of semantics*. CUP
– (1977) *Semantic theory*. CUP
Krámsky, Jiři (1972) *The article and the concept of definiteness in language*. Mouton: The Hague
Kretschmer, Paul (1947) *Objektive Konjugation im Indogermanischen*. Österreichische Akademie der Wissenschaften: Vienna
Kuno, Susumu (1976) 'Subject, theme, and the speaker's empathy: a re-examination of relativization phenomena', in Li (1976) 417–44
Kunze, Jürgen (1975) *Abhängigkeitsgrammatik. Studia Grammatica* XII. Akademie-Verlag: Berlin
Kuroda, S.-Y. (1971) 'Two remarks on pronominalization', *FL* 7, 183–98
Kuryłowicz, Jerzy (1964) *The inflectional categories of Indo-European*. Carl Winter: Heidelberg
Lakoff, George (1968a) 'Pronouns and reference'. Parts I + II. *IULC*, July
– (1968b) 'Counterparts, or the problem of reference in transformational grammar', *IULC*, November
– (1970) *Irregularity in syntax*. Holt, Rinehart & Winston: New York
Lakoff, Robin (1969) 'Some reasons why there can't be any *some–any* rule', *Lg*

45, 608–15

Langacker, Ronald W. (1966) 'On pronominalization and the chain of command', in Reibel & Schane (1969) 160–86

Lawler, John M. (1973) 'Tracking the generic toad', in Claudia Corum, T. Cedric Smith-Stark & Ann Weiser (eds.) *Papers from the 9th Regional Meeting, Chicago Linguistics Society*, 320–31

Leech, Geoffrey N. (1969) *Towards a semantic description of English*. Longman: London

Lees, Robert B. & Klima, Edward S. (1963) 'Rules for English pronominalization', in Reibel & Schane (1969) 145–59

Li, Charles N. (ed.) (1976) *Subject and topic*. Academic Press: New York

– & Thompson, Sandra A. (1976) 'Subject and topic: a new typology of language', in Li (1976) 457–90

Linsky, Leonard (1967) *Referring*. Blackwell: Oxford

Lyons, John (1966) 'Towards a "notional" theory of the "parts of speech"', *JL* 2, 209–36

– (1968) *Introduction to theoretical linguistics*. CUP

– (1970) (ed.) *New horizons in linguistics*. Penguin: Harmondsworth 1972

– (1973) 'Deixis as the source of reference', in Keenan (1975) 61–83

– (1977) *Semantics* (2 vols.). CUP

Matthews, Peter H. (1972) *Inflectional morphology*. CUP

– (1974) *Morphology : an introduction to the theory of word-structure*. CUP

McCawley, James D. (1971) 'Where do noun phrases come from?', in Steinberg & Jakobovits (1971) 217–31

Mey, Jakob L. (1960) *La catégorie du nombre en finnois moderne. TCLC* 13, Nordisk Sprog- og Kulturforlag: Copenhagen

Miller, James E. (1975) 'The parasitic growth of deep structures', *FL* 13, 361–89

Moore, George E. (1936) 'Is existence a predicate?' in *Proceedings of the Aristotelian Soc.*, Suppl. 15, 175–88

Mortensen, Arne Thing (1972) *Perception og sprog*. Akademisk: Copenhagen

Mustanoja, Tauno F. (1960) *A Middle English syntax*. Part I. *Mémoires de la Société Néophilologique de Helsinki* 23. Société Néophilologique: Helsinki

Nilsen, Don F. (1972) *Toward a semantic specification of deep case*. Mouton: The Hague

– (1973) *The instrumental case in English*. Mouton: The Hague

O'Connor, D. J. (1975) *The correspondence theory of truth*. Hutchinson: London

Okell, John (1969) *A reference grammar of colloquial Burmese*. OUP

Partee, Barbara H. (1970) 'Opacity, Coreference, and pronouns', *Synthese* 21, 359–85

Pears, D. F. (1963) 'Is existence a predicate?', in Strawson (1967) 97–102

Perlmutter, David M. (1969) 'On the article in English', in Bierwisch & Heidolph (1969) 233–48

Pilch, Herbert (1968) 'Modelle der englischen Wortbildung', in Brekle, H. E. & Lipka, L. (eds.) *Wortbildung, Syntax und Morphologie : Festschrift zum 60. Geburtstag von Hans Marchand*. Mouton: The Hague

- (1970) *Altenglische Grammatik*. Hueber: Munich
Popper, Karl R. (1963) *Conjectures and refutations: the growth of scientific knowledge*. Routledge: London 1969
- (1972) *Objective knowledge*. OUP 1974
Porzig, Walter (1934) 'Wesenhafte Bedeutungsbeziehungen', *BGdSL* 58, 70–97
Postal, Paul M. (1964) *Constituent Structure: a study of contemporary models of syntactic description*. Mouton: Bloomington & The Hague
- (1966) 'On the so-called "pronouns" in English', in Reibel & Schane (1969) 210–24
- (1971) *Cross-over phenomena*. Holt, Rinehart & Winston: New York
Quine, W. V. O. (1953) *From a logical point of view: logico-philosophical essays*. Harper & Row: New York 1963
Quirk, R., Greenbaum, S., Leech, G. N. & Svartvik, J. (1972) *A grammar of contemporary English*. Longman: London
Reibel, D. A. & Schane, S. A. (eds.) (1969) *Modern studies in English: readings in transformational grammar*. Prentice-Hall: Englewood Cliffs, N.J.
Reichenbach, Hans (1947) *Elements of symbolic logic*. Macmillan: New York 1966
Rischel, Jørgen (1972) 'Derivation as a syntactic process in Greenlandic', in Kiefer, F. (ed.) *Proceedings of the KVAL Sea-borne Spring Seminar*, April 9–10. Stockholm – Turku
Robbins, Beverly (1968) *The definite article in English transformations*. Mouton: The Hague
Robinson, Jane J. (1970a) 'Case, category, and configuration', *JL* 6, 57–80
- (1970b) 'Dependency structures and transformational rules', *Lg* 46, 259–85
Rosenbaum, Peter S. (1967) *The grammar of English predicate complement constructions*. MIT: Cambr. Mass.
Ross, John Robert (1967) *Constraints on variables in syntax*. IULC, Fall
Royen, Gerlach (1929) *Die Nominalen Klassifikationssysteme in den Sprachen der Erde. Linguistische Bibliothek Antropos* 4. Mödling bei Wien
Russell, Bertrand (1905) 'On denoting', in Lackey, D. (ed.) *Essays in criticism*, 103–19. Allen & Unwin: London 1973
- (1940) *An inquiry into meaning and truth*. Penguin: Harmondsworth 1973
Sampson, Geoffrey R. (1969) *Towards a linguistic theory of reference*. PhD diss., Yale University. Unpubl.
- (1975) *The form of language*. Weidenfeld & Nicolson: London
Schachter, Paul (1976) 'The subject in Philippine languages: topic, actor, actor-topic, or none of the above', in Li (1976) 491–518
Schibsbye, Knud (1961) *Engelsk Grammatik* III. Naturmetodens Sproginstitut: Copenhagen
Searle, John R. (1969) *Speech acts*. CUP 1970
Seuren, Pieter A. M. (1969) *Operators and nucleus*. CUP
Sommerstein, Alan (1972) 'On the so-called definite article in English', *LI* 3, 197–209
Sørensen, H. Steen (1958) *Word-classes in Modern English with special reference to proper names: with an introductory theory of grammar, meaning, and*

*reference*. Gad: Copenhagen

- (1959a) 'The function of the definite article in Modern English', *ES* 40, 401–20
- (1959b) 'An analysis of "to be" and "to be true"', *Analysis* 19.6, 121–31
- (1963) *The meaning of proper names*. Gad: Copenhagen
- (1967) 'Meaning', in *To honor Roman Jakobson* III, 1876–89. Mouton: The Hague

Sparkes, Ivan G. (1975) *Dictionary of collective nouns and group terms*. White Lion Publications: London

Steger, H. (ed.) (1970) *Vorschläge für eine strukturale Grammatik des Deutschen*. Wissenschaftliche Buchgesellschaft: Darmstadt

Steinberg, D. & Jakobovits, L. (eds.) (1971) *Semantics*. CUP

Stempel, W. D. (ed.) (1971) *Beiträge zur Textlinguistik*. Wilhelm Fink: Munich

Sten, Holger (1949) 'Le nombre grammatical', *TCLC* 4, 47–59

Stockwell, R. P., Schachter, P. & Partee, B. H. (1973) *The major syntactic structures of English*. Holt, Rinehart & Winston: New York

Strawson, P. F. (1950) 'On referring', in Strawson (1971) 1–27

- (1953/4) 'Particular and general', in Strawson (1971) 28–52
- (1959) *Individuals: an essay in descriptive metaphysics*. Methuen: London 1974
- (ed.) (1967) *Philosophical logic*. OUP 1973
- (1971) *Logico-linguistic papers*. Methuen: London 1974

Sussex, Roland (1974) 'The deep structure of adjectives in NPs', *JL* 10, 111–31

Tesnière, Lucien (1959) *Eléments de syntaxe structurale*. Klincksiek: Paris

Thompson, Laurence C. (1965) *A Vietnamese grammar*. University of Washington Press: Seattle

Thrane, Torben (1976) *A study in the referential functions of English noun phrases*. PhD diss., Univ. of Edinburgh. Unpubl.

Vater, H. (1975) 'Toward a generative dependency theory', *Lingua* 36, 121–145

Weinrich, Harald (1966) *Linguistik der Lüge*. Verlag Lambert Schneider: Heidelberg

Wienold, Götz (1967) *Genus und Semantik*. Anton Hain: Meisenheim a. Glahn

# Index